Identity, Citizenship, and Political Conflict in Africa

Identity, Citizenship, and Political Conflict in Africa

Edmond J. Keller

Indiana University Press
Bloomington and Indianapolis

This book is a publication of

Indiana University Press
Office of Scholarly Publishing
Herman B Wells Library 350
1320 East 10th Street
Bloomington, Indiana 47405 USA

iupress.indiana.edu

Telephone orders 800-842-6796
Fax orders 812-855-7931

© 2014 by Edmond J. Keller

⊖ The paper used in this publication meets
the minimum requirements of the American
National Standard for Information
Sciences—Permanence of Paper for Printed
Library Materials, ANSI Z39.48–1992.

Manufactured in the
United States of America

Library of Congress
Cataloging-in-Publication Data

Keller, Edmond J. (Edmond Joseph), [date]
   Identity, citizenship, and political conflict
in Africa / Edmond J. Keller.
   pages cm
   Includes bibliographical references and
index.
   ISBN: 978-0-253-01178-7 (cloth :
alk. paper) — ISBN: 978-0-253-01184-8
(pbk. : alk. paper) — ISBN: 978-0-253-
01189-3 (ebook) 1. Africa—Politics and
government. 2. Citizenship—Africa.
3. Group identity—Africa. 4. Identity
politics—Africa. 5. National characteristics,
African. 6. Nationalism—Africa. 7. Nation-
building—Africa. I. Title.
   JQ1879.A15K45 2014
   305.8096—dc23

                                    2013030356

1 2 3 4 5   19 18 17 16 15 14

If you don't know your history, if you don't know your family, who are you?
—Mary Pipher

Contents

Summary and Conclusion: Identity, Citizenship, and Social Conflict · 147

Preface

When I first entered graduate school and decided to, fell into, or was drawn by my mentors into the study of African development and change, the continent was at the earliest stages of its sociopolitical transitions from colonial rule to democracy. I can recall that at the time, there was a great deal of optimism that—despite what looked like a rocky road ahead—independent African states would slowly but surely transform themselves into liberal democracies similar to those found in the West. One of the primary assumptions of scholars at the time was that Africa needed both national and regional political integration; however, national integration was the most immediate objective. In other words, scholars believed that highly ethnically diverse states could be transformed into multiethnic or multitribal political systems comprised of individuals and ethnic communities that would see the nation states to which they belonged as terminal communities—the community to which one owed her/his political primary allegiance. The key was thought to be getting institutions right. Democratic political institutions and liberal economic and social institution were thought to be the panaceas necessary and sufficient to move Africa toward this destiny.

However, after a half century of independence, the goal of national political integration is as elusive as ever. Nations have been built, and the African citizens in those nations appear to accept that they have allegiance to the particular nation-states to which they belong; but, the allegiance of their citizens tend to be more often than not divided between the nation-state and the ethnic communities to which they claim ancestry. In some cases, attachment to the subnational community is more fiction than reality, but is clung to as though it were primordially based. The question I was thus confronted with is, "Will the nation-building project in most African states be under construction forever?" Or, secondarily, "How necessary is it for the persistence and consolidation of African states for there to be developed an exclusive sense of national identity that is the primary political identity for citizens?"

Over the years these problematic questions have consumed me. Rather than continue to live with this puzzle, I decided to attack it head on through my research. What my research reveals is that no matter what the answers to these questions are, one of present-day Africa's most burning political issues is the establishment of widely accepted notions of national citizenship that apply equally across ethnic communities. Citizens themselves want to solidify their rights as individuals and as ethnic groups to belong to a particular national community. States that seek to reduce incidents of ethnic conflict to create the political stability needed for economic development also would like to resolve this issue. Yet, the right formulas for achieving this end have not been identified and widely accepted. This conundrum led me to begin this project on re-thinking identity, citizenship, and social conflict in Africa.

Needless to say, the ideas and arguments contained in this book are my own, and I alone am totally responsible for any errors of fact or interpretation that might occur in the following pages. At the same time, my work has benefited greatly from my extensive field experiences and travels throughout Africa, particularly in Kenya, Ethiopia, Sudan, Tanzania, South Africa, Nigeria, and Uganda. Each step along the way, I encountered examples of why citizenship is so valued by the average citizen and why conflicts over this issue are at the root of so much political instability. My research has continued to force me to grapple with this issue.

I owe a great debt of gratitude to colleagues who are too numerous to count, but some deserve special words of thanks—those who especially encouraged me along the way or commented on earlier articulations of my ideas, including the late Don Rothchild, Edith Mukudi Omwami, Ruth Iyob, Crawford Young, Georges Nzongola-Ntalaja, Lahra Smith, Peter Little, Abubakar Momoh, Richard Ralston, Eghosa Osaghae, Kamal Sadiq, and Beth Elise Whitaker. A number of students were subject to my poorly formed ideas about this topic. They read my work and gave me comments, which I took very much to heart. Special thanks go out to Cynthia Ugwuibe, Benjamin Musuhukye, George Ofosu, and Sybille Nyeck. Aline Hankey was the research assistant who was with this project from beginning to end. I could not have come to this point without her constant input, feedback, and studious efforts to uncover the research sources used to put the work together. Other research assistants who helped immensely and deserve my deepest appreciation are Munga Julia Njeri, Elaine Blakeman, Denise Liu, and Annalisa Zox-Weaver.

Edmond J. Keller
Los Angeles, California
January 15, 2013

PART 1
Citizenship and Political Conflict in Contemporary Africa

1

Identity, Citizenship, and Nation Building in Africa

"Nigeria is not a nation. It is a mere geographical expression."
—Chief Obafemi Awolowo, *Path to Nigerian Freedom*

"We feel dissatisfied and unhappy when people tell us that we are not of this place. We have been here for over two hundred years. . . . We know no other place other than here . . . so we have nowhere else to go."
—Zangon-Kataf, Warri, Nigeria, Human Rights Watch interview, November 16, 2005

From their very inception as independent polities, African states have struggled to manage identity politics. Following the European Scramble for Africa that began in 1884–1885, colonial powers imposed their own artificial criteria to create states in Africa. Over less than a century, African peoples were grouped according to the rules of competing European powers that had formed their colonial African possessions and established effective control over them. As a matter of administrative convenience, the colonialists organized their African subjects according to assumed ethno-linguistic characteristics. Initially, they gave little—if any—thought to the notion of "independent" African states; however, this attitude began to change around the time of the Second World War and, by the mid-1960s, almost the entire African continent was again free of European rule. Rather than returning to their original forms of political organization, however, African societies found themselves facing the need to form viable multiethnic and multicultural nation-states comprised of "citizens" rather than mere "subjects." As they approached the challenge of nation building, African nationalist leaders aimed to create among what had until then been a multiplicity of parochial communities referred to as "tribes, a sense of "national" unity, transforming them so that they would now have primary attachment to the newly created multiethnic nation-states. A common phrase of that time was, "We must die as tribes and be born as a nation!" This effort proved to be a formidable challenge for the leaders of these newly independent states, and became the subject of intense scholarly discourse.

A common assumption of modernization theorists, as well as of third world political activists of that era (the 1960s), was that the process of modernization would lead inexorably to the breakdown—and the ultimate demise—of traditional institutions based upon communalism.[1] This process was often described as "national political integration" and involved downplaying social, cultural, and economic differences, and strengthening or fostering a sense of national unity—or a sense of unity within the context of diversity— among the inhabitants of a particular polity. The newly created, multiethnic or multicultural nation replaced parochial entities of conjugal or extended families—or the so-called tribe[2]—as the terminal community. The expectation among scholarly and policy analysts at the time was that nations would produce modern liberal institutions characterized by democracy and individualism. In short, some observers assumed that Western political institutions could simply be grafted onto African polities and that the transition to political modernization would be relatively smooth.[3] Moreover, there was a prevailing belief that, as a result of the combined weight of modernization and conscious national government policies of political integration, cultural diversity would give way to more homogenous national cultures.[4] Nonetheless, five decades later, in many parts of the developing world such assimilation has not completely happened. In fact, as Crawford Young asserts, the most recent wave of democratization in Africa has, in effect, ended the national integration project.[5] In other words, nation building is still a work in progress. As Craig Calhoun notes, "Neither nationalism nor ethnicity is vanishing as part of an obsolete traditional order; both are part of a modern set of categorical identities invoked by elites and other participants in political and social struggles."[6] In a similar vein, Benjamin Barber contends, "The planet is falling precipitously apart and coming reluctantly together at the very same moment."[7]

In many parts of the developing world, the challenge facing state and nation builders was to construct viable multiethnic or multinational states, or as some have suggested, "new nations." And, indeed, over time, the citizens of these new states have come to see themselves as "nations."[8] In many cases, nations with origins in nineteenth-century Europe emerged organically as collections of people who shared the same territory, language, history, and culture—or some combination of these factors—and felt the need to move to more complex and effective forms of sociopolitical organization.

The terms *state* and *nation* are often conflated, but in reality are quite different. Nations are based upon abstract normative attachments and are, in large measure, moral communities that in the mid- to late nineteenth century came to acquire legal definition and fixed geographic boundaries in the form of states.[9] In that sense, these nation-states were the product of a process of reform and modernization. By contrast, nation-states that formed after the end of colonialism in Africa have, in large measure, been the result of efforts to conservatively preserve the polities that were artificially constructed by European colonialists.[10] Notably, however, the concept of "nation" that took hold in Africa was not the same as the concept of "nation" that emerged in the creation of such entities in nineteenth-century Europe.

In Africa, even though deep parochial identities have been eroded, traditional values, institutions, and mores continue to exert considerable influence over various segments of social life. For example, even though national governments routinely seek to instill in the general population a sense of citizenship that transcends parochial identities and to organize political life accordingly, long-standing traditional identities—or even some newly invented identities that are treated as though they are from the ancient past—are often at odds with such objectives.[11] This reality presents particular problems in deeply divided societies, in which national governments attempt to minimize the perception among some religious, ethnic, or nationality groups that they have been and continue to be systematically discriminated against at the expense of other more favored groups.[12]

These dynamics must be understood in the context of how national identity has been defined in modern Africa, a process that has involved accepting both the legitimacy of the physical boundaries of the state and the legal command of state institutions of national governance.[13] Individuals and groups that occupy given territories are considered, and consider themselves, citizens with rights and obligations.[14] I shall return to this point later, but for the moment suffice it to note that much of the national civil conflict occurring in Africa today can be attributed to perceived grievances relating to citizenship rights.

We have reached a point at which understanding the politics of contemporary Africa requires that we rethink our original assumptions and reformulate our perceptions of the political transitions currently taking place on the continent. The quest for national political integration has been replaced by the need to create mostly multiethnic and multiracial societies in which all citizens and social groupings have equal citizenship rights—rights that are applied according to a nondiscriminatory rule of law. Jeffrey Herbst focuses on the emergence of a salient concept of citizenship in Africa as politically vital to the process of fixing colonial boundaries.[15] As colonialists established effective control up until the nationalist period, they changed the patterns and rhythm of population movements on the continent, which over time came to affect claims to citizenship in the resulting nation-states. However, until recently citizenship per se did not form the basis for sociopolitical conflict. Crawford Young and others correctly note that democratization has considerably raised the import of group identity within the context of multiethnic societies characterized by historic inequalities.[16] In a similar vein, Peter Geschiere argues: "Throughout the continent the new wave of democratization of the early 1990s seemed to bring initially a promising turn toward political liberalization. Yet in many countries it inspired in practice and quite unexpectedly especially determined attempts toward closure in order to exclude fellow-countrymen from their full rights as national citizens."[17]

Scholars have found that the sources of many domestic political conflicts in Africa today are rooted in ethnically based grievances among constituent groups. As mentioned, modern states on the continent are comprised of a multiplicity of ethno-linguistic groups that were gathered into particular states as a matter of administrative convenience, not by free will.[18] Ironically, these domestic conflicts are occurring at the very moment that African societies are attempting to liberalize and democratize their political systems to a greater extent than ever before. In some cases, these grievances and resulting conflicts relate to alleged irregularities in multiparty elections, or to the denial of citizenship rights of certain groups to vote or of some individuals to run for political office. In other cases, complaints relate to a rejection of or encroachment on the land claims of particular groups.[19] In still other cases, conflicts are rooted in historic injustices visited upon certain groups by a more dominant group that now controls the reins of state. In all such cases, we see the emergence of a more communitarian sense of citizenship. The question is: What qualifies an individual or group to claim land in particular areas? Or, rather, who has the right to claim legitimate inclusion in the postcolonial state or even a relevant subnational community?

Even though we can identify two analytically distinct bases of political identity in Africa today, these identities should not always be perceived as conflicting. In fact, these two notions of citizenship can and do coexist in time and space on a regular basis. Empirical evidence indicates that people accept that subnational citizenship and national citizenship identities are not inevitably at odds.[20] Employing *Afrobarometer* data, Robinson found that 70 percent of the respondents from sixteen Sub-Saharan countries viewed their national identity as more—or equally—important than their ethnic identities.[21] Data from the Values Survey Databank (VSD) clearly demonstrate this finding as well. VSD surveys in ten selected African countries between 1999 and 2001[22] showed that in cross-country comparisons consistently just over 95 percent of the respondents saw no conflict in being proud of both their national citizenship and their identity group. In other words, people can be proud of both their ethnic affiliation *and* their national citizenship. These findings indicate the need to rethink the assumption that the forces of modernization and globalization are undermining parochial loyalties. Similarly, in a 2003 survey in Ethiopia, Keller and Omwami[23] found that although respondents strongly identified with their own ethnic groups, they were supportive of the idea that all ethnic groups in the country have equal rights. In spite of strong ties to their own ethnic groups, they accepted that other groups deserve to have their citizenship rights respected and protected.

Although we cannot attribute all incidents of state-level civil conflict in modern Africa to any one particular origin, in many cases citizenship and its associated rights are clearly at the forefront. The complexity of this issue can be seen in all parts of Africa; however, the immediate stimuli and opportunities for conflict based on various aspects of citizenship rights, claims, and related grievances, in fact, vary from place to place. Given its diverse and complex nature, how are we to understand this phenomenon? What are the theoretical and substantive aspects of contemporary incidents of citizenship-based and identity-based political conflicts? History is replete with fraught claims to and conflicts over citizenship rights. What gives these incidents their character? It is assumed in these pages that we cannot understand such conflicts out of context. How citizenship is defined has changed over time and has varied from place to place. Moreover, the concept of "citizen" may look one way in theory and another way in practice. How do we understand this distinction?

The contemporary legal definition of citizenship is largely derived from the legacy of former colonial powers that governed particular territories.[24] All African states today have laws relating to citizenship and citizenship rights that are based largely on the legal codes of former colonial powers. But because disputes over citizenship rights often occur, these laws are in constant flux. Some of these disputes are local in nature but others, as we shall see, take on national relevance. Again, because it has legal command, the state can decide who is and is not eligible for citizenship. Today, it is not uncommon for those living in a particular country to be required to possess and to carry identity cards stating their birthplace. Not having a proper identity card may result in the loss of individual rights normally accorded to legitimate citizens.[25]

Although concerns around identity and citizenship in contemporary Africa are complex and varied, developing a framework for analysis of these issues will help us make sense of their growing importance on the continent. In some cases, ethnically based conflicts related to grievances grow out of electoral competition in national elections; others are triggered by long-standing claims relating to land ownership and other property rights; still other conflicts are linked to failure on the part of national or local governments to deliver public goods to ethnic communities in an equitable manner.

This study is grounded in the assumption that any attempt to make sense of these issues of identity and citizenship requires an understanding of three primary factors: (1) the context in which politics takes place; that is, the weight of history; (2) the institutions or structures that shape politics in particular circumstances; and (3) the perceptions and cultures of individuals and groups involved.[26]

The Context of Politics

All politics take place within the context of a particular political culture, whether we are speaking of national or subnational politics. To explain political change, one must understand not only the relevant context of political culture but also the structures that are found in that culture and the human agents that influence—and are influenced by—those particular structures. Relevant structures and human agents can be both domestic and international. At the same time, it is necessary to acknowledge that even with the necessary structures and agents present, political accelerators or precipitating events must be there to initiate change. Precipitating events may or may not be part of a formal political process, such as elections or other forms of political contestation. Ethnic communities can also be provoked to behave in certain ways by ethnic entrepreneurs who rhetorically link cultural grievances to a denial of the basic rights of their particular groups. Depending on the nature and context of the interaction among certain structures and human agents, change can be peaceful or hostile. For instance, in national elections, if minorities or opposition groups see the results as "free and fair," or at least not worth fighting over, then the likely direction of change will be peaceful; should this perception not be the case, political protest, and even violence, can be expected. (A full articulation of this analytical framework will be presented in chapter 3.)

Despite the differences in the political culture from one African state to the next, and despite the variability in precipitating events, at a very fundamental level we can identify relevant political agents, political institutions, and structures that shape and are shaped by actors interacting within a particular political culture. By tracing these relationships as they develop and change, we can better understand citizenship conflicts based on ethnic identity.

Roots of the Crises of Identity and Citizenship

Some critics suggest that state failure is at the heart of the crises of identity and citizenship that we find in Africa today. For example, Robert Bates ascribes African state failure in the late twentieth century to the fact that "rents" in the form of development assistance or proceeds from the sale of African resources began to dry up in the 1980s.[27] When this happened, he argues, many African leaders resorted to predation and abandonment of policies intended to spread the greatest good to the greatest number. Faced with states that could not or would not attempt to satisfy their demands, the African masses in such places could either accept their increasing poverty and misery—or turn to protest and violence. Bates draws a link between this turn of events and ethnic violence, arguing that the ethnic diversity found in African states does not cause violence but is, in fact, the result of state failure.[28]

In addition to facing the challenge of nation building, at independence, the leaders of African states became consumed with the idea of "development," a concept thought to have economic as well as social and political dimensions. As suggested, at the time of independence, outside observers, as well as African political elites, assumed that grafting institutions found in European democracies would be an easy thing to do, and that the challenges of economic development were the most formidable. However, a reasonable question to ask would be: How difficult a task would this transformation be, particularly given that the new states of Africa had not gone through the same or even similar processes of socioeconomic development as had the countries of the North that they sought to emulate? Some argued that this effort would be difficult because colonialism had not really ended but had simply morphed into "neo-colonialism."[29] Though they had withdrawn politically, former European colonial powers continued to control Africa via multinational corporations and their own forms of "remote control."[30] Moreover, rather than adopting bureaucratic structures similar to those characterizing Northern states at the time, the institutions borrowed only some of the structural characteristics, while continuing to be influenced by the patrimonial systems similar to those that were a part of traditional societies. The tendency was for African leaders to institute systems of personal rule that patrimonialized the states left to them by the colonialists;[31] in the process, official corruption became a "coin of the realm." This trend had a profound effect not only on economic development, but also on sociopolitical development. As such, any effort to understand the origins of Africa's ongoing crises of identity and citizenship must consider the weight of this history.

Colonialism, Neopatrimonialism, and State Failure

Despite the fact that the departing European powers left administrative institutions in place in their former colonies, these institutions were quickly refashioned so that rather than operating by formal-legal bureaucratic principles, they functioned on the basis of the personal wishes of the elites controlling government. In other words, the bureaucratic forms left at the end of colonialism were injected with an expanded and restrictive form of patron-clientelism, thus undermining Western-style democracy in most independent states. For example, democratic, multiparty systems—where they remained—were transformed into de jure or de facto single-party systems; in other places, military regimes replaced competitive party systems. In either case, democracy gave way to autocratic rule.

By the mid-1980s, 60 percent of Africa's fifty independent states had fallen under military rule; among the remaining civilian regimes, only seven had competitive party systems (Botswana, Gambia, Mauritius, Senegal, Swaziland, Namibia, and Zimbabwe). Even where civilian regimes existed, national elections tended not to present voters with clear policy choices, but merely served to present the illusion of democracy. Denial of basic citizenship rights and human rights became common, as these new governments often operated as though their sovereignty provided them with the legitimacy they needed to rule in ways that were most beneficial to them personally.

In the context of few political and economic resources for securing legitimacy, the African state had the tendency—no matter what its ideology—to preoccupy itself with the struggle to establish security, control, and autonomy.

This situation gave rise to intense struggles among various segments of society to control and exploit the offices of the state. Graft and corruption became part and parcel of everyday political life at all levels. At the same time, because the most developed sociopolitical intuitions at the time were based on communal affinities, politics followed suit, and party politics became tinged with ethnic loyalties.

Beginning in the mid to late 1980s, poverty, underdevelopment, economic dependence, ethnic and class conflict, lack of political practices prioritizing equal citizenship rights, and fragile political and economic institutions all came to be structural handicaps from the legacy of European colonialism. Colonialism was not the source of *all* of Africa's problems, but it was a significant contributor. What has to be borne in mind is that despite the negative legacies of colonialism, human agents—namely African political leaders—must also be understood as having contributed to contemporary problems through bad choices they willingly or unwittingly made; factoring in what some have called "the revolution of rising expectations"[32] among the African masses, the result is a recipe for postcolonial state failure and ethnic conflict. Because the concept of "national citizenship" had to be developed through the nation-building effort, subnational affinities became the most common way for members of the African populace to define their identities.

Whereas Western societies had taken hundreds of years to move from autocracy to more democratic forms of governance and equitable safety nets for their populations, newly independent African state governments abruptly faced demands by their populaces to improve their life circumstances. Western societies, by this time, had benefited from passing through periods of political liberalism and the industrial revolution, with states becoming stronger relative to other interests in society, including those of the growing capitalist classes. These states had figured out ways to regulate and reign in the excesses of capitalist development in order to protect the interests of workers and the poor.[33] They imposed taxes and regulations on industrial and commercial enterprises and used the income the state derived from this effort to strengthen themselves, while implementing welfare systems to provide social safety nets for the population at large. Also, Western societies—having passed through the industrial revolution—gave their state leaders a firm basis on which to build democratic political institutions. Michael Lofchie has noted that in the earliest days of independence, African leaders did not have the option of gradually introducing liberal democracy or returning to traditional forms of governance.[34] Also, they could not import and impose the same types of technological capacities that had grown out of the industrial revolution in the West and apply them wholesale to their own countries. Instead, they confronted what they saw as the need to rapidly catch up with the West. They seemed to feel that the realities of the existing political environment, fueled by the development of ethnically based neopatrimonialism, would not allow them to go through the same developmental processes, at the same deliberate pace, as had the West. Even though independent African states had neither the revenue sources nor the technological capacity of Western states, when they first began to take form, African states were expected to perform welfare functions to satisfy expectations by the general population that independence would usher in a new era of equitably based prosperity, particularly for their own groups.

Unable to cope with these demands, new states began to drift away from democracy and social equity, toward autocracy and neopatrimonialism that most benefited their own groups. Authoritarian regimes between 1960 and the mid-1980s closely controlled politics, ostensibly in the name of national unity. Although some observers saw these developments as a real tragedy, others looked on the bright side, contending that because Africa had drifted toward chaos and possible collapse, some form of political stability was necessary for sustainable development to be realized. Instead of democracy, they suggested, in the short term Africa most needed "developmental dictatorships" that prioritized economic growth above all else; genuine liberal democracy would be suitable for some time in the future.[35] Robert Bates has argued that the primary objective of many African leaders at this time was to maintain a steady flow of rents for themselves and their most loyal supporters. In the process, others in society, although they could not rely on the national governments for much, were spared the state's predation.[36]

Today in Africa, politics at all levels have become more like business. Political power is widely understood as a vehicle to economic power, and political resources tend to be reduced to economic ones. Politicians and nonpoliticians alike recognize this reality, and many common citizens accept this situation, tending to believe that resources distributed by those they vote into power will be used to help themselves personally, and their group more generally. The identity that seems to matter most is attachment to one's ethnic community.[37] Under such circumstances, political power is sought not just for its own sake, but also for the material advantage it promises.

Elected political officials have come to view state resources as their own personal resources, to be distributed to satisfy their own personal needs. Richard Joseph, for example, identifies what he terms "prebendalism" at the center of Nigeria's national politics, as those in power saw political office as a means through which to satisfy the demands of their most important constituents.[38] The original meaning of *prebend* refers to offices of feudal states that could be obtained in recognition of services rendered to a noble person, or through outright purchase, which could then used to generate income for the holders of such offices. This system existed in imperial Ethiopia, but Joseph claims that the same principle applies to the way politics worked in Nigeria's Second Republic. Offices of the state would be competed for and then used to the personal benefit of officeholders and their supporters. This arrangement would ordinarily not be seen as a problem if office holders did not discriminate on the basis of the group identity of their regions or individual constituents. However, when they appeared to be making decisions on how to distribute the resources at their disposal almost exclusively on the basis of ethno-regional identities instead of the common good, this partiality caused groups that were left out to become discontent. Others have described a situation in which Nigerian citizens cast their votes in elections in terms of potential opportunities to get their own share of the "national cake."[39] In sum, ethnic citizenship and conflicts over citizenship rights tend to coexist with an emerging sense of national citizenship in Africa today. While these two conceptions are not always at odds, in many cases of conflict over citizenship rights they are; in other situations, ethnic tensions are heightened as a result of historic ethnic claims to land and power.

Organization of the Book

The major part of this book attempts to apply this modest analytical framework to five cases: Nigeria, Ethiopia, Côte d'Ivoire, Kenya, and Rwanda. At least in part, each of these cases represents some aspects of exclusionary nationalism or citizenship based on "indigeneity." Following this general introduction, the book is divided into two main parts with a final concluding chapter. Part I traces the evolution of the concept of citizenship in present-day Africa from a theoretical and a legal perspective. This section consists of two chapters. The first substantive chapter, chapter 2, considers the theoretical and legal dimensions of the concept of citizenship, and demonstrates how current conceptualizations of this phenomenon in Africa are similar to, or different from, classical theories of citizenship. The chapter goes on to briefly consider the various ways in which African states established the legal basis for national citizenship, the different ways in which average African citizens understand what it means to be a citizen of a particular polity, and how their understanding relates to other individuals and groups in society. Chapter 3 spells out a new framework for analysis of the relationship between the state and citizenship and the differential basis of citizenship-based conflicts. Though mixed, the methodology used for this study is mainly comprised of ethnography and a variant of social process tracing. Part II is made up of five chapters, chapters 4 to 8. These chapters focus on the five case studies, Nigeria, Ethiopia, Côte d'Ivoire, Kenya, and Rwanda, and represent the different ways in which citizenship and identity conflicts outside formal political institutions manifest themselves in Africa today. In this study, a modest analytical framework is utilized in considering the case studies.

Nigeria's *Federal Character Principle* has meant that, since independence, in order to access certain social services and other rights of citizenship, individuals have had to prove that their ancestral village was within the particular jurisdiction in which they made the claim to their rights and privileges. In some cases, the immigration of groups from one Nigerian state and subnational jurisdiction has led to conflict over land and access to certain social services. Migrants in states that border on the north or the south of the country are regularly seen as aliens, and thus without claim to citizenship rights in their new area of residence. Recently, this prejudice has been conflated with religion, and conflicts have emerged between Christians and Muslims.

Notably, since introducing the Federal Character Principle in the late 1960s, Nigeria has been actively pursuing an affirmative action policy to address the historically based grievances of ethnic groups. Indeed, institutions have been created for this express purpose. However, this effort is fraught with problems, ranging from the low capacity of administrative agencies assigned to implement these policies to official and unofficial corruption.

Like Nigeria, Ethiopia since 1991 has been a state based on the principles of federalism; however, it is unusual for a nation-state to be explicitly organized around the concept of "ethnic federalism." There are nine federal states, six of which are organized on the basis of the culture of the region's dominant ethnic or nationality group. The other three federal states are multiethnic. The 1994 constitution states: "Any woman or man, either of whose parents is an Ethiopian citizen, shall be an Ethiopian citizen."[40] There is a provision for naturalization, but the constitution is not specific about a beginning date for establishing the indigeneity of persons residing in the country and not considered by the state to be foreigners.

Modern Ethiopia was founded during the process of imperial state building, beginning roughly around 1885. The empire state was constructed through conquest and was comprised of a multiplicity of nationality groups, but was politically dominated by the Amhara. The process of nation building did not begin until the reign of Emperor Haile Selassie I, following the Second World War. The emperor's approach was top down: he simply declared that all of his subjects were part of the "Ethiopia family." Throughout Haile Selassie's forty-four-year rule, various nationalities continued to cling to their own indigenous cultures and to express their objection to being included in the Ethiopian state. To some extent, this discontent sowed the seeds for the collapse of the empire, which ended in a military coup d'état in 1974.[41] Realizing that the nation-building process was incomplete, the military junta declared its commitment to Marxism-Leninism and scientific socialism. Ethnic identity was declared antirevolutionary and was replaced with various cross-ethnic social classes; however, popular frustration about exclusion and marginalization on the part of nondominant groups endured. A civil war ensued, and the regime was again transformed in 1991, when the Marxist-Leninist regime was swept away.[42] The new regime, headed by an umbrella political movement, the Ethiopian Peoples' Revolutionary Democratic Front (EPRDF), declared its intentions to rectify the state-building failures of the past and to celebrate the country's ethnic diversity rather than attempt to crush it. Since that time, struggles over citizenship and identity in Ethiopia have not waned.

In contrast to Nigeria, Ethiopia has no specific national policy of affirmative action, but rather leaves such matters to the states. The constitution gives the states the right to self-determination up to and including secession. By most accounts, the experiment in ethnic federalism has been a failure. The question is, *why?*

During processes of political change, conflict can occur at all levels of a community. From the beginning of the postcolonial period, Côte d'Ivoire has seen conflicts over citizenship relating to rights to land in certain parts of the country. As in Nigeria, the situation in Côte d'Ivoire eventually led to a definition of citizenship based on autochthony, or the ancestral birthplace of the families of individuals. This arrangement later involved questions relating to the actual ancestral village of presidential candidates, based on whether it was inside or outside the country. Further complexity thus led to interregional conflict that conflated with religious conflict and lasted for almost a decade (2002–2011).

The case of Kenya illustrates how citizenship claims have entered into the realm of party politics, resulting in intense social conflicts. The most recent interethnic conflicts that have taken on national proportions in Kenya grew out of grievances among different groups about electoral rigging. These precipitating events compounded frustrations related to historic disputes over immigration, land, and property rights. The conflicts themselves were instigated by cultural brokers and ethnic entrepreneurs bent on power, or by those who felt they had been the victims of vote rigging and other electoral violations in the 2007 national elections. These events occurred after more than a decade of pressure from civil society and formal political parties to transform Kenya from a one-party system to a multiparty democracy. When conflict relating to the elections broke out, long-standing tensions over immigration and land ownership, particularly in the Rift Valley, erupted. Yet again, immigrants were accused of being alien—"strangers"—and thus were fair game for ethnic cleansing by groups who claimed the Rift Valley as their ancestral home.

Although the two major groups in Rwanda, the Tutsi (14 percent) and Hutu (85 percent) account for 99 percent of the population and historically belonged to the same ethnic group, colonialists had manufactured a racial distinction between the two groups. During the struggle for independence, the Hutu simultaneously engaged in a revolution against the Tutsi monarchy and, through democratic elections, came to dominate politics in the country. More than 100,000 Tutsi were driven from Rwanda, and those remaining were not accorded full citizenship rights. When the second wave of democratization began to spread over Africa in the late 1980s and early 1990s, exiled Tutsis, particularly in Uganda, decided to fight their way back into Rwanda to reclaim their birthrights. In large measure, then, the Rwandan civil war in the early 1990s was a clear attempt by the Tutsis not only to return to their country of origin but also to claim full citizenship rights in the process.

The final section of the book offers a summary and discussion of the implications of the argument and findings for Africa in general. Special emphasis is placed on the importance of good governance, democracy, and the rule of law for creating an enabling environment for the consolidation of citizenship rights in Africa today. As rules governing identity, citizenship, and group relations become more institutionalized and firmly established, it is reasonable to expect that citizenship rights will be applied and upheld in a more equitable manner. However, for now, these issues are in their earliest stages of being worked out. Any high expectations that nation building in the former colonial states of Africa would be a relatively smooth process have been proven to be far from the case. In fact, throughout the continent, nation building continues to be very much a "work in progress." Richard Sklar has noted that in Africa democracy is everywhere under construction and everywhere in doubt.[43] This is also true of the nation-building project on the continent.

2

Theoretical and Formal-Legal Dimensions of the Concept of Citizenship in Africa

"The construction of 'nationhood' therefore implies a constant redefinition of who is part of the political community, and who is not. On the legal level, processes of inclusion and exclusion rely on two basic regulative mechanisms, nationality and citizenship."
—Bachmann, Staerklé, and Doise, *Re-Inventing Citizenship in South Caucasus*

"Are you a Mumbala or a Mupende?"
—Angry policeman (Zaire 1962) quoted in Young, *The Politics of Cultural Pluralism*

The concept of citizenship can be traced back to Western philosophers such as Aristotle, Machiavelli, Locke, and Rousseau, but over time this idea has acquired different meanings that have been deemed appropriate to particular times and places.[1] As a consequence, citizenship has always been a contested concept. Before I proceed with a discussion of the idea of citizenship in present-day Africa, I will examine the origins of this concept and how it has changed and adapted over time. Although there is no organic connection between the concept as it was first articulated in the ancient Greek city-state of Athens and the way it is understood today, there is no doubt that later conceptualization of citizenship and its role in politics and governance throughout the world have had a lasting influence.

Western Origins of the Concept of Citizenship

Aristotle held that human beings are political animals and that to acquire the status of "citizen" is to be designated a responsible member of a political community, or *polis*.[2] In Aristotle's time, the "citizen" was a "free man" who held the right to participate with others in his class in political and judicial affairs. Originally, the concept of the citizen referred to leaders of city-states in ancient Greece and to their responsibility to make political decisions on behalf of the community. Importantly, emphasis was on the responsibilities of a small number of community members to virtuously represent the best interests of the polis. Members of the community itself, except for the leaders of the polis, were not sovereign. In that sense, although it espoused self-rule, this system was an elitist, republican form of citizenship. Not all members of the community were accorded the opportunity to participate in the leadership of the polis: women, children, individuals foreign to the community, some laborers, and slaves were denied the possibility of ever being citizens. Responsibilities of citizens in ancient Greece included eligibility for public office, voting in the assembly of citizens, military service, and the ability to participate in all aspects of a binding legal system.

The idea of liberal citizenship first surfaced during the Roman Empire, a period in which the liberal tradition was born. Property ownership, particularly land ownership, became a factor that determined the status of the citizen. The more land one owned, the higher his status. The Romans, in other words, created social ranking based upon property ownership, and they enacted laws to protect the property of individual citizens.

What distinguishes the liberal tradition from the ancient republican notion of citizenship is an emphasis on the *rights* of citizens as opposed to their virtues, and the negation of a political community that is separate from the rest of the community. By law, all people considered to be legitimate members of the community were now citizens. In order to exercise their full citizenship rights, individuals had to participate in civic affairs, including voicing their opinions as to who should govern and what public policies should be followed by those whom they supported for office. In this way, individuals distinguished themselves as true citizens rather than as mere subjects. This system did not mean that citizens had to participate directly in deliberations and decision making, only that they had the right to vote to delegate their representation in such matters. Foundations such as constitutions were introduced in order to protect individual rights, and to guard against the excesses of those who govern.

Over time, the concept of citizenship was broadened, assuming a liberal cast. In the process, it came to mean any constitutionally legitimate member of the community who had rights, privileges, and obligations to that community. Citizens were still expected to maintain a civic ethos, but were no longer an exclusive, small group of "men" chosen by their peers. Beginning with the ideas about citizenship expressed by John Locke in the seventeenth century, notions of the collective sovereignty of all members of the political community began to predominate. Citizens became defined by laws and were protected by constitutions that enshrined the notion of equality for all citizens before the law.

Perhaps the most important historical foundation for a liberal citizenship rooted in a republican form of government can be traced back to the French Revolution (1788–1789) and to the political philosophy of Jean-Jacques Rousseau.[3] This period firmly established the collective sovereignty of all who were considered part of the French nation, broadly conceived. The impetus for the French Revolution was economic crisis and widespread discontent over the system of governance in France, which at the time was ruled by a monarchy and its aristocratic supporters. Rogers Brubaker argues that the French Revolution invented not only the nation-state but also the modern institution and ideology of national citizenship.[4] The French state and French identity had been constructed over a long period of time, but society was governed by two classes ("Estates"), the nobility and the clergy; everyone else was considered nothing more than subjects. Rather than being based on social equality, then, citizenship was based on legal inequality. Theoretically, all French people had rights before the law, but these rights were in fact stratified according to the location of their group in the hierarchy of privilege. Foreigners had no guaranteed rights and, most importantly, could neither inherit nor bequeath property. However, by the late eighteenth century the laws had gradually changed so that individuals who previously had been automatically considered foreigners could become naturalized French citizens.

The French Revolution called for a sweeping away of the privileged classes and a leveling for the equality of all—the invention of one equal class of "citizens." In other words, the "Third Estate" was to go along with the First and Second Estates, the nobility and the clergy. Moreover, this new estate was declared sovereign and could thus make rules and decisions on behalf of the entire community. Citizenship, then, was thought to be based on the common rights and obligations of the residents of the nation, thus excluding those considered aliens.

France had been in turmoil for more than thirty years when the final push of the French Revolution began in 1788. In April of that year, food riots took place in Paris, and a month later the Estates General, an assembly of all citizens, convened for the first time since 1614. In June, the Estates General declared itself the National Assembly. In late August, the Assembly issued the Declaration of the Rights of Man, which lay out the principles and ideals of the Revolution. Among its pronouncements were the complete destruction of absolutist privilege and the declaration of a new republican regime. Furthermore, it asserted the inalienable rights of liberty and equality for all citizens in clear and forceful language. The result was an expansive view of citizenship. However, within a short time even those who had led the Revolution began to parse the idea of citizenship to narrow its meaning without completely returning to the old notions of privilege. For example, even as the Revolution was in its most intense phase, Abbé Sieyès, one of the main theorists of the Revolution, delivered a report to the National Assembly in July 1789, proposing a twofold distinction between citizens: active and passive citizens and active and passive rights.[5] All citizens should have passive rights that were inalienable and universal; however, not all citizens should have the right to play an active role in the formation of governance institutions. Active citizens were claimed by Sieyès to be the true "stakeholders" (*actionnaires*).[6] This view of citizenship characteristics was adopted by the National Assembly and enshrined in the Declaration of Man and Citizen (1789), but was excluded from the constitution of 1792 in favor of a more inclusive sense of citizenship.[7]

At a very fundamental level, the concept of citizenship has withstood the test of time. Today, at its very essence, particularly in democracies, citizenship simply defines who is and is not a member of a particular community. Moreover, it is a regime of rights, obligations, and privileges accorded to individuals in a community. In its original formulation, the designation of citizen afforded the individual the right to participate in deliberations over the rules governing society and in the exercise of the power to implement and enforce those rules.[8] Also, citizens were accorded certain rights and privileges within the community. Today, all of these duties, rights, and privileges tend to extend across the particular polity as long as groups and individuals are deemed legitimate members of the community.

T. S. Marshall identifies three basic elements of citizenship: (1) the civil element, (2) the political element, and (3) the social element.[9] The civil element relates to the individual's right to freedoms and to the protection of those freedoms according to a particular rule of law. The political element involves the rights that individuals have to participate in the exercise of power. In modern times, participation is usually not direct, but rather tends to be through designated or elected representatives. In the process, individuals are supposed to willingly accept membership and all that it entails in the community, and to accord it their loyalty. Beyond that expectation, every member of the community is due the respect of every other member on an equal basis. In other words, because of the social element, individuals have the right to a prevailing quality of life and to the full enjoyment of the culture of their community.

The Emergence of National Citizenship and the Persistence of Subnational Citizenship in Africa

In most of colonial Africa—even after the partition of the continent among European powers—Africans could not claim to be "citizens" of particular colonies. (Exceptions to this rule could be found in French Africa after 1946 and in Lusophone Africa beginning in 1961.)[10] Instead, they were considered "natives" or subjects distinct from Europeans who were the citizens of the colonizing metropolitan country.[11]

Sovereignty of European colonial possessions was, by definition, denied.[12] The indigenous peoples of Africa did not attain citizenship in a nation-state until the end of colonialism, at which time Africans residing in a particular former colony theoretically became its citizens.[13] Up until then, all but the African chiefs and African nobility through whom the Europeans ruled were merely "subjects." Even then, local elites were still the subjects of their metropolitan rulers. In the case of imperial Ethiopia, which took on the role of an internal colonialist around the beginning of the European colonial presence in Africa, not until the drafting of the 1974 constitution did the concept of citizen for most of the population become relevant.[14]

Mahmood Mamdani makes this point eloquently in his path-breaking book, *Citizen and Subject: Contemporary Africa and the Legacy of Late Colonialism,* in which he traces the origins of ethnic identity in colonial Africa, then weaves this thread into the contemporary problem of citizenship on the continent. He analyzes two related phenomena: how power is organized, and how it tends to fragment resistance in modern Africa. Colonialism is said to have divided African societies on the basis of ethnic categories and to have superimposed "nonnatives" on top of the indigenous people they found in a particular territory. Ethnicities were demarcated horizontally and governed by customary laws. Each ethnic group had its own distinct customary laws. Under colonialism, indigenous Africans did not have citizenship rights or obligations; they were subjects. Therefore, they could not be a part of civil society.

The colonialists organized their rule in Africa to buttress the policy objective of keeping indigenous people of the colonies separate and under political control. Mamdani meticulously exposes the myth of indirect rule, revealing it as a common approach to colonial rule no matter who was the colonial ruler. The colonialists usually created chiefs who interpreted and applied customary laws in an arbitrary and capricious manner. In South Africa, because they were categorized above indigenous Africans, whites were accorded citizenship status even during the colonial period. This categorization was the reality until the Apartheid Regime ended in the early 1990s.

Mamdani argues that the colonial politicization of indigeneity was the greatest crime of colonialism.[15] Politicized ethnicity is the source of much of the sociopolitical conflict we find in Africa today. Though conflicts generally manifest around issues of elections and land, they are at their core about citizenship and citizenship rights. To a large extent, this phenomenon can be traced back to the decision by European colonizers to divide the indigenous population based on their *assumed* ethno-linguistic affinities; therefore, during the colonial era a widespread sense of individual identity with the nation-state never developed. In fact, parochial loyalties among Africans were cultivated and thereby deepened. When independence arrived and the need arose for Africans to organize for political contestation at the national level, the tendency was toward the expanded politization of the "ethnic community." This response has had a long-lasting impact on contemporary African politics; in popular discourse relating to political matters, citizenship rights tend to be defined in group terms rather than individual terms, with identities being exclusionary rather than inclusionary.[16] Moreover, in part because states are seen as the providers of public goods, over time groups as well as individuals have readily accepted their citizenship within the nation-state.[17] Secessionist movements in modern Africa have been rare, and when they have occurred have usually been based on a desire among aggrieved groups to separate regions that were carved out during the colonial period (for example, Somalis in Ethiopia; ethnic groups in Kivu and Katanga, DRC; Biafra in Nigeria) from the multiethnic state.[18] Evidence suggests that in most cases when ethnic groups become mobilized around group grievances and direct their protests toward the state, they tend to demand equal citizenship rights rather than separation.

Whereas in the West the tendency has become to equate citizenship identities with the individual, in many parts of Africa it is common to base such rights and expectations on the group or ethnic community. At the national level, in accordance with the liberal tradition, political discourse suggests that all individuals in all ethnic groups are citizens in the nation-state, with equal rights, privileges, and obligations in all parts of the country; but at the level of the ethnic community, depending on the circumstances and the stakes involved, parochial identities and assumed rights often trump liberal identification with the nation-state. The saliency of two sets of citizenship identities, two publics, one at the national and the other at the subnational level, is an important artifact of African politics today.[19]

It is important to stress that in Africa, as elsewhere, individuals have multiple identities that are mostly socially constructed and not always politically salient. Such identities are fluid, intermittent, and largely dependent upon situations. An identity may or may not be politically important to a person or group, depending on the circumstances in which the individual or group finds itself at any given time.[20] Despite this reality, in identifying with their own group or by distinguishing their group from other groups, individuals often treat this type of identity as though it were "fixed," primordial, and unchanging.

A good illustration of the dual nature of politically significant group identities is offered by Steven Ndegwa, who builds on the work of scholars such as Peter Ekeh and Richard Sklar.[21] Ndegwa identifies the basis for sociopolitical conflict in Kenya in the first two and a half decades of independence, but his work has relevance to the larger study of the relationship between ethnicity and citizenship in Africa. Liberal citizenship rests on formal-legal bases; but in traditional ethnic groups, citizenship was based on custom and cultural practice. Even though it can be exaggerated, tradition is often invoked when certain groups attempt to claim their citizenship rights. Along these lines, Bayart argues that "the demand for, and if necessary, the fabrication of, authenticity are dear to culturalists, who claim to preserve the original purity of their identity from external pollution and the aggressions of the 'Other' by reconstituting, in an authoritarian manner, 'their' culture, at the end of a regressive process."[22] For good historical examples of this attitude, one need only hearken back to the "authenticity" movement under the Mobutu regime in Zaire or, more recently, to the *Ivorité* movement in Côte d'Ivoire.

Despite its recent and artificial nature, politicized ethnic identity that is regarded as equal to one's citizenship identity is instrumental in shaping individual interests and actions in modern Kenya, and elsewhere in Africa. A claim to the existence of ethnic citizenship must rest on evidence of identity, authority, and legitimacy for members of an ethnic group. In other words, individuals must at least theoretically, and sometimes legally, be able to establish that they have roots in that particular national—and sometimes local—community. Essentially the difference between ethnic and nation-state citizenship lies in the Weberian legal, rational, and bureaucratic frameworks that uphold identity, legitimacy, and authority in the nation-state, as opposed to the social customs, social practices, and nonbureaucratic structures that define and uphold citizenship in ethnic groups.[23] Ethnic identity rests on a socially—as opposed to a legally—constructed definition of belonging.

In postcolonial Kenya, the socially enacted relationship among ethnic identity, authority, and legitimacy competes with the legally sanctioned membership, authority, and legitimacy of the nation-state.[24] Because neither entity has been able to erase the other, most individuals assume contingent and hierarchical allegiance depending on the area of competition in which they find themselves. The situation often determines the repertoire chosen for action by individuals within the context of their own ethnic group.

According to what has become a widely accepted view in Africa, liberal citizenship qualifies one to participate in her or his national community. As we shall see in the next section, citizenship is legally defined as membership in a nation-state. In the ethnic community, citizenship can best be described as illiberal and republican. That is, everyone in the community is considered equal according to custom and tradition, but he or she agrees to a system of governance characterized by the representation of identifiable segments of the community by delegates. This approach is quite in keeping with African traditions in all parts of Africa. For example, in most African traditions elders or certain age grades were expected to perform certain governance functions.

The idea of belonging to a significant traditional authority system is referred to by Ndegwa as *civic republican citizenship*. Liberalism, by contrast, is centered on the individual. At the same time that an individual centers himself on the parochial unity of his own ethnic group, because of the equality across groups implied in the notion of national citizenship, he cannot legitimately claim rights that would infringe on any other groups' rights.[25]

The illiberal, republican citizenship prescribed by allegiance to one's ethnic group has the potential to undermine the liberal citizenship assumed in the national community in two ways. First, the rights of the individual in the national community can be, given the right circumstances, at least in the eyes of the individual, subordinated to those of the ethnic community. Second, even as they act in the national arena, individuals are free to form and revise their aims and ambitions within their experiential life in parochial communities. For example, among the Maasai and Kalenjin of Kenya's Rift Valley, a significant number of indigenous people who live there feel that land that is rightfully theirs was alienated from them by force and duplicity during the colonial era, and that the current African regime perpetuates, rather than resolves, this situation.[26]

Even though we can identify two analytically distinct bases of political identity in Africa today, it is important to note that these identities should not always be perceived as in conflict. In fact, these two notions of citizenship can and do coexist in time and space on a regular basis. Empirical evidence supports the nonviolent coexistence of subnational citizenship and national citizenship identities.[27] In other words, people can be proud of their ethnic affiliation while being proud of their national citizenship.

Since the independence of many African countries, the issue of indigeneity has fueled conflicts over citizenship in one form or another.[28] It is under such circumstances that we can clearly see the different levels—and contingent nature—of citizenship on the continent. In some places, communal identity is described as "indigeneity" or "indigenous"; in other places, most notably in Francophone Africa, one may see a veritable claim to rights by groups in a particular area of their country based on their "autochthony."[29] In either case, such individuals are asserting that they, in a primordial sense, "belong to the soil," their place of origin. In its strictest form, autochthony links the group or individual to the place it claims as the origination of its ancestry. Such cases are thought to represent virtually irrefutable and primordial rights to membership in a community, conveying not only obligations to the community but also rights. A less strict form of indigenous identity might involve claims of primordial attachment to the place in which they themselves were born. In this work, when discussing the basis for claims of "indigeneity" or "autochthony" or "indigenous," I base my analysis on the context of the particular national or local community. Because *autochthony* is the most commonly used term, I employ it in my analysis of Francophone countries.

According to Bambi Ceuppens and Peter Geschiere, the concept of autochthony can be traced to classical Greek history; however, it was first introduced to Africa during the period of French colonialism in West Africa and the Soudan (the present-day Sahel region of Africa) in the nineteenth century. At the time, the concept of autochthony was used as a mechanism for categorizing Africans who inhabited those regions into manageable groups for administrative purposes. In this way, the colonialists could monitor the movement of their subjects both inside and outside of their territories of residence.[30]

As it is used in popular discourse in Africa, autochthony is often contested and means different things to different people. It originated from a Greek term that literally means "from the soil itself."[31] Today, on the one hand, it could mean having "arrived first"; on the other hand, it could signify having "arrived second."[32] Thus, Jackson characterizes autochthony as a "slippery" concept. The myth surrounding the notion of the autochthony of a group is based primarily in tradition and custom, but as we shall see, a sense of national belonging has come to be determined, in most cases, by law. Therefore, the question is: When was the nation actually formed (the exact date)? Despite this application, it is useful to attempt—for analytical purposes—to categorize the predominant meanings of autochthony or indigeneity that prevail in Africa today. Three meanings stand out: autochthony based on ethnicity, autochthony based on a group's claim to being represented in a nation-state when it was first formed, and the autochthony of national public figures. It is important to note that in many cases, the constitutional definition of citizenship is not clear as to the relationship of citizenship identity and the date of the exact founding of the nation-state.

Autochthony Based on Ethnic Identity

As suggested, one's social identity is fluid, intermittent, and experiential. At the same time, it is important to keep in mind that there are generally two forms of citizenship that regularly exist in the consciousness of African people in their daily lives: a form of communitarian citizenship and a form based on residence in a national community largely created as a by-product of colonialism. These forms of identity need not be in competition with one another—but they can be.

At the time of independence, the leaders of most multiethnic nation-states in Africa felt the need to engage in nation-building projects. To a large extent, these projects remain incomplete to this day. In fact, they may never be completed because of the tension that arises out of the "two publics" in Africa. Geschiere has noted that in such circumstances autochthony can be a threat to national citizenship and to the idea of a democratic society based upon freedom, justice, and equality for all individuals.[33] This threat is realized when communal groups emphasize their exclusive right to belong to their subnational communities to the exclusion of those whom they consider "strangers." This dynamic has implications for the free involvement of so-called strangers in local politics and in their access to whatever social services are controlled by the local authorities. Locals may surmise that "only autochthonous groups belong in this place; strangers only have citizenship rights in their place of origin." In some cases, even when a national constitution and public rhetoric itself proclaim the rights of all members of a nation to protection by law, in practice this right might not be accorded. The assertion of exclusive citizenship rights in a local community may be articulated from within, or could be pushed by ethnic entrepreneurs in opposition at the national level—or by an incumbent regime.

Take the case of Cameroon. At independence in 1960, President Ahmadou Babatoura Ahidjo emphasized nation building, and this aim became a normal part of the national political discourse. However, in the early 1990s, this attitude began to change, perhaps in part because of the double pressure of intense economic crisis that characterizes the newest age of globalization and of internal and external pressures on President Paul Biya's regime to democratize. These developments triggered a series of changes that led to a rise in tensions between national and subnational citizenships.

Even as many counties in Africa were democratically opening up their political systems, President Biya resisted and, in order to shore up his personal rule, began to actively play the autochthony card. Geschiere and Francis B. Nyamnjoh argue that Biya capitalized on a growing fear among residents of Southwest Province and the city of Douala of being swamped by increasing immigration from other parts of the country.[34] They trace a particular conflict over the exercise of voting rights by groups thought to be alien to the region. In the 1996 municipal elections in Douala, amid economic instability, the indigenous population of the city was outvoted by immigrants from the Northwest and West Province (Bamenda and Bamileke). After these elections, Biya's government is known to have encouraged and supported large and violent protests on the part of those who considered the city to be their domain. Biya fueled these flames by pointing out that the rights of minorities were guaranteed in the 1996 constitution, and that the people should protect them. Slogans such as "Immigrants do not belong here and they should go to their home regions in order to vote" were common.[35]

Similar examples could be found in Nigeria, Kenya, and the Democratic Republic of Congo, where groups have either claimed their own autochthony to a region or have denied the autochthony of groups they considered strangers.

In many places on the continent, conflicts based on autochthony or ethnicity are often couched in terms of land rights.[36] Georges Nzongola-Ntalaja, for example, notes: "Given the fact that for the most part land was held in common for all members of the community, and was not a commodity for private appropriation . . . only indigenes could be considered rightful heirs to this property. This is why across the continent, groups identified as strangers or settlers may live in an area for over one hundred years and still be considered as having no legitimate rights in the land they occupy."[37]

In traditional society, then, attachment to one's community was traced through the soil of ancestors. During the colonial period, the colonial regime either compromised traditional systems of land rights by making all land the property of the authority (e.g., the Crown in Kenya) or it influenced indigenous authorities to deal with land issues in a manner favored by the colonial regime (e.g., Côte d'Ivoire, Kenya). Following independence, national authorities dealt with such rights in ambiguous and arbitrary ways, favoring their own objectives of accumulating power and aggrandizing personal resources. In some cases, they operated in collaboration with indigenous local authorities already in place. In the process, even when one's indigeneity to a community was affirmed, this objective worked to negate any claims to land without the endorsement of local authorities, giving national authorities enormous power over who had the right to—at the very least—use the land.

The land issue in Africa remains complex. In general, during the colonial era, ruling regimes utilized pluralistic systems of land tenure based on both common law and customary law. In some areas, customary law was the rule; other areas utilized imported common law or statute. Where the interests of European settlers were concerned, common law was applied. Since independence, ruling regimes have often relegated customary law—where it still exists—to second-class status. At the same time, these customary laws have not been replaced by clearly defined legal arrangements.[38] Although customary law is not often, if at all, mentioned in national legislation, in some places it continues to be integral to the ethos of local rural communities. As such, conflicts that have recently occurred in places such as Kenya, Côte d'Ivoire, and Nigeria have highlighted the importance of the gap between practice and perceptions on the ground and in the letter of the law. In some cases, local communities may not even be aware of actual national laws relating to land rights; in other cases, often at the encouragement of cultural brokers, they might be aware but choose to flout the law.

Autochthony Based on a Group's Representation in the Nation-State When It Was Initially Formed

What groups can rightfully claim to belong to the nation? The thorniness of this issue was clearly demonstrated during the emergence of sovereign national conferences in parts of Africa in the early 1990s. For example, the Hutu of Rwanda and Burundi (who account for 84 percent of the population in both countries) claim to have been, along with the Twa (1 percent), the original inhabitants of the two countries. Anyone from those two groups residing in the respective countries is considered an autochthon to the country. However, excluded from this equation were the Tutsi (14 percent).[39] By contrast, the Rwandophone of Kivu Province in the Democratic Republic of Congo are denied authentic citizenship in that region because they are said to have arrived after the creation of what is present-day DRC.[40] Today, one's national citizenship is, to a large extent, enshrined in law—a subject that will be dealt with more fully in the next section of this chapter.

The French Revolution served as an indirect model for the notion of autochthony based on a legal claim to belonging to a nation-state. In many parts of Africa, both in Francophone and non-Francophone regions, beginning in the late 1980s the idea of a sovereign national conference took root. In Francophone Africa, the first country to move in this direction was Benin in early 1990. The idea of a national convention patterned on the French Estates General gained popular appeal.[41] Although this movement is most closely associated with Francophone Africa, as early as the late 1980s, non-Francophone countries on the continent—such as Ethiopia, Namibia, and South Africa—engaged in very similar processes.

Pearl Robinson does an excellent job of showing how ideas generated in the French Revolution served as a template for efforts some two hundred years later in Africa, involving a wide array of citizens in the process of ushering in multiparty democracy after a long period of authoritarian rule.[42] Like the delegates to the Estates General in the late eighteenth century, African delegates made it one of their first orders of business to suspend the constitution and to declare the conference sovereign. In general, the conferences were hastily organized and not structured so as to mimic exactly the pattern of the Estates General. They were simply linked in a vague sense to the French Revolution.

National conferences lasted from a few as ten days (Benin and Madagascar) to as long as seventeen months (DRC). Delegates were not elected in a democratic manner, but were said to represent their particular group interests.

The aim of these gatherings was, like that of the Estates General, to renegotiate the "social contract" (constitution).

As will be noted in the next chapter, in the DRC, Mobutu manipulated the organization and functioning of the national conference by insisting on representation by regions and subregions. The delegates were supposed to represent the predominate interests of their own ethnic groups. Minority groups tended to be underrepresented. As might be expected, this reality created intergroup tensions over who constituted legitimate representatives of particular regions and ethnic communities. Charges of a failure to establish autochthony within the nation-state became common. For example, most groups claiming autochthony considered Rwandophones "latecomers," and thus not real citizens.

Another emerging source of social conflict relating to a sense of exclusionary citizenship is represented in the escalation of xenophobia in Africa.[43] This phenomenon could be attributed to the pressure being placed on local economies in the process of globalization and to the increased immigration of people who have been made refugees by war or by widespread economic difficulties in their own countries. Xenophobia, which refers to discrimination against foreign nationals, occurs both in rhetoric and in practice. For example, whereas during the apartheid era South Africa maintained strict control over population movements, and relied on migrant laborers to staff mineral mines, since the end of the apartheid system, the new government has been pressured by indigenous citizens to expand and protect their labor rights. Similar fears by nationals in Botswana, Nigeria, Uganda, Gabon, and elsewhere have resulted in a trend towards xenophobia. In places such as Côte d'Ivoire, Zambia, and the DRC, politicians have used xenophobia to limit their competitors in elections.[44] Given that historically ethnic groups were not limited by the geographic boundaries imposed during the colonial era, groups had been free to move and settle over wide areas. Following independence and particularly since the onset of recent trends toward political liberalization, groups with kin outside a particular polity are sometimes accused of not being indigenous to the country in which they reside, making them ineligible for any citizenship rights.

The Autochthony of National Public Figures

Although the citizenship of national political figures did not generally present itself as an issue during the period of nation building in Africa, it was not immune from discourse in the popular culture. Jackson notes, for example, "Everyone from President Kasavubu to Mobutu (DRC) himself was, at some point, dubbed a 'quarteroon,' 'son of a coolie,' 'Rwandan.'"[45] In the Côte d'Ivoire, President Houpouet Boigny was accused of being some sort of foreigner.[46] However, as the second wave of democratization spread on the continent in the late 1980s, challenges to the citizenship of presidential candidates became an issue in some places. For example, Kenneth Kaunda had led Zambia to its independence in 1964, but was ousted in 1991. He attempted to make a comeback five years later but was constitutionally barred by the high court from running because, even though he was born in Zambia, his parents were Malawian. In a similar vein, Rupia Banda, who had served in various national posts in Zambia since independence, including the presidency from 2008 to 2011, was challenged by an opposition party based upon his citizenship. He claimed that both of his parents were Zambian, but his opponents claimed he was, in fact, a Malawian. The courts eventually refused to hear the case.

The most notorious recent incident of this kind was an effort by successive Ivorian presidents from the south of the Côte d'Ivoire to derail the presidential candidacy of the northerner and Muslim Alassane Ouattara in the national elections of 1995 and 2000. Even though he had served the country in various positions, Ouattara was disqualified from candidacy based on his alleged citizenship. A high court declared that he was not eligible to run for the presidency because his mother was from Burkina Faso. By this time, the country had come to identify all groups from the north of the country as nonautochthonous.

However, in 2002, the courts declared that Ouattara was, indeed, eligible to run in the 2005 elections. Those elections were eventually postponed because of the first phase of the country's civil war. Ouattara did run for the presidency in 2010 and received enough votes to be elected but was prevented from assuming office by the Constitutional Council, which declared his main opponent, Laurent Gbagbo, the winner. The civil war intensified and eventually ended in 2011, making the way for Ouattara to take office. This event will be addressed in greater detail in the case study in chapter 6.

The Legal Basis for Citizenship in Africa

Because of the realities of perceived dual citizenship in Africa, progress toward liberal democracy is handicapped[47]—despite the efforts of national governments to foster an atmosphere that replaces parochial loyalties with allegiance to the national community. In an excellent account of how informal local institutions in Ghana and Côte d'Ivoire have been shaped over time by the postcolonial governments, Lauren MacLean provides empirical evidence of how communal practices of reciprocity have shifted largely because of the influence of national government policies relating to social services. This shift is also related to the differences in state-society relations in the two countries.[48]

In some places, the legal definition of a citizen is often murky. In others, even when laws are clear, incumbents and even parochial communities tend either to flout these laws or to be unaware of them and thus to arbitrarily define who does and does not belong to a particular community. To understand this reality, it is helpful to gain an understanding of the formal-legal basis for citizenship in Africa and of the institutions designed to deal with this issue.

The legal definition of citizenship is enshrined in international law and, in Africa today, is largely based on the legacy of colonial powers that governed particular territories.[49] Citizenship not only determines who is a member of a particular national community, but also generally guarantees the equal rights of all to whom it applies. However, as Derek Heater correctly notes, "Members of ethnic or religious minorities can feel that they are truly citizens only if they perceive an underlying fairness in the social, legal and political systems."[50]

As understood, legal definitions of citizenship tend to be conflated with nationality.[51] On the ground in Africa, people are perceived as having a national citizenship that exists alongside a more communal sense of citizenship. These identities may not always be in conflict with one another, but when a person or a group chooses to emphasize one identity over the other, discord often occurs.

Just over a decade ago, in one of the first efforts to codify African citizenship laws, Jeffrey Herbst found that of the forty countries he identified and coded, fourteen countries traced citizenship primarily to descent—that is, where the individual was born[52]—and twenty-six to the birthplace of their ancestors.[53] The former attribution is commonly referred to as *jus soli* (place of birth) and the latter as *jus sanguinis* (the birthplace of the ancestors). Theoretically, jus soli does not depend on the birthplace of the parents, but rather on where an individual was born. Individuals are automatically considered citizens of the country in which they are born. However, in present-day Africa, this definition is often translated to mean the place of origin of one's ancestors. In some places, location of birth might relate to a traditional community within a particular state, or to the state at the time of its creation, or thereafter. For example, the constitution in Africa's newest state, South Sudan, states that anyone residing in the territory prior to January 1, 1956, or whose "father" was resident at that time, has the right to citizenship in that country. A person not of one of the ethnic groups that originally inhabited the territory of South Sudan, but who has lived in the territory consistently since January 1, 1956, may also choose to become a citizen.[54]

Jus sanguinis is supposed to establish the citizenship of an individual based on the citizenship of her or his parents. In most of Africa, traditional systems have been based on patriarchy, which dictates citizenship primarily on the citizenship of the father. In some places, depending on the circumstances, the location of birth might relate to a traditional community within a particular state, or it might relate simply to the state at the time of its creation or thereafter. A person can also acquire citizenship through naturalization, which can occur either by marrying a citizen of a particular country, living in a country over a specified period of time, or registering with the national government as the foreign-born dependent of a citizen.[55] In some cases, only the foreign-born wife of a male citizen can acquire citizenship through marriage. Should a female citizen marry a foreign male, the husband would not be recognized as a citizen, because the system of patriarchy dictates that he would be a citizen of the country in which his father was born.[56]

In most of Africa, although it is legally possible for a person to acquire citizenship through naturalization, in practice this process rarely occurs.[57] Moreover, incumbent regimes, because they possess sovereignty, legal command, and the declaratory power of the state, might arbitrarily declare groups and individuals to be noncitizens.[58] Such a fiat was handed down in 1998, when the Ethiopian government declared that despite the fact that thousands of Eritreans, and even their parents, had been born in the country or had lived there for generations dating back to when Eritrea was considered nothing more than a province of Ethiopia, all Eritreans were noncitizens. Prime Minister Meles Zenawi justified himself by saying that he could make such a decision if only because he "did not like the color of their eyes."[59]

This form of exclusionary citizenship can play out at the subnational and national level.[60] For example, much of the ethnic conflict in parts of Cameroon and Kenya over the past two decades has been based on the efforts of groups not originally from the Douala area of Cameroon or the Western Rift Valley of Kenya to exercise their liberal citizenship rights in those regions either by running for public office, voting, or purchasing property and otherwise establishing domicile in the particular region. More recently, in Nigeria, regional conflicts have emerged in the center and north of the country based at least in part on the claims of indigenous populations and of those perceived as "foreign" or otherwise having their citizenship questioned. At the national level, the most notable recent examples of serious conflicts growing out of the practice of exclusionary citizenship have been the Ivorité movement in Côte d'Ivoire and the Hutu rejection of Tutsi claims to Rwandan citizenship, as brutally represented in the genocide of 1994.[61]

In present-day Africa, traditional citizenship identification with parochial communities exists side by side with the modern notion of citizenship that is enshrined in law. The latter relates to membership in a national community. In some case, membership is determined by the status of groups and individuals at the time a particular nation-state is founded. Other times, the right to national citizenship is less clearly defined in legal codes. In almost all places, one can acquire national citizenship through naturalization, but this practice is uncommon. In any case, citizenship confers on individual groups certain rights and obligations to the nation-state. At the same time, individuals have certain rights and obligations related to their particular parochial community. These identities, national and subnational, can peacefully coexist, but in many cases they clash, causing varying degrees of social conflict. This dynamic will be demonstrated in the case studies in Part 2.

3

Toward an Analytical Framework of Identity and Citizenship in Africa

"Disputes over national and local belonging and differing conceptions of citizenship are at the heart of many of the most intractable conflicts in Africa."
—International Refugee Rights Initiative, "Citizenship: Developing New Approaches to Citizenship and Belonging in Africa"

"Rather than the state (in Africa) providing a common bond for the people through the tie of citizenship, with equal rights, privileges and obligations, both in precepts and practice, people's loyalties are bifurcated."
—Said Adejemobi, "Citizenship, Rights, and the Problem of Conflict and Civil Wars in Africa."

Social conflict in Africa has many sources; however, this work focuses on conflicts rooted in disputes over citizenship and citizenship rights. How are we to understand the recent sources and consequences of citizenship-based conflicts in Africa? In some cases, ethnically based conflicts relating to such grievances grow out of electoral competition at the national level; in others, they are triggered by long-standing claims involving land ownership and other property rights; in still others, these types of conflicts concern the ethnic composition of one level of government or the other and/or its perceived failure to deliver public goods to ethnic communities in a nondiscriminatory manner.

No extant general theory or analytical framework can help us explain these conflicts. Oftentimes, they have social-psychological roots and cannot be elucidated through theories of rational political behavior or primordially based interethnic animosities. The difficulty of explaining such conflicts analytically derives from the dynamics of politics, particularly the politics of contention, which are often uncertain.[1] I would suggest, however, that developing a framework for analysis that could be applicable in *certain* circumstances is possible, as is tracing social processes in the evolution of individual African countries to identify factors that seem the most relevant to explaining conflicts based on ethnic identity and citizenship rights.[2] In some cases, conflicts in two different polities may appear very similar, but in fact idiosyncratic features of the different countries must be factored into any analysis of them. The purpose here is not to take an approach that determines a dependent variable, but to test competing explanations for why certain events occurred the way they did in certain places and not in others; and to provide at least partial clarification of the sources and patterns of conflict that occurred in certain instances.

The Utility of Process Tracing

This study's methodological approach is generally qualitative, relying mostly on descriptive analysis of specific social processes and drawing inferences from systematic evaluation of this qualitatively derived data. This method is commonly known as process tracing. In some cases, process tracing focuses on a single significant event, in others it concentrates on recurrent events over time. Process tracing involves what is termed "causal-process observations."[3] This approach contrasts with the data set observations heavily relied upon (if not exclusively relied upon) in quantitative approaches. The goal is to engage in a diagnostic analysis of evidence that is not always readily quantified, or when it is quantifiable, the data do not present as complete a picture as is desired. For example, we can empirically record incidents of conflict, but relying exclusively on structural indicators and the resulting human action does not inevitably get at the motivations behind human action. I contend that the process-tracing approach can help us understand the fundamental essence of events, which might be missing when a quantitative approach alone is used.[4] It might also help us to carefully consider certain anomalies in social science data that depart from one's original theories or hypotheses.[5]

This approach has proven to be highly useful in the analysis of macro historical events, such as war and peacemaking, as well as of more micro events at the subnational level. Ethnic conflicts in particular regions of a country, or across regions of a country, might create national crises even though the root causes of the conflicts might be based in different sets of factors. To be sure, making causal inferences from observational data is not easy, particularly because of the complexity of the political process under observation. But by assuming the role of diagnostic investigator, however difficult this may be, one may gain a better understanding of the causes of particular political conflicts. For instance, careful process tracing ask such questions as, "Who knew what, when, where, and why, and how did they respond?"[6] The goal here is to establish that the model is suitable for understanding the case studies that make up the major portion of the book. There is a systematic attempt in the process to sift through evidence relating to the context of politics, the relevant social structures, the human agents involved (e.g., ethnic entrepreneurs/politicians, civil society), the interaction of these variables, and the resulting outcomes. Each case study begins with the assumption that the incidents to be addressed represent tensions or conflicts that can be traced to citizenship-rights claims and expectations. Special attention is devoted to understanding the sequencing of relevant events that led up to—or have had the potential to lead to—a national crisis. In some cases, local clashes over land rights and land use between ethnic groups, conflicts growing out of the conflation of electoral politics and ethnic representation among competing parties, or disputes over the rights of groups to be represented in local governance structures could all, under the right circumstances, escalate into crises of national proportions.

Bases for Conflicts over Citizenship Rights in Africa

In many cases, conflicts over citizenship rights are based on multiple factors, and thus present analytical problems. For example, the many ethnic conflicts that have occurred in Kenya over the past two decades have related to elites performing as cultural brokers who encouraged their ethnic kin to strike out against the state and against groups allegedly infringing on their citizenship rights. In some cases, these disputes have been based on claims of voting irregularities; other times, they have erupted over land and other property rights. In Nigeria, some recent communally based conflicts have been rooted in ethnic as well as religious and regional identity.

The Case of Rwandophones in the DRC

The most intense recent conflicts in the Democratic Republic of Congo (DRC) have been based on long-standing exclusionary citizenship claims in the northeast of the country and have involved groups that claim to be indigenous to the

Kivu area and Tutsi immigrants from Rwanda and Burundi.[7] Georges Nzongola-Ntalaja roots this conflict in the effort by certain groups in the region to claim land based on traditional communal principles.[8] Under these traditional customs, land could not be privately owned, bought, or sold, but could only be passed down and divided among descendants of families deemed indigenous to the community. Certain groups were excluded from claiming indigeneity because the community considered them "strangers," as they had migrated from other places and settled in the Kivu area. In some cases, immigrant groups that may have resided in the community for hundreds of years were still considered outsiders.[9] The issue of indigeneity became an acute problem in the early 1970s, as the notion of *authentic* national "citizenship" became more important. Even though some ethnic Rwandan immigrants had lived in the Kivu area for decades, because their families had migrated there more recently—around the time of the social revolution in Rwanda, in the late 1950s and early 1960s—they were not considered indigenous to the area. Although assessments of ethnic groups were based on autochthony, other laws excluded Rwandese immigrants as nonindigenous Congolese.

Many Rwandese immigrants had become involved in civic and economic life and, over time, came to consider Kivu their rightful community. However, groups claiming indigeneity still regarded them as strangers and as threats to the rights of descendants of the region's original inhabitants. This tension resulted in periodic outbreaks of violence and ethnic cleansing directed toward Rwandese in northeastern DRC.

The origins and, indeed, intensity of these most recent conflicts can be traced to the immediate postindependence period. For example, in 1962 the independence government carved up the province of Kivu into three sectors: North Kivu, South Kivu, and Maniema.[10] In the process, Rwandophones were denied a cohesive territorial space for their group and were thus deprived of political leverage in provincial administration, particularly in North Kivu. Facing the marginalization of the Rwandophones and the denial of their citizenship rights, elites from the Rwandese immigrant community vigorously protested. Tutsi immigrants, over time, fought to have their citizenship rights in the country legally codified. Though they achieved limited success from time to time, in the end Tutsi were still considered "strangers."

The plight of the Rwandophones in Kivu became particularly grave in the late 1980s and early 1990s, when the ruling regime of President Mobutu sese Seko, of what was then *Zaire*, agreed to the creation of a Conférence Nationale Souveraine (sovereign national conference) in order to chart the transition to democracy.[11] Importantly, in identifying potential participants in the Conference, the country was divided up into geopolitical regions on the basis of which delegates were chosen. Disagreements immediately arose in the different regions over who could legitimately represent the interests of the authentic inhabitants of particular regions. Delegates from each province had to establish not only that they were autochthonous to the regions they claimed to represent but also that their group was indigenous to Zaire. A fierce debate raged around the country over who could legitimately claim citizenship, in some places resulting in interethnic violence.

The tensions over citizenship that accompanied the transition to democracy in the country were a culmination of problems that had been building since independence. Significantly, the 1964 constitution stated that "There is only one Congolese nationality. It is granted, beginning from the date of 30 June 1960 to all persons having now, or at some point in the past, as one of their ancestors a member of a tribe or the part of a tribe established on the territory of the Congo before the 18th October 1908."[12]

This classification excluded Rwandophones whose ancestors had arrived in later waves. Since independence, in Zaire and, indeed, all over Africa, questions of the autochthony of a group or a particular political leader have been common, but have rarely resulted in violence. However, in this case, violence against Rwandophones became common and intensified. Significantly, although violence was historically sometimes directed toward Rwandophones, they themselves were not known to resort to violence to demand citizenship rights. Until the beginning of the most recent period of democratization, Rwandophones had in fact not only participated in the economy in Zaire, but also served militarily and even occupied political offices at both the local and national level. One such person was Berthelemy Bisengimana, a Congolese Tutsi, who became the so-called director of the office of the president early in the Mobutu regime. From that vantage point, he took the lead in attempting to clarify confusion over the citizenship of Rwandophones. In 1971, largely because of the leadership of Bisengimana, a law was enacted that would accord nationality explicitly to "Persons originating from Rwanda-Burundi established in Congo since 30 June 1960."[13] In 1972, Bisengimana played a pivotal role in introducing a law that would move the cutoff date for establishing ancestral roots within the country from 1908 to January 1, 1950, effectively allowing the majority of Rwandophone descendants and immigrants—who had migrated in large numbers during the 1930s—to gain rights as full citizens.[14] This law, however, was not enshrined in the constitution, and opponents fought to have it repealed. In 1981, it was annulled, and the constitution was amended, pushing the qualifying date for established ancestral lineage from the updated 1950 point back to August 1, 1885, the year that European powers agreed on a strategy for partitioning the African continent among themselves at the Berlin Conference. As a result of this legislation, most Rwandophones were completely excluded from citizenship qualifications; in order to confirm nationality, individuals now would have to prove that they had had an ancestor living within the territory of the Congo before 1885.

In contrast to the peaceful efforts of Rwandophones to establish their legitimate rights to citizenship in the DRC, since the mid-1990s some Rwandophones have participated in civil wars in the country, largely driven by their exclusion from national and regional communities that they see as their ancestral homelands. Most recently in 2012, civil conflict in northeast DRC erupted again. This time, rebellion was sparked by a mutiny within the national army by Rwandophone troops (referred to as M-23) who proclaimed their dissatisfaction with the way they were treated in the military as well as with the way their ethnic kin were being threatened by the remaining Rwanda Hutu Interwahanwe operating in and around refugee camps in the region.[15] Such tensions only highlighted Tutsi assumed alien status in the DRC, and they sought not unification with Rwanda, but DRC citizenship rights including government protection of their human rights.

In an effort to make sense of the complex interactions among the structural, human agency, and contextual variables that form the basis for conflict over citizenship and citizenship rights, the remainder of this chapter provides an analytical framework.

A Framework for Analysis

Any attempt to understand political dynamics must include an understanding of three primary factors: (1) the context in which politics takes place; that is, the weight of history; (2) the institutions or structures that shape and are shaped by politics in particular circumstances; and (3) the individuals and groups involved.[16] This claim holds for peaceful and violent political processes.

The Context and Parameters of Political Dynamics

All politics—national and subnational alike—take place within the context of a particular political culture; it thus seems reasonable to suggest that objective conditions and structural relationships at a particular point in time, along with a country's political culture, set the parameters of political dynamics. Adam Prezworski has noted that in the process of political transitions during the Third Wave of Democratization, incumbent leaders and the manner in which they responded both to their structural environments and to the shifts taking place in their country's political culture were instrumental in shaping the course of political change.[17] In order to explain political change, as well as to understand a group dynamic in a particular community, one must appreciate not only the relevant context of political culture but also the structures that are found in that culture and the human agents that influence and are influenced by those particular structures. Relevant structures and human agents can be both domestic and international. In the domestic arena, class structures, ethnic relations, religious groups, civil society, governing institutions, labor relations, and other factors have varying roles and varying degrees of involvement in the ebb and flow of politics. In the international system, state–state relations, globalization processes, multinational institutions (both public and private), international organizations, and various treaties and procurement contracts may all be relevant to understanding political dynamics in certain instances.

As important as they are, structural variables alone cannot trigger the process of change in any direction or fully explain the causes of social conflict. Human actions as catalyzing agents are essential before the full implications of politics are apparent. Perceptions among individuals and groups about the opportunities and constraints presented by particular structural patterns are integral.[18] In some cases, mass social mobilizations are contagious; for example, groups in one country might be inspired by the successful political mobilization of similar groups in other countries. Such a chain reaction seems to have been the case in countries in North Africa and the Middle East when they, in rapid succession, erupted in protest demanding regime change during what was known as "The Arab Spring." A dramatic set of events that spread over the whole region began in Tunisia in December 2010, when a street vendor named Mohammed Bouazizi set himself on fire to protest an oppressive government and eventually died. Out of this event emerged a popular uprising, which led to the collapse of the Zine Abidinde Ben Ali regime. The unrest in Tunisia was followed in January 2011 by a popular uprising in Egypt by protesters bent on regime change. Over the next year and a half, popular uprisings erupted in other North African and Middle Eastern countries. Some of these protests, such as those in Yemen and Libya, resulted in regime change; in others, autocratic regimes, such those as in Bahrain and Syria, cracked down on opposition groups and tenuously clung to power. In still other countries, such as in

Morocco, Saudi Arabia, Jordan, and Algeria, incumbent regimes were able to pacify protesting groups with limited reforms.

As significant as contagion might be in certain instances, most groups simply become emboldened when they perceive that the risks of collective action are less than they have been in the past, and that prospects for yielding a desired outcome have improved. For example, when it loses its cohesion or is otherwise weakened, an incumbent regime may send a signal to potential opponents of the regime that they can form an effective alliance with regime "softliners" (as was the case in South Africa with the demise of the "Apartheid Regime"). Alternatively, opposition forces may simply feel that the time is right to successfully act on their own,[19] as was the case in Kenya, where in spite of their long history of ineffectiveness and weakness, opposition parties coalesced in 2002 and effectively ousted the autocratic regime of Daniel arap Moi.[20]

Under such circumstances, clear vision and good timing are everything. Should opposition groups be disorganized or misread the situation, their movements could fail to achieve their objectives. This possibility holds whether we are considering the actions of formal opposition groups that want to engage in regime change, or are focused on the claims of certain groups in civil society that are most concerned with establishing and protecting their citizenship rights relative to those of other groups in their national community. The nature and context of interactions among certain structures and human agents can lead to conflict or peaceful change. For instance, if minorities or opposition groups perceive the results of national elections as both "free and fair," or at least not worth fighting over, the likely direction of change will be peaceful. Should this not be the case, political protest and even violence could be expected. As recently as 2008, in Kenya and Zimbabwe, widespread violence following national elections erupted in part because of claims of voting irregularities. These events eventually led incumbent regimes and their most important opponents to strike power-sharing deals. By contrast, in Senegal in 2012, President Abdoulaye Wade, after having lost a runoff election, peacefully conceded to his opponent, Macky Sall.

Civil Society and Agency

In considering the importance of human agents in the study of politics, until recently, scholars have focused to a great extent on the role of elites in inspiring and leading social movements. Before turning to a brief discussion of opposition elites as leaders in political movements, considering the civil society factor is important. The case studies that follow explore the actions of elites as well as of civil society. Popular grievances relating to infringements upon— or the denial of—citizenship rights often emanate from the grassroots level of civil society. What is civil society?

The Nature of Civil Society

The term *civil society* often refers to groups that emerge spontaneously in protest against a particular regime or its policies.[21] Rather than wanting to separate from a particular state or to displace a regime and seize political power for themselves civil society organizations generally mobilize around a particular issue or set of issues with the objective of improving conditions for their own group. They are often attracted to formal political organization and to particular leaders whose views and objectives they see as alternatives to incumbent regimes or whom they support for other political or personal reasons. Members of formally organized interest associations might be incorporated into civil society once it is mobilized; yet, they are not civil society writ large.

In contrast to formally organized and institutionalized groups, such as trade unions that regularly confront management or the state around economistic or welfare concerns, civil society organizations are usually spurred to action by social or sociopolitical grievances that have reached crisis level. Grievances may relate to food and commodity prices, irregularities in elections, ethnically or religiously based discrimination, or any variety of government policies.

In a seminal article, Jean-Francois Bayart defines civil society as the political space between the household and the state.[22] Civil society is outside the formal political arena, but can be drawn upon when a political crisis occurs. However, civil society should not be conceived as necessarily associated with autonomous voluntary associations or with all social movements. It, like more formal and institutionalized interest associations, is a subset of society writ large. What defines civil society is the focus of its agenda. It is not an institutionalized interest association that exists for articulating and defending the civil and political rights of its members on a day-to-day basis, even when there is no obvious crisis. Instead, civil society is ephemeral, emerging over a limited period of time in response to a particular political issue. After a crisis has passed, civil society disappears from view and lies dormant.

Besides their primary missions, organized interest associations, including trade unions, are often prime candidates for casting their lot with a civil society organization when certain salient issues become a concern that transcends the individual concern of institutionalized interest associations. These groups may not have been born civil society organizations, but are moved by circumstances to engage in social movements catalyzed by civil society. For example, both the National Christian Council of Kenya and the Uganda Joint Christian Council are primarily ecumenical organizations, but in the 1990s they developed political wings that made them significant national-level political players in their respective countries.

Groups that initially make up civil society are usually intellectuals, artists, professionals (such as lawyers, teachers, and doctors), organized labor, and women's and students' associations. However, it has become increasingly common for ethnic associations concerned with protecting the citizenship rights of their social groups to also be involved. During the drive for independence, these types of groups provided the support base for nationalist parties. Crawford Young suggests that the vital associational life in the buildup to independence in the immediate post–World War II period could be considered the "Golden Age" for the evolution of civil society in Africa.[23] Just following independence, autonomous civic associations were either co-opted by the state or by mainstream political organizations or were repressed by autocratic regimes. Consequently, it can be said that civil society was forced into dormancy, where it bode its time, waiting for openings in the political and economic systems that would allow it to once again mobilize. In some cases, when civil society did later become mobilized, it was clear that what have been termed "civic republican citizenship" interests were at issue. For instance, widespread complaints over rigged elections or other forms of voter fraud in places such as Kenya, Egypt, and Zimbabwe in the past decade set the stage for groups with other long-standing grievances to rise up and demand justice at subnational levels for their particular ethnic or religious groups. Land crises in Kenya and Côte d'Ivoire are clear examples.

Sidney Tarrow has noted that under normal circumstances, rational people do not confront an obviously stronger opponent when they perceive their opportunities for success to be minimal.[24] However, when the risk of collective action appears to be significantly reduced, social movements, such as those represented in civil society, are likely to emerge spontaneously. This response often takes place when a group experiences a widespread sense that unless it asserts itself, its lot will not change—and may even worsen. Such was the case for Muslim migrants living in northern Côte d'Ivoire from the late 1990s until 2010. The grievances of the general population in that region merged with the interests of military elements, catalyzing the most recent civil war. This situation will be addressed fully in the case study of Côte d'Ivoire.

Civil society is a mélange of social groupings that come together in crisis to protest or otherwise take action based on grievances that either go beyond the purposes for which they were initially organized or draw them together as a social movement involving others who have the same or similar grievances. Perceived crisis over a particular issue serves as a catalyst for either nonviolent mass protest or for various other forms of violence, ranging from riots to war. Once they have either achieved their objectives or have been defeated by their opponent, civil society groups usually once again retreat to a condition of dormancy.

Mobilizing Civil Society

Notably, political stimuli or precipitating events must occur before change is initiated. These actions are not always part of a formal political process, such as elections or other forms of political contestation. Ethnic communities can also be prompted to join a heretofore dormant civil society and to behave spontaneously in certain ways; or, they can be mobilized by cultural brokers and entrepreneurs who rhetorically link ethnic grievances to the denial of basic rights to their particular groups. To a great extent, the character of any mobilization is based on the interaction of extant political structures in a given polity, the ideas and actions of certain human agents (such as incumbent elites, the leaders of civil society, and ethnic entrepreneurs), and the context in which the politics surrounding a particular issue takes place.

In general, civil society cannot be effectively imported from one polity to another. Under most circumstance, it organically develops within and emerges from the local context. Consequently the relative scope and strength of any given civil society varies from one context to the next. Civil society organizations can also draw their inspiration from groups outside of their own communities. They might even be supported directly and indirectly by similar organizations elsewhere, but, they usually emerge around issues that are a part of their everyday existence.[25]

Elites and their Roles in Articulating and Instigating Claims of Citizenship Rights

Relevant political identities are not only socially constructed, but also fluid, intermittent, and experiential. In addition to their roles as cultural brokers calling their groups to action, ethnic entrepreneurs may be moved to take the lead in an ethnic protest movement in the aftermath of spontaneous upheavals in their particular communities.[26] In examining why people follow cultural brokers and put their lives on the line, David Laitin and James Fearon found that in some cases leaders are simply attracted to social movements that are already in motion. Local communities may be interested in pushing their own agendas and elites, and formal political organizations appropriate their spirit and action for their own political purposes. For example, in order to build a following, elites may frame issues in ethnic terms, recruit followers based on imagined threats or discrimination, or take advantage of preexisting ethnic tensions. Often a primary motivation for mass action on the part of ethnic communities is fear of marginalization or exclusion.

A foremost instrument used by elites attempting to mobilize supporters is hortative language that encourages followers to take action in favor of or against some situation. Murray Edelman has described language as "a necessary catalyst of politics."[27] Followers may be reminded of the past glories of their group or past injustices against them; or they might be encouraged to take action to change their unfavorable condition. Manipulation through verbal communication was clearly in evidence during the build-up and execution of the Rwanda Genocide in 1994. Hutu extremist leaders and publicists utilized speeches and the media to incite followers to engage in genocidal atrocities.[28]

The agendas of ethnic groups may have little to do with communal tensions per se, but might relate to acting on grudges or material concerns. In some cases, conflicts may be local in origin but involve claims of infringement on a group's civic republic citizenship rights being elevated to a level of national import. For example, civic republican citizenship rights claims might be directed toward the national state on the basis of perceived discriminatory policies in favor of one group at the expense of the particular aggrieved group. In Nigeria, particularly since the last days of the colonial era, incidents of tension and conflict between the Junkun and the Tiv in Tabara State have led to political instability. The initial trigger in these conflicts related to either land or to fear by the Junkun of possible marginalization as a result of the rapidly growing Tiv immigrant population in the state. Junkun ethnic entrepreneurs cited the negative consequences of allowing the Tiv the same rights to land as the indigenous Junkun. Because of the growing tendency of Tiv to migrate to Tabara State, the accordance of such rights would ultimately lead to the marginalization of the Junkun in the politics of their indigenous homeland.[29] This situation will be more fully discussed in the Nigerian case study.

Following the 2007 national elections in Kenya, violence was fueled by rampant rumors of vote rigging on the part of the ruling Party of National

Unity (PNU). Prominent political leaders are thought by many to have been responsible for encouraging an escalation of the violence. Consequently, charges were brought before the International Criminal Court in the Hague against two sitting members of the Kenya National Assembly, Uhuru Kenyatta and William Ruto. These two men are believed to have been instrumental in inciting much of the violence in the Rift Valley following the elections. Kenyatta is a Kikuyu and the son of Kenya's first president, Jomo Kenyatta, the architect of Kenya postindependence policy of privatizing land throughout the country.[30] He represents the politically and economically dominant Kikuyu, who claim the Central and parts of Eastern Province as their ancestral homeland. However, these regions have historically been characterized by overpopulation and land pressures. The policies initiated by Jomo Kenyatta's regime opened the door for Kikuyu entrepreneurs and other land-hungry members of that group to acquire land in the highly agriculturally productive Rift Valley.

Ruto is a Kalenjin from the western Rift Valley and represents groups that futilely resisted the alienation of their ancestral land to European settlers at the turn of the twentieth century. During the struggle for independence, the Kalenjin supported the Kenya National Democratic Union, comprised mainly of minority groups drawn together in support of a federalist solution (*majimboism*) for independent Kenya. Kalenjin eventually were co-opted into the ruling Kenya African National Union (KANU) a year after independence, agreeing to the transformation of the country from a federal system to a republic. Nonetheless, fear of domination by the Kikuyu and their allies, the Luo, continued, at times escalating into ethnic violence. Some ethnic elites among the Kalenjin fueled popular discontent among their constituents over what they characterized as an invasion of nonindigenous settlers into their homeland leading to the further erosion of their own rights to land. Since independence, this depiction has proved to be an effective mobilizing tool for Kalenjin politicians seeking electoral support.[31]

As important as claims to indigenous rights to land may be, ethnic elites, in their personal quest for power, influence, and wealth, might seek to lead already-mobilized ethnic kin by claiming that their citizenship rights are being threatened. Depending on the political context and the scale of mobilization by the discontented group, incidents such as elections, unpopular government policies, or escalations of state repression in areas represented by the cultural broker may initiate nonviolent or violent movements. In such cases, the role of the ethnic entrepreneur/politician is critical.

PART 2

Identity Politics and Selected Cases of Conflict over Citizenship Rights in Africa

4

Nigeria

Indigeneity and Citizenship

"Bitterness due to political differences will carry Nigeria nowhere and I appeal to all political leaders throughout the country to try to control their party extremists. Nigeria is large enough to accommodate us all in spite of our political differences."
—Alhaji Abubakar Tafawa Balewa, "First Speech as Prime Minister" (1957)

"Ethnicity as a crucial determinant merged earlier and more forcefully in Nigeria than anywhere else in tropical Africa."
—Crawford Young, "Comparative Claims to Political Sovereignty"

Nigeria is the most populous country on the African continent, with more than 150 million people. It is an extremely diverse country, with between 250 and 400 distinct ethnic groups. The largest ethnic groups are the Hausa of the northwest (making up around 28 percent), the Yoruba of the southwest (around 18 percent), and the Ibo of the southeast (around 14 percent). The remaining ethnic groups number from a few thousand to several million in population. In addition to its ethnic diversity, Nigeria is religiously diverse. About half the population practices some form of Islam; Christians make up another 40 percent; and the remainder of the population practices various traditional religions. Notably, only about 35–40 percent of the Muslim population is concentrated in the northwest of the country, whereas 55–60 percent of Nigeria's Muslims is clustered in enclaves throughout the rest of the country.

The British colonized what is present-day Nigeria in a piecemeal manner, beginning in the mid-nineteenth century. A British presence was initiated through private commercial interests along the Atlantic coast and later along the Niger River. However, the British government did not establish an effective presence in the region until after the Conference of Berlin (1884–1885). Before 1900, the region was controlled by three different agencies: the Royal Niger Corporation, located along the Niger River valleys and surrounding areas; the Foreign Office of the United Kingdom, in the Niger River Delta; and the British Colonial Office, in what was known as Lagos Colony. Between 1900 and 1914, the Colonial Office gradually took control of all of these possessions and brought them under one colonial administration.

In this context, the seeds of Nigeria's current problems relating to citizenship and identity were sown.[1] The early twentieth century was the first time that the disparate ethnic groups of this extremely large colony were brought under one administration. Indeed, the practice of cobbling together European colonies in Africa out of extremely culturally diverse territories was common. However, the sheer size and complexity of the Colony of Nigeria presented particular challenges. Not overcoming these issues during the process of state building would make the problem of nation building all the more difficult in the future. The British arbitrarily divided the colony into three cultural zones, centering its administration on the numerically dominant ethnic groups found in each of these areas. In the north, where the largest ethnic group was the predominately Muslim Hausa-Fulani, the colonialists chose to rule indirectly through traditional centralized rulers. However, in the southwest, where the largest ethnic group in the region was the Yoruba, the colonialists pursued a mixed direct and indirect rule strategy; in the southeast, with hundreds of distinct ethnic groups with no history of centralized rulership, the British's administrative approach was mainly indirect rule.

Nigeria became a quasi-federal state in 1951 and a full-fledged colonial state in 1954. The colonialists recognized that Nigeria's size and diversity meant that they had to find an effective way to manage affairs. The 1954 constitution was an attempt to reconcile and accommodate regional and religious tensions that had already begun to surface throughout the colony. This constitution made the separation between the federal and state governments clear, explaining that any powers not delegated to the federal government were under the purview of individual states. Importantly, it did not create a strong central government and left the states in an extremely strong position in their dealings with the federal government. The tendency, then, was for states to focus on the identity of citizens within their respective regions, and to continue to accept the strong attachments of ethnic groups to their own communities. As such, by the time it achieved independence in 1960, Nigeria had no strong sense of national unity. At the same time, national leaders—at least publically—professed that, despite limited institutional basis, their goal was to create "national unity out of diversity."

Following independence, regional tensions escalated, as did intraregional tensions. Nationally, these tensions grew out of efforts by the northern leadership group to assert dominance in national politics. In large measure this struggle over which ethnic elites would dominate national politics is what led to the declaration of Nigeria as a republic in 1963. The creation of the Republic of Nigeria only served to heighten interregional tensions. At the regional level, minority groups and political factions engaged in ongoing protests over political domination by other groups and being denied rights to self-determination. This dissent clearly indicated that the issue of "indigeneity" would have a central role to play in both national and subnational polities for some time to come. Some minorities were placated when a fourth region, the Mid-West, was created in 1963, but rather than satisfying the pent-up demands of minority groups outside, and even inside that region, this modification only exacerbated tensions. Intraregional tensions were particularly high in the southwest, which immediately after independence in 1963 became embroiled in a complex mix of ideologically and ethnic-based conflicts. These problems continued until the military coup of 1966, which led to the collapse of Nigeria's First Republic.

Background to the Biafra War

Under colonialism, governance in the north was characterized by a form of indirect rule. The British had allowed traditional religio-political authorities to manage their own affairs, which enabled northerners to remain true to their traditions and, to a large extent, to stem the tide of modernization and its accompanying secular formal education and urbanization.[2] On the other hand, the southwest had maintained—and greatly expanded—its contacts with Western countries, becoming the commercial center of the territory. This development was not lost on the residents of the southeast, and they—like the Yoruba to the west—embraced secular formal education and commerce, particularly after the Second World War. During that time, in the southeast, Ibo leaders who had seen the value of Western education as early as the 1930s, came to believe that their group was so far behind that extraordinary measures had to be taken in order for the Ibo to "catch up" with the Yoruba.[3]

Notably, throughout the colonial period, Iboland was what Donald Horowitz would term an economically backward region.[4] It was very populous; even when the region began to vigorously pursue the development of its human capital after the Second World War, the dearth of economic opportunities for its residents at home meant that the region had to become a labor-exporting enclave. Educated and skilled Ibos migrated to urban areas throughout the country and, as they did, set up Ibo cultural self-help associations to provide a sense of support and security to Ibo migrants from the southeast. The Ibos had never been a coherent ethnic group organized into a large political unit such as a state, empire, or sultanate, yet the pressures of competitive communalism during the process of modernization had led to the development of an expanded sense of Ibo identity.[5]

As Nigeria moved toward independence, and began to rapidly urbanize and develop economically, Ibos came to see themselves in terms of their regional identity, in competition with the Yoruba, who had long taken advantage of employment and business opportunities throughout the entire country. This kind of thinking and behavior carried over into the political arena during the nationalist period. Whereas in the past, Ibos had viewed their extended families, towns, or parochial regions as their terminal political communities, many came to view Iboland in general as their terminal political community. In the process, a pan-Ibo identity was socially constructed.

The first signs of the serious interethnic conflict that would come to characterize Nigeria after independence can be traced to an incident in 1945 in the northern city of Jos.[6] At that time, a deadly riot targeting Ibo migrants erupted, resulting in the loss of a number of lives. In 1953, an even more deadly ethnic riot occurred in the northern city of Kano, and again Ibo migrants were targeted by northerners. As the nationalist period unfolded, ethnically based parties emerged, but, for a time, given the federal character that independent Nigeria would assume, there was a tendency to form cross-ethnic political alliances. All parties had to compete for votes in all regions, which led to efforts by parties to join in what they perceived would be minimum winning coalitions. In this environment, federal elections in 1959—leading up to independence—contributed to high expectations, at the same time that intense inter- and intraethnic political competition created an aura of fear and anxiety, particularly among the Ibo.

In the wake of independence, the Ibos continued their attempt to exercise national citizenship rights and to take advantage of economic opportunities as well as opportunities in the civil service throughout the country. The north lacked educated, skilled people in both the public and private sectors. Ethnic elites in the north constantly emphasized the need for their group to take the lead in *Africanizing* all aspects of society; northern leaders translated that to mean *northernizing*. Not only was there a fear of being swamped and marginalized by Ibo migrants to the north, but also the Yoruba in the west feared the penetration of Ibo migrants into their homeland. For instance, federal universities were sites of intense competition between the Ibo and the Yoruba. While the paramount Ibo political leader, Nnamdi Azikwe, preached national unity based upon a sense of a common Nigerian identity, many in the north as well in the southwest came to see a hidden Ibo agenda aimed at dominating all aspects of Nigerian life.

By the time of federal elections in 1964, Nigeria's federal political system was clearly on the brink of collapse. Rigged regional elections in late 1965 in the western region were the direct precipitating cause of the coup on January 15, 1966. Rigging had been common since the last days of the colonial period, but this election was particularly remarkable for the amount of ballot stuffing and the manipulation of the vote-counting process on the part of the region's ruling party, the Nigerian National Democratic Party (NNDP). This deceit set the stage for ethnic tensions within the region, and pressures culminated in a coup led by J. T. U. Aguiyi-Ironsi, an Ibo. Moreover, most of the coup leaders were Ibo officers of roughly the same age and educational background; in other words, they were friends who trusted one another. Initially, the country greeted the coup with jubilation, but it soon came to be seen as an ethnically based coup, heightening fears that the Ibo were positioning themselves to finally and completely take over the country. In the days that followed, mostly non-Ibo military officers and leading politicians were assassinated.[7]

Fewer than five months after taking power, Ironsi issued a decree calling for the abolition of the regions and for the transformation of Nigeria into a unitary state. On May 27, 1966—three days after the decree—ethnic riots targeting the Ibo again broke out in northern cities. Hundreds of people died. Out of fear and insecurity, Ibos began to flee the north, returning to their homeland. Simultaneously, a secessionist sentiment emerged in the north. At the federal level, discussions were underway about the possibility of partitioning Nigeria.

Although the southeast had always been Nigeria's poorest region, by the mid-1960s it was evident that Iboland and its environs had the potential to be an economically productive and advanced region. Oil had been discovered in 1956, prompting some elites to believe that the region could manage independently and not have to rely on economic opportunities and remittances from other parts of the country.

Amid tensions and growing insecurities throughout Nigeria, a second coup was staged on July 29, 1966. This time the coup was headed mostly by northern officers, who proceeded to kill Ironsi and his closest supporters. They initially chose a Yoruba brigadier general to head the new government, but he declined, and the group finally settled on Yakubu Gowan, a northern Christian from a minority group, to assume executive leadership.

The Biafra War

The first six months of 1966 saw an escalation of pogroms against Ibos in the north, forcing many of them to return to Iboland. Along with former Ibo migrants, Ibo military personnel returned home. Given that Ibos in the north no longer seemed to have the protection of their citizenship rights, and the only safe place for them was in their home regions, their very survival dictated that they leave the north.

Among Ibo intellectuals, the fact that Ibos were being forced to return home en masse made the idea of regional secession from Nigeria an all-the-more attractive option. The final decision for the southeast to secede from the rest of Nigeria came on May 30, 1967.[8] At the time, Lt. Colonel Chukwuemeka Ojukwu announced that the eastern region would now be known as the independent Republic of Biafra. This decision was justified by the fact that the citizens of the eastern region were being regularly discriminated against in other parts of Nigeria, which made remaining a part of the republic untenable. For its part, the federal leadership in Nigeria took the position that, given its strong commitment to nation building, its only option was to resort to war in order to preserve the union.

Among intellectuals, motivation for secession was clearly economic, but was also in part based on cultural and political considerations. The latter was particularly true among average Ibo. Notably, however, the Ibo were by no means monolithic. Within Iboland itself, there were intraregional differences of opinion about secession. Lack of unanimity was intensified by the significant number of minority groups, such as the Efik, Ibibio, and Ijaw, living throughout the eastern region. The Ibo tend to be concentrated inland, whereas other minorities are largely found along the coast, where the petroleum wealth of the east is also found. Crawford Young has convincingly argued that Ojukwu made a gross miscalculation when he assumed that he would have the backing of every group in the region.[9] For example, the Ibos of the Mid-West region were initially ambivalent about supporting the secession. They had declared their neutrality, in the hope that both the federal government and the Biafra regime would leave them out of the fight. That they could not remain above the fray became readily apparent when the Mid-West was invaded by the Biafra army, which occupied the region for a month.[10]

Remarkably, at one point during the war the Biafra army penetrated deep into the western region. Eventually, the tide turned and the federal army began to push the Biafra forces back into their own territory. By early 1969, it was clear that the secession would fail, but the fighting continued mostly due to widespread fear among the Ibo that if they lost, they would become the victims of genocide. The war came to an abrupt end on January 6, 1970, when Ojukwu fled to Côte d'Ivoire. Resistance ceased almost immediately.

The State-Creation Exercise

Having won the civil war, the Nigerian government not only had to establish a rhetorical commitment to nation building but also had to set in place institutional mechanisms to achieve this objective. Under the leadership of the military regime of Yakabu Gowan, the federal government attempted to strengthen its own position while reorganizing the country administratively. A key element in this strategy was the creation of an ever-increasing number of states. One of Gowan's first acts as the country's chief executive was the creation of twelve states to replace the previous four. The objective was to "multiply the points of power,"[11] so that more communal groups would feel invested in the federal system and would be in a position to exercise their rights to self-determination. In 1976, on the eve of a return to civilian rule, the number of states was expanded to nineteen. After a brief four-year interlude of civilian rule, the military returned and, by 1993, had expanded the number of states to its present thirty-six, along with the Federal Territory of Abuja.[12]

Some critics charge that despite these efforts, an institutional foundation for effective nation building has not been built.[13] In fact, some critics assert that this process has only served to exacerbate ethno-regional and even local tensions, evidence of which can be seen in ongoing inequalities in education and employment. Moreover, the three largest ethnic groups continue to dominate politics and economics at the national level. Rotimi Suberu contends that the state-creation exercise had more to do with the redistribution of political power for political reasons rather than for economic and social development. He goes on to draw a link between the desire of successive military regimes to shore up their own power and the state-creation process; as a result, the exercise has been inconclusive and, in some cases, repressive.[14]

Since 1966, in contrast to the first half decade of independence, the federal government had become much stronger relative to the state governments. In fact, Suberu and Larry Diamond argue that Nigeria has come to be characterized by "hyper-centralization."[15] That is, the central state now dominates and, over time, has come to function like a unitary state, while maintaining a hierarchical, multi-tiered system in which the federal constitution makes the central government sovereign when differences occur within any other levels of government. In spite of occasional digressions from this path, the central government has devolved powers and resources to the states, rather than the other way around, and states, in turn, have come to monitor and fund local governments. For a brief time, the federal government tried to bypass the states in providing and monitoring resources to local governments, but this effort proved unwieldy, and today resources flow from the center to local government indirectly through state governments.[16]

Indigeneity and Citizenship in Perspective

Since independence, apart from the Biafra War, several regional and subregional conflicts have occurred involving claims by aggrieved groups alleging the denial of basic citizenship rights to either ethnic or religious communities. To a large extent, these conflicts could be attributed to issues relating to autochthony (born from the soil) or indigeneity.[17] That is, groups now commonly claim primordial rights to a particular geographic location, and therefore arrogate the right to determine who is a citizen of that place and to assert the legitimacy to compete for land in the area. More importantly, this definition of citizenship has been enshrined in the Nigerian constitution. At the same time, individuals maintain their rights (as is the case with every Nigerian) to their national citizenship. As in other parts of Africa, this process has raised the possibility of tensions and conflicts between the two conceptualizations of citizenship.

The end of the Cold War coincided with the beginning of a second wave of democratization in Africa, calling for an abandonment of autocratic one-party systems and military regimes in favor of competitive multiparty systems. Beth

Whitaker and Pierre Englebert clearly show the link between this change and the shift in immigration policies of countries such as Côte d'Ivoire, which deny voting rights to immigrants, although they had had those rights prior to that time.[18] The claim to indigenous rights—or the denial of such rights in some cases—is extended to nonagricultural property as well as to access to public goods. Peter Geschiere, in a very creative comparison between Cameroon and the Netherlands, argues that the ending of the Cold War and the ripple effects of change led to anxiety over migration and immigration not only in Africa but also in other parts of the world.[19] In this context, as has been argued above, certain triggers have occurred at particular times and in particular places, leading to conflicts largely justified through assumed rights by communal groups claiming to be indigenous to the area and thus excluding those who could not "prove" they had the same rights. This notion applies not only to African ethnic groups but also to the current status of immigrant groups from other countries. For example, in the case of Tanzania, although Asians (those of south Asian descent) had been despised by the indigenous population for the privileged economic position that their race had acquired during the colonial period, with the onset of multiparty democracy and neoliberal reforms, indigenous African opposition politicians often claimed that they should be denied full citizenship rights not because of their race but because they were not indigenes. The ruling party, Chama Cha Mapinduzi, orchestrated a counter-interpretation based not on race but on the fact that Asians were "foreigners."[20] They could, as a consequence, be considered candidates for naturalization. In other places that had had significant settler populations during the colonial era—such as Zambia and South Africa—race has not become a significant factor in the denial of basic citizenship rights.[21] In still other places, special efforts have been made either to accommodate long-residing residents or other marginalized groups within the ambit of constitutionally protected citizenship rights, or at least to think about doing so.[22]

The 1999 constitution spells out the requirements of citizenship in Nigeria. Every person born in Nigeria before October 1, 1960, the date of independence, either whose parents or grandparent belong or had belonged to a community deemed indigenous to the country is automatically a citizen. Also, a person born after that date but whose grandparents or parents were citizens at the time of independence can claim national citizenship in the country. If a person is born of Nigerian parents who reside outside the country, she or he, too, has the right to claim Nigerian citizenship.[23] Citizenship can also be acquired through naturalization, but only Nigerians can be considered for public office at the state and federal levels. If a person emigrated from one state in Nigeria to another, he or she might face local resistance from political leaders in the community if only based on the fact that he or she was not an indigene.[24]

The institutionalization of indigeneity in Nigeria was a direct outgrowth of the Biafra War and the intense inter- and intraethnic conflicts that occurred in the immediate aftermath of independence. Shortly after assuming the office of the presidency in October 1975, Brigadier General Murtala Mohammed, on the occasion of announcing a constitutional drafting committee that would pave the way for a return to civilian rule, indicated that Nigeria should base its policies on the "Federal Character Principle."[25] He claimed this basis was necessary if the country was to develop a sense of national unity and political stability. When the constitution of the Second Republic was announced in 1979, it stated that "the composition of the Government of the Federation and its agencies and the conduct of its affairs shall be carried out in such a manner as to reflect the federal character of Nigeria and the need to promote national unity and also command national loyalty thereby insuring that there shall be no predominance of persons from a few states or from a few ethnic or other sectional groups in that government or in any of its agencies."[26] The document went on to extend this requirement to state and local governments, mandating that they take into account "the diversity of the peoples within their areas of authority and the need to promote a sense of belonging and loyalty among all peoples of the Federation."[27]

Over the next twenty years, this concept was extended and refined, always emphasizing that all policies flowing from the constitution were meant to promote national unity. For example, in 1996, the Federal Character Commission (FCC) was established and, in 1999, was institutionalized in the new constitution. The stated purpose of the FCC is to ensure the fair and equitable distribution of social services, infrastructure, and economic opportunities. Moreover, the FCC has the authority to prosecute any public officials who do not faithfully apply the Federal Character Principle in the conduct of their office. However, the implementation of affirmative action policies in accordance with the Federal Character Principle has been fraught. Despite their legal requirement to follow the letter of the law, public officials have been known to engage in nepotism and corruption in making appointments and distributing social services, and in other aspects of development policy. On the face of it, the objectives set out by the FCC are very wide in scope and extremely complex, which in part explains the difficulty of implementing the policy.[28] Other factors to consider are that prosecuting violators of the principle would involve one federal agency charging another in court and that the political will to follow the letter of the law is not always guaranteed.

Even though the Federal Character Principle operates in an imperfect manner, evidence indicates that its objectives guide many of the affirmative action policies followed by different levels of government. Also, the influence of the Federal Character Principle can be seen in the requirement that, in order to run for the presidency, a person must belong to a political party, but that party cannot be organized around religion or ethnicity. To be elected, a candidate must secure at least 25 percent of the vote in two-thirds of the states. In presidential elections, an informal rule of the game has to do with what is known in Nigeria as "zoning." The country is divided into zones within the constituent states, and the country is divided into a north and a south zone. For presidential elections, a so-called gentleman's agreement about the division dates back to the earliest days of independence. Formalizing a constitutional provision calling for the rotation of the presidency between the north and the south has been considered from time to time, but has never happened. Nonetheless, an understanding exists that the presidency of a person from one region should be followed by the presidency of a person from the other region. The 1999 constitution decrees that a person can hold the presidency only for two successive terms of four years each. The informality of regional representation in the office of the presidency was put to the test in 2011 with the death in office of President Alhaji Yar'Ardua, a Muslim from the north, and the succession as interim president of Goodluck Jonathan, a southerner. A controversy arose when Jonathan decided to run for the presidency on his own, and won. He is supposed to be eligible for two four-year terms, but controversy will likely ensue if he decides to run again in 2015.

In keeping with the Federal Character Principle, the federal civil service is supposed to allocate resources and jobs at its disposal to individuals from constituent states on an equitable basis.[29] At the same time, as noted above, regional states and local authorities can decide who is indigenous to the community and who is not.[30] This system, then, is quota driven. Quotas for federal jobs or admission to universities, for example, are set for each state, and only individuals indigenous to the particular state can qualify against the quota for that state from which the individual originates.[31] If they are identified as meeting the quota, individuals qualify for civil service jobs or university positions in a state where the quota is yet to be met.

A recent World Bank report indicated that try as it might, the FCC has been unable to meet its numerical equality or equal representation quotas at both state and zonal levels.[32] At the federal level, problems have been attributable to the vast differences in educational development from state to state. States in the southwest and in parts of the south center tend to be much more educationally developed than some of the poorer states in the north. The educational discrepancy exposes the difficulties of trying to apply national citizenship principles while remaining true to the Federal Character Principle. Some critics complain about discrimination against legitimate citizens of the country when they try to exercise their national citizenship rights in areas outside of their home areas. Other critics assert that adherence to the Federal Character Principle promotes mediocrity rather than equity.[33]

Nigeria consists of almost eight hundred local governments that have a major role to play in determining indigeneity. Eighty percent of Nigeria's gross domestic product flows through local governments, which are responsible for the distribution of public goods among people living in their jurisdiction. These local administrations control such resources as revenues they receive as a result of taxation and the federal revenue-sharing system, access to land and other property, admission and scholarships for schools and universities, health care, and other types of social services. One need only prove that he or she is a citizen of the country in order to vote; however, it is not uncommon for individuals deemed nonindigenous or settlers in communities where they now reside to be denied participation in other aspects of public life, such as running for political office.[34]

To prove indigeneity to a particular community or state, individuals must possess a "certificate of indigeneity." These certificates are issued by local government authorities, and must be signed by ward and district heads; however, no clear agreement exists on the criteria for determining indigeneity. This ambiguity gives local authorities significant power in determining who is a legitimate citizen of the community or state. One critic has suggested, "where the kinship system (or clan organization) has a great deal to do with the organization of social life, it can be a source of nepotism and corruption in public life; especially in the recruitment and promotion of men in the public service."[35]

Under normal circumstances, determining the indigeneity of an individual does not lead to widespread intergroup conflict in Nigeria. Popular discontent with certain aspects of government policy—such as the application of affirmative action policies—is more often expressed rhetorically than through violence. Rather than being strictly based on clashes over the indigeneity of one group over another, communal conflicts often stem from political issues of representation. One group might feel that local governing institutions are not representing its traditions and values because other groups with different traditions and agendas control these governmental entities. Such has been the case in the Ife–Modakeke conflicts that have intermittently erupted in western Nigeria since independence.[36] Similar incidents have occurred elsewhere, but clashes over indigeneity issues are increasingly the source of conflicts, particularly in the southeast and south central parts of the country.[37]

Tiv–Junkun Conflict and Indigeneity

A notable recent conflict that has contributed significantly to debates around indigeneity and citizenship has been between the Tiv and Junkun people of east central Nigeria. For the most part, the dispute has related to land rights and has involved the Junkun, who claim to be indigenous to the area they inhabit in Tabara State, and the Tiv, whom they consider settlers with no traditional rights in the region. For the Junkun, land has traditionally been a symbol of prestige, and they have cherished this notion within their traditions. Although they welcomed the Tiv when they arrived in the late eighteenth century, and agreed to allow them to farm land in the area, this grant was considered no more than a courteous loan. In more recent times, the Junkun have become suspicious that the Tiv have been conspiring to control all of the land they share with the Junkun. This fear of marginalization was particularly heightened in the early 1990s when Tiv politicians sought to take leadership roles in the local government in the community of Wukari. In doing so, the Junkun began to feel that "outsiders" were violating their traditions, institutions, and rights. In response, the Tiv claimed that the land they shared with the Junkun belonged to both groups, and that they had as much right to it as did the Junkun. The Junkun claimed exclusive indigenous rights to the land, arguing that they had been there well before the Tiv arrived.[38]

The Tiv claim that they have lived in the area for generations and therefore have full citizenship rights, including political rights and the right to land ownership. In fact, the two groups have had relations for centuries. At the time Nigeria became a colony, both groups had established themselves in the Benue Valley. Initially these relations were cordial, but during the latter part of the British colonial presence in the area, interactions changed. Moses Aluaigba, basing his conclusions on interviews he conducted in 2008, suggests that this shift was in part due to politics and in part due to ecology.[39] The population growth of the sedentary Junkun had not been dynamic—a sharp contrast to the rapid population growth of the Tiv. In addition, the Tiv practice a form of shifting agriculture that requires they utilize enough land to allow for periodic use and fallowness.

As population increased, the Tiv felt the need to expand their settlement territories into new parts of Tabara State, where some Junkun lived. Periodic conflicts between the two groups had always occurred, but beginning in 1959 these conflicts intensified, becoming more frequent. The present day has seen some of Nigeria's most violent interethnic clashes based on the denial of basic citizenship rights.[40] Notably, this development has coincided with the emergence of the independence movement and of national political competition.

The trigger for the most recent round of intense Tiv–Junkun conflicts occurred over a two-year period, beginning in 1990. This crescendo in part related to escalating fear held by Junkun of their possible complete marginalization as a result of elections in which Tiv politicians sought to dominate representation on the Wukari Local Government Council and the Wukari Traditional Council. The Junkun claimed that Tiv were not eligible for the Traditional Council, as they were not indigenous to the region. On their part, the Tiv rejected this charge and claimed equal citizenship rights based on their indigeneity. The Junkun feared that Tiv success in dominating local politics would further threaten their traditional claims to the land in the area. The Junkun claimed that the electoral numbers of the Tiv had been inflated by the influx of migrants who had no citizenship rights in their community. Tensions continued to rise with the creation of Tabara State in 1992, which included the two groups.[41]

The land question involved in this most recent flare-up directly related to claims by Tiv farmers over land that had been designated by their Junkun counterparts as their legal ancestral land. The Junkun felt compelled to defend and repossess their land from the Tiv—or face becoming irrelevant.

In some cases, other sources of conflict, such as property rights or identification with a particular region or religion, have been conflated with issues of citizenship.[42] One example—found in the conflict within Plateau State—is between original Berom inhabitants and Hausa and Fulani immigrants from the Muslim North. This conflict has been particularly intense in the urban and rural areas around the city of Jos. Given that indigeneity is so closely tied to economic and social opportunities, the competition over inclusion and exclusion has occasionally resulted in violent confrontations between those who consider themselves indigene and those whom they consider as migrants.

Most inhabitants of Plateau State are Christian, and the social conflicts that have recently emerged have not been strictly among those who consider themselves indigenes and Hausa and Fulani newcomers, but also between Christians and an alien religion, Islam.[43] The Muslims had sought to establish themselves in local government so as to gain access to certificates of indigeneity, which would qualify them for civil service jobs and educational opportunities. Also, the influx of migrants from the north has resulted in serious pressure on the arable land in the area.

The Biafra War was spurred on by pogroms in the north against southern settlers who had migrated there to take advantage of economic opportunities. Most of the victims were Christians from the southeast. After the war, intermittent violence in northern cities against southerners continued. However, following the year 2000, ethnic and sectarian violence spread south and to the middle-belt region, particularly to the very ethnically and religiously diverse Plateau State. Jos and Plateau State in general have, since independence, been the source of both Christian and Muslim proselytization. As proselytization has intensified so has discourse relating to citizenship claims. The Christians of Plateau State see the Muslim newcomers as a threat based on both their ethnicity and their religion. Muslims fear being discriminated against by Christians, and have recently attempted to assert their claim to citizenship rights. That these migrants now outnumber the original inhabitants around the area of Jos has served as an increasingly keen source of conflict.

The resulting unsettled politics have made Plateau State a prime candidate for the spread of ethno-religious conflict, which in large measure is at the root of the anti-state movement. *Boko Haram* began in the north and, between 2009 and the present, spread south to places such as Plateau State.

Boko Haram, a group whose name translates as "Western education is sin," is an Islamic sect that began in the northern city of Maiduguri in Borno State in 2002.[44] It views the Nigerian secular state as corrupt and prone to oppressing Muslims. Some of its followers point to the summary execution of the group's founder, Mohammed Yusuf, in 2009 as a clear example of the anti-Muslim stand against the group.

Boko Haram would like to establish Nigeria as an Islamic state based on a strict interpretation of Islamic law (*Sharia*), where only Muslims are "true citizens." Although twelve of Nigeria's thirty-six states already have legal systems based on Sharia law, Boko Haram adherents do not feel that the brand of Islam practiced in those states is pure enough. Should the sect's more stringent Sharia interpretations take hold, the current conception of what it means to be a citizen of Nigeria would completely change. This notion would introduce a form of exclusionary citizenship that would be at odds with Nigeria's efforts to reconcile civic republic identities with the identity tied to the Nigerian nation-state. Before 2009, the Boko Haram movement did not see itself directly at war with the state, but beginning in 2008 this attitude changed. Since then, the movement has become more violent—targeting police, politicians, and public institutions. Members of Boko Haram feel that both Christian and Muslim clerics do not respect the movement's own religious views. Since the 2011 national elections, the group's violence has intensified, spreading farther to the south, including to the national capital, Abuja. On Christmas Day 2011, Boko Haram went so far as to bomb Christian churches in several parts of the county. Such attacks continue. Boko Haram has warned Christians to completely leave the north. It is unclear if their efforts seek to reconstitute Nigeria as an independent northern and Islamic state and a southern non-Islamic state.

In large measure, assertions by Boko Haram followers that they and other Muslims are being discriminated against and repressed amount to nothing more than claims of violations of their constitutionally established national citizenship rights. Some observers suggest that much of the current violence in Nigeria is being perpetrated by criminal gangs that claim to be associated with Boko Haram. Others assert that the radical Islamic group has reached the point of feeling that its enemy is the state and therefore that perpetrating violence against that enemy is legitimate.

In terms of population, Nigeria is one of Africa's largest states. It is also among Africa's most diverse countries. The institutions that British colonialists bequeathed to the governance of independent Nigeria quickly proved to be flawed. They were simply grafted onto Nigeria without taking into consideration the extreme ethnic diversity of the country, and the related need to carefully tailor governance institutions down to the grassroots level. Following independence, successive regimes attempted to make administrative adjustments to the governance structures of Nigeria so as to accommodate ethnic, regional, and religious diversity, but their effectiveness was limited. The number of states was expanded from three to thirty-six, and affirmative action policies based upon the Federal Character Principle have been constitutionally enshrined. The federal state has held together for more than fifty years, but tensions and conflicts over citizenship, ethnic, regional, and religious discrimination continue to plague the country. The nation-building project continues to be a work in progress, thus raising the question: "Will the nation-building project in Nigeria ever be complete?"

5

Ethiopia

The Politics of Late Nation Building and the
National Question

"We remind you . . . that all of you are by race, blood and custom, members of
the Ethiopian family. Although there may be local dialects, we must always
strive to preserve our unity and our freedoms."
—Emperor Haile Selassie I, "Speech in the Ogaden, Ethiopia,
August 25, 1956"

The contemporary state of Ethiopia traces its history back some three thousand years, but did not begin to take its modern form until the mid-nineteenth
century.[1] Four emperors in succession pursued the modernization of the state:
Tewodros II, 1855–1868; Yohannes, 1872–1889; Menelik II, 1889–1913; and Haile
Selassie I, 1930–1974.[2] Notably, the construction of modern Ethiopia did not
begin until the eve of the European Scramble for Africa. Rather than fall vic-
tim to European colonialists, Ethiopia's emperors felt the need to update their
militaries and engage in wars of conquest in order to establish and defend the
territorial integrity of the state.[3] The modern state was built on a semifeudal
economy, but in an effort to compete with and fend off European powers, even
before the beginning of the Second World War, Emperor Haile Selassie engaged in a defensive modernization of his military and in the construction of
a centralized bureaucratic apparatus centered around the notion of royal absolutism.[4] The leadership in these processes was provided by elites from the Amhara and Tigre ethnic groups that populate the central highlands of the terri-

tory. The right to rule was conferred upon those deemed fit to serve as King of Kings by the authority of the Ethiopian Orthodox Church. Emperors were declared direct descendants of King Solomon and the Queen of Sheba. Ethnic groups that inhabited the periphery were considered mere subjects of the crown rather than integral members of the community. Over the years, this hierarchy proved to be a major challenge to successive Ethiopian leaders who sought to build a viable multiethnic nation.

From the time he assumed the emperorship, Haile Selassie felt that he had time to create a sense of national unity and to have Ethiopia accepted into the world community of nation-states. In the international arena, he presented Ethiopia as a unitary, multiethnic state characterized by a common sense of national identity. Domestically, however, Haile Selassie's regime followed a policy of top-down control and total domination over subject nationalities. As a result, his domestic policies were generally a failure. Internationally, the emperor came to be seen as the epitome of African independence—viewed as the only African leader to have successfully rebuffed the colonization efforts of the European powers and to have his state internationally recognized alongside the major world powers at the time.

By 1974 most, if not all, of the myths of stability and national unity that Haile Selassie had attempted to cultivate were being challenged. The country, though independent, was at risk of being Balkanized as the emperor's authority was being vigorously questioned from within. The most severe challenges came from Eritrean nationalists in the north, certain segments of the Oromo in the south-central part of the country, and Ogaden Somali irredentists in the southeast. Between 1973 and 1974, Haile Selassie proved unable to resolve the cumulating challenges confronting his regime. Opposition movements constantly disputed the very integrity of Ethiopia's national boundaries, while drought, famine, unemployment, and a generalized economic crisis created a destabilized political environment.

Although Ethiopia's modern leaders have always faced the difficult task of constructing a viable multiethnic nation out of disparate ethnic groups— and with creating a sense of national belonging among these groups—none has succeeded. The question is, *why?* To understand why this failure had been the case, one must put the emergence of modern Ethiopia into historical context, and critically examine the policies followed by Emperor Haile Selassie and the two regimes that succeeded his: the Marxist-Leninist regime, 1975–1991; and the autocratic Ethiopian People's Revolutionary Democratic Front regime, which has ruled since that time. Each of these regimes was characterized by flawed policies of national political integration and nation building. Each failed to address the "national question."[5]

Imperial Ethiopia: State Formation without Nation Building

Throughout his reign, Haile Selassie tried to present the public image of a modernizing autocrat who had the best interest of *all* his subjects at heart; however, critics both inside and outside Ethiopia saw him as more committed to reforming how his bureaucratic empire was organized and operated, and thus preserving royal absolutism, than to modernizing it. For example, rather than engaging in democratic reforms after he came to power in the 1930s, the emperor strengthened the authority of the bureaucratic center and developed a multiethnic cadre of young educated professionals whom he expected to do his bidding even without democratic reforms. However, it was this very nascent educated class that sowed the seeds of royal absolutism's demise.

By all indications, 1960 was a watershed year in the evolution of modern Ethiopian polity. In that year, the specter of revolution first surfaced with an attempt to overthrow Haile Selassie's regime. This coup attempt failed, but was important in having exposed contradictions in the emperor's policies of modernization. Its leaders were several young Western educated civil servants who had tried unsuccessfully to work within the system to make it less corrupt and more democratic. Notably, they did not gain the support of the clergy or the military, and Haile Selassie's support at the center held firm. However, even in its failure, the coup had a profound effect on the course of political developments after 1960.[6] Prior to this time, the emperor had been insulated from the grievances of various groups in society. From this point on, protests from workers, students, and ethnic self-help associations became commonplace. As in the coup of 1960, grievances centered on such issues as land, tax administrative reform, low wages, and the lack of democratic reform.

In 1965, a group that came to be known as the "student movement" engaged in a mass demonstration before parliament, calling for democratic and land reforms. Also, various ethnic groups began to organize nationally to challenge the foundations of the imperial regime: It was becoming very clear that Haile Selassie was not committed to genuine national political integration. He dealt with various nationality groups by attempting to pacify them—either gently or harshly—rather than by satisfying their demands for social equity. Rather than condemn and deal firmly with public corruption, he cultivated the image of a benevolent father figure, disassociating himself from such activities. No specific policy of national political integration ever existed under Haile Selassie's rule except for the priority he gave to developing a small multiethnic cadre of young elites to serve in his administration. John Markakis notes that authors of the emperor's official governmental documents consciously avoided any reference to ethnic, linguistic, or religious diversity.[7] Most of the government's efforts were devoted to discouraging or destroying the language, religion, and culture of subject populations.

During the 1960s, the emperor did engage in a form of ethnic patronage, incorporating some ethnic elites into his administration; however, Amhara political representation and dominance remained unchanged. Moreover, development activities remained concentrated in the central part of the country— the Amhara homeland. The rest of the country suffered from abject poverty and very little development activity except for import-substitution industries controlled by the central government.

The policies of Haile Selassie's regime did little to change Ethiopia's devastating poverty, widespread illiteracy, and lack of social services in the countryside. Moreover, students in peripheral areas were required to be educated in a language other than their own. For example, at the elementary grade levels, students were taught in Amharic, and at the high school and university levels, the language of instruction was English. Many people in peripheral areas despised this language policy, not so much because it did not foster the social mobility of local populations, but because of the implications it had for the destruction of their indigenous culture. In such cases, rather than serving as an agent of national political integration, the language and education policy further alienated ethnic minorities.[8] This pattern of neglect and inequality in peripheral areas could also be found in social services, such as formal health care and public works, further contributing to poverty and underdevelopment in areas of the rural periphery.

Perhaps as important as the poverty and underdevelopment of peripheral areas were grievances relating to land. Following the Second World War, Haile Selassie attempted to undercut the power of the traditional landed classes by concentrating more on power and authority at the center, thus creating hope among the peasantry and landless classes that they would benefit from his land reform policies. However, a key element in the emperor's strategy of winning elite support had been imperial grants of land based on freehold tenure. Anyone receiving such a grant was allowed to hold the land in perpetuity. Individual landholders could pass such land down in the form of inheritance.

Rather than ceasing after 1960, this practice increased as the government attempted to benefit from foreign development assistance for the expansion of agricultural production. In the process, peasants and tenants were evicted from land in order to make way for new landlords. The new policy of freehold tenure tended to directly conflict with traditional communal tenure practices in place. The resulting social instability exacerbated popular discontent, particularly in the southern parts of the country. Now, not only was the region's poverty and underdevelopment attributed to the domination of the Amhara and their relatives, the Tigre, but it was also associated with the social classes involved in the spread of a reformed land tenure system and capitalized and mechanized agriculture.

Failed Nation Building during the Imperial Period: Citizenship and the National Question

Haile Selassie was never able to develop an effective policy of national political integration. As mentioned, he concentrated mainly on incorporating a small number of ethnic elites into the ruling classes, rewarding them with material benefits and other trappings of privilege. This policy promoted the adoption of the Amhara language, culture, and Orthodox Christianity and the denigration of all other cultures. Rather than conveying a sense of national citizenship among the majority of peripheral populations, Haile Selassie's policies instilled a sense of resentment not only among the masses but also among the very elites that he was attempting to cultivate. Such responses were particularly pronounced among the Eritreans, Ogaden Somalis, and Oromo, and contributed significantly to the emergence of a nationalist movement among these groups. In the remainder of this subsection, I will trace the development of such sentiments among the Eritreans, Ogaden Somalis, and Oromo.

During the Scramble for Africa, Italy claimed what is present-day Eritrea, which lies next to the Red Sea. Initially, a treaty between Emperor Menelik II and the Italian government legitimized this claim. The treaty was written in both Italian and Amharic—but the two versions differed. The Ethiopian version suggested that Ethiopia could rely on Italy in the event of threats from other powers. The Italian version declared Ethiopia a "protectorate" of Italy. The differences in the two versions caused a serious rift between the two countries.[9] When Ethiopia abrogated this treaty, war ensued. The result was the resounding defeat of Italian forces by the armies of Menelik at the Battle of Adowa in 1896.[10] Subsequently, Ethiopia entered into diplomatic agreements with France, Italy, and Britain, which resulted in most of Ethiopia's present-day boundaries. Italy was allowed to keep Eritrea on the condition that it not threaten the Ethiopian heartland.

Both Menelik and Haile Selassie had attempted to establish the legitimacy of Ethiopia's claim to Eritrea in the international community. However, during the Second World War, the Italian Fascists again attempted to invade and control the Ethiopian highlands. In 1936, they succeeded in driving Emperor Haile Selassie into exile and proceeded to occupy Ethiopia for five years. They were eventually ousted from the territory by a British Commonwealth force in 1941. Haile Selassie was restored to the throne and assisted by the British in reasserting his authority in the country both administratively and politically.

Eritrean Resistance and Independence

Following the war, Haile Selassie attempted to secure international support for the unification of Eritrea and Ethiopia.[11] The official claim of the Imperial government was that Greater Tigre, including Eritrea, had been an historic part of the Aksumite Empire.[12] During the war, the British seemed to favor the idea of an independent Eritrea, but once hostilities ceased they gradually shifted to the Ethiopian position. At the Paris Peace Conference—less than a year after the United Nations was formed—a formula was worked out by delegates to the conference for the disposal of the former Italian colonies. Regarding Eritrea, after several study commissions, in 1950 the UN Security Council passed a resolution calling for an autonomous Eritrean government to be federated with Ethiopia. Furthermore, the two political entities were to negotiate a federal constitution. Between 1950 and 1952, a constitutional debate ensued. For at least four years prior to this decision, Eritrean political groupings had voiced both favor and opposition to such an arrangement. In parliamentary elections in 1952, Unionists secured thirty-two out of sixty-eight seats, the Democratic Party garnered eighteen seats, and the Muslim League gathered fifteen. Unionists then formed a coalition government with the Muslim League. Assuming that Eritrean autonomy would be preserved, the new legislature voted to ratify the federal constitution. Eritrea was allowed to fly its own flag and to retain Tigrinya and Arabic as the national languages, rather than Amharic.[13]

During constitutional discussions, the emperor had made it clear that he supported the Unionists, and once they were in power, he worked subtly but systematically to cultivate Eritrean support for a closer relationship with Ethiopia. In the same year it was inaugurated, the Eritrean constitution was suspended. A year later, all trade unions were banned. By 1956, the National

Assembly had been temporarily suspended and all political parties had been barred. By 1958, the Unionists, who were firmly in control of the National Assembly, abandoned the requirement that both the Eritrean and Ethiopian flags be flown in public places. Now, only the latter was required. Moreover, the Ethiopian code of laws replaced the Eritrean code of laws. This move was followed in 1960 by a name change—from the Eritrean Government to the Eritrean Administration, thus making the way for Ethiopia's total annexation of Eritrea in late 1962.[14]

Almost immediately, low-intensity warfare began, involving a liberation movement that called itself the Eritrean Liberation Front (ELF) and was comprised mostly, but not exclusively, of Muslim supporters. By 1967, the ELF had gained significant support among the masses, particularly in the northern and western part of the country. The emperor attempted to undermine the movement by making personal visits to the region, ostensibly to assure Eritreans that they were, indeed, equal members of the Ethiopian community and would be treated accordingly. He dispensed political offices, titles, and other resources, hoping to buy off would-be elite opponents.[15] However, from this point, resistance only intensified.

In 1970, the ELF, riven by internal disputes, split. Thus was born the Eritrean People's Liberation Front (EPLF). Differences between the two groups continued into the 1980s, until the EPLF emerged as the most effective Eritrean opposition movement. The EPLF clearly demonstrated its strength in 1974, when its forces resoundingly defeated a peasant force dispatched to the region to support the efforts of the newly installed junta, the Dergue, to completely crush the Eritrean movement. The new regime responded by stepping up its efforts to suppress the movement militarily. This action failed and, by the late 1980s, the EPLF had captured most of Eritrea and entered into a united front with other ethnic movements, such as the Tigre People's Liberation Front (TPLF) and the Oromo Liberation Front (OLF), united in their commitment to militarily overthrow the Ethiopian regime. In the end, the remnant of the Dergue regime was overthrown in the summer of 1991. I shall return to this point.

The Somali Nation in the Ogaden and Haud

The origins of Ethiopia's troubles in the Ogaden region can be traced to its incorporation into the Ethiopian state between 1887 and 1955. As indicated, Ethiopia had secured its claim to the region through treaties with Britain, France, and Italy in the late 1800s. Until that time, the area had never been a part of historic Ethiopia, except for brief periods during wars of conquest.[16] Even with international recognition, Ethiopia was only able to secure tenuous control over the Ogaden region. The crown gained some control by establishing garrison towns staffed by regional armies with the objective of protecting Ethiopia's international borders, and secondarily of maintaining law and order. However, the full impact of Ethiopia's colonization of the Ogaden was not evident until after the war.

In contrast with Eritrea, which is comprised of thirteen distinct ethnic groups, the Somali trace their sense of nationhood to antiquity. This national identity is not based on a shared history of oppression, but instead on a distinct culture that is shared by people who presently inhabit the Republic of Somaliland, Puntland, Djibouti, northeast Kenya, the remnants of the Republic of Somalia, and the Ogaden. As such, they are bound by language, custom, religion, and traditional sociopolitical organization. This nation was divided among Ethiopia, France, Britain, and Italy during the process of alien colonization.[17]

The colonial period had seen Somali resistance, but Somali nationalism did not come fully into view until the war. The Italian Fascists had attempted to create an Italian East Africa, including "Greater Somalia." During this war, the Western powers seemed committed to unifying the Somali nation once peace was restored to the Horn of Africa. However, this commitment proved to be hollow. Instead, through diplomatic maneuvering at the UN, and with the support of the United States, Ethiopia was able to have fulfilled its claims over the Ogaden and another Somali inhabited territory to the southeast, the Haud. It took administrative control of these regions in 1948 and 1955, respectively. Somali resistance was immediate, and Ethiopia was not able to establish effective control until 1955.[18]

Between 1955 and 1960, Haile Selassie made several publicized attempts to bring the Somali regions into the Ethiopian fold. During this period, urban administration and social services such as schools and clinics were set up to convey the appearance of effective administration and concern for the integration of Somali residents of the region as citizens. Some Somali were even co-opted into the administration of the region. Nevertheless, resistance continued.

Illustrative examples of Haile Selassie's approach to the Ogaden and the Haud during this period are his trip to the region in 1956, where he delivered a speech intended to assure the Somali that despite their cultural heritage they were, indeed, citizens of Ethiopia.[19] Noting some of what his regime had done for the Somali of the Ogaden, the emperor asserted that the Somali people were related to all Ethiopians by blood and custom. He stated, "We remind you . . . that all of you are by race, color, blood, and custom, members of the

Ethiopian family. Although there may be local dialects, we must always strive to preserve our unity and our freedom."[20] Clearly, the emperor considered the union between the Ethiopian state and the Somali of the southeastern part of the country justified on both spiritual and practical grounds. He suggested that without Ethiopia, the region was not economically viable. Indeed, a 1963 official press release stated, "Ethiopia will not part with one of her children because of any alleged linguistic, religious, or tribal affinity; nor will Ethiopia permit one single inch of Ethiopian soil to be separated from the motherland on such specious grounds."[21]

Despite token attempts to develop modern infrastructure in the Ogaden and other Somali regions, the emperor seemed to equate Somali integration with nothing more than economic and political domination. To have a place in Ethiopia, then, Somalis would have to submit to assimilation while accepting the political hegemony of the Amhara. Just across the border, British Somaliland and Italian Somaliland achieved their separate independences in 1960, and quickly united to establish the Somali Republic. This merger only served to fuel the aspiration of Somalis living outside of the republic for unification into a Greater Somalia.

The primary impetus for militaristic irredentism in the Ogaden was the founding of the Western Somali Liberation Front (WSLF) in 1960. The movement's objective was to separate a major part of southeastern Ethiopia from that country and join it with the Republic of Somalia. For most of the 1960s, the WSLF relied heavily on Somalia for military and logistical support, but following a military coup the junta leader, Mohammed Siad Barre, withdrew this support, preferring to invest in the modernization of Somalia's regular army. Having been rejected by Siad Barre, the leadership of the WSLF shifted the organization's headquarters to Aden, in Yemen. From there, the WSLF attempted to pursue a guerrilla war from abroad. However, when Aden entered into a treaty with Ethiopia in 1976, the WSLF returned to Somalia. By that time, Siad Barre, having built a very effective national army, seemed not to feel threatened by the WSLF's presence in his territory. At the time, Ethiopia was in the midst of what would be known as the Red Terror Campaign, an operation against opponents of the Marxist regime's attempt to transform Ethiopian society.[22] This extremely violent period has been characterized as a civil war. In this context, Siad Barre decided to attempt an appropriation of southeast Ethiopia, thereby to recover one piece of the divided Somali nation.

Somalia launched an invasion into Ethiopia in the summer of 1977—a period in which the superpowers, the Soviet Union and the United States, were switching their alliances from one country to the other. Whereas it had been allied with Ethiopia until early 1977, the United States now switched to a tentative alliance with Somalia. The Soviet Union, by contrast, switched from Somalia to Ethiopia. However, Somalia's decision to invade Ethiopia was not undertaken in concert with the United States, who remained out of the conflict between the two countries. The USSR, however, provided massive amounts of military equipment and logistical support to Ethiopia. The conflict lasted until March 1978. Over a six-month period, Somali forces occupied vast tracts of land in southeast Ethiopia. With the assistance of the Soviets and their allies, Ethiopia was finally able to beat back the invasion.

Since the end of the Ogaden War, two successive regimes in Ethiopia have attempted to integrate Somalis in the southeastern part of the country more fully into the multiethnic nation.[23] Nonetheless, low-intensity Somali resistance has continued.

The Oromo and National Identity

The Oromo is the single largest ethnic group in Ethiopia, comprising 40–50 percent of a population of just over 80 million. This group is disproportionately represented in the southern parts of Ethiopia, which were the object of nineteenth-century wars of conquest mainly by the emperors Tewodros, Yohannes, and Menelik. This territory came to be valued for its rich agricultural capacities.

The Oromo and the Amhara have a long history of contact. Intermarriage and assimilation, especially among elites, were not uncommon. However, according to Oromo accounts of that history, beginning with the reign of Tewodros, highland Ethiopians (e.g., Amhara and Tigre) undertook a systematic effort to economically exploit the Oromo and to destroy their culture.[24] Prior to this offensive, the Oromo people were organized in a relatively loose confederation of clans that shared a common language and culture, and were believed to have been the descendants of a common ancestor.[25]

From the time of Tewodros and Menelik, the Ethiopia government established effective control over the Oromo periphery by establishing garrison towns controlled by military officers charged with administration and maintaining political order. For their service, the military officers were provided land as well as the authority to collect in-kind contributions from small-scale farmers or sharecroppers who cultivated in their areas of responsibility. This system was, by all indications, a form of feudalism. Initially, the Oromo did not regard the terms of these arrangements as excessively exploitative, but as capitalism during the Haile Selassie regime began to take hold, land was privatized and demands on its tillers became increasingly exploitative.[26] This situation, coupled with the global effort to end colonialism and increasing nationalistic sentiments, led to the emergence of an Oromo nationalist movement.

Haile Selassie attempted to secure Oromo fealty through alliances with certain Oromo leaders. The most favored elites were those who chose to become totally assimilated into Amhara culture, often adopting Christian names and becoming fluent in the Amharic language. From the Ethiopian perspective, assimilated Oromo were fortunate compared to the Nilotic groups in the southwest of the country. Though they had been the object of Amhara slavery, the Oromo were seen as civilizable and therefore able to be assimilated into Amhara culture. This perception contrasted sharply with the Amhara view of the Nilotic groups, who were viewed as *shakilla,* or pariahs, destined to a fate of slavery. According to the dominant group, the Oromo could rise to legitimate citizenry in Ethiopia, but only if they abandoned close attachment to their traditions and culture, and assimilated.[27]

P. T. W. Baxter has argued that the destruction of Oromo culture under the imperial system was systematic.[28] In elementary school, as in Eritrea, the language of instruction was Amharic; at the upper levels, it was English. For a brief period during the Italian occupation, the Oromo language was promoted in school; but once he returned to power, Haile Selassie banned the language from public use. In addition, traditional culture was denigrated, and the Amhara culture and Coptic Christian religion were privileged. Traditional religions continued to be accepted but were relegated to no more than ritual status.

The inferior status assigned to the Oromo and to Oromo culture must be taken into account in explanations of this group's resentment of Amhara political dominance. Occupied by the Oromo, the peripheral areas of the south were the backbone of Ethiopia's agriculturally based economy. They cultivated such valued export crops as coffee, oil seeds, hides, and skins. Moreover, rather than exercising their traditional rights to land, the Oromo were mere peasants, sharecroppers, or pastoralists on the land they occupied. The landlord–tenant relationships became increasingly inequitable as capitalism took hold in the countryside.[29]

In the early part of the twentieth century, Oromo rebellion against the central government became endemic. The process sharpened the sense of ethnic Oromo national identity.[30] However, a definite movement for self-determination or for equal citizenship rights did not clearly surface until about 1965, when an Oromo cultural organization emerged and became nationally prominent. The organization was named Mecha-Tulema, after two major

Oromo clans from the historic Oromo Federation. Leadership of the organization mostly consisted of Oromo intellectuals who had been assimilated into Amhara culture and became involved in government and business; most prominent among them was Tadesse Biru. Speeches at mass meetings promoted galvanizing Oromo unity and reclaiming Oromo dignity and culture. The tone of these rallies was often hortative and critical of the central government's policies toward the Oromo. Yet, initially demands were for first-class citizenship rather than separation from the Ethiopian state.

By late 1966, Haile Selassie was extremely concerned about the Mecha-Tulema movement, and thus banned the organization. Tadesse Biru was tried for sedition and condemned to death, but the sentence was later changed to life in prison.[31] From this point on, the seeds of nationalistic resistance among the Oromo had clearly been sown, but no serious militancy emerged until the Oromo Liberation Front (OLF) was formed in 1973. Over the next three years, the OLF began to engage in armed (although limited) activity, mostly in the southeastern part of the country.

Revolution, Afro-Marxism and Nation Building: The Enduring National Question

In early September 1974, a military coup brought an end to Ethiopia's modern imperial regime. Coup members were not guided by an elaborate ideology, instead claiming that they were mainly motivated by a sense of patriotism. Initially, the new regime adopted as its motto *Ethiopia Tikdem* (Ethiopia First); however, within three years, it had detached from this African nationalist ideology and began to pursue a variant of "scientific socialism."

From the very beginning, the regime, or the Dergue (committee) as it came to be known, was confronted with popular discontent, as several ethnic groups made demands for equal citizenship rights and/or self-determination. In some cases, autonomy entailed decentralization and a modicum of regional autonomy, but in the case of the Eritrean Liberation Movement, self-determination implied separation and independence from Ethiopia. The Eritrean People's Liberation Front and other nationalist movements in that region had been waging a civil war against Ethiopia for more than a decade. The Dergue initially tried to quash this movement militarily, an effort that not only was unsuccessful, but also served to intensify the conflict. In an effort to find a political solution to bids for self-determination by Eritreans and others, the Dergue established its Program for the National Democratic Revolution

(PNDR) in 1975. It declared its commitment to creating a political system and government based upon the principles of "scientific socialism" and political and administrative decentralization, allowing local communities to have more of a say in governing their own affairs.

A significant part of the reforms first introduced saw the nationalization of all rural and urban property. Land once owned by the ruling classes and the nobility became state property in the name of the people. The repossessed land was redistributed to local communities and governed by local development councils called *kebeles*. This system marked an effort to secure the support of groups that had historically been dominated and exploited under the semifeudal imperial system. Significantly, although the land was in the name of the "people," the people could not own the land in the strictest sense, which meant that grievances relating to the destruction of traditional social structures and custom remained unresolved. The new regime envisioned the creation of a stateless, classless society that leveled intergroup relations among nationalities. Rather than promote the restoration of traditional values and culture, the goal was to make such institutions irrelevant.

In spite of great efforts over its first decade of rule to create conditions for widespread acceptance, the Dergue, by 1976, was confronted with persistent civil unrest throughout the country. Its tendency to respond with violence against those who challenged the regime led to international exposure of gross human rights problems in the country. For instance, in the U.S. presidential campaign of 1976, candidate Jimmy Carter pledged to cut off military aid to several countries guilty of gross human rights violations—including Ethiopia. He did precisely that when he assumed office in 1977. By November 1976, the Dergue was desperate, and had already turned to the Eastern Bloc for military, economic, and political assistance. Relations between the United States and Ethiopia were almost completely severed in late April, and the Soviet Union stepped in to fill the void. At this time, Ethiopia demanded that the United States close down the Kagnew Naval Air Station in Eritrea, all U.S. military assistance and advisory group operations, the Naval Medical Research Unit, and the Unites States Information Service. Also, personnel at the U.S. Embassy and Agency for International Development had to be greatly reduced.[32]

In addition to military and economic aid, the Soviets and their allies attempted to encourage the Dergue to create institutions to assist in pursuing its scientific socialist development strategy. By 1984, the Workers' Party of Ethiopia (WPE) had been created, with a mandate to be the vanguard of the revolution. This action came when Ethiopia was in the midst of a catastrophic drought and famine. Despite the widespread social problems the country faced, the Dergue forged ahead with its socialist policies and preparations for inaugurating a Marxist-Leninist constitution. It diverted resources that could have been used for famine relief and poverty alleviation to military purposes, and relied heavily upon the international community for humanitarian assistance.

In its role as the vanguard of the revolution, the WPE had as a primary task laying the foundation for a socialist constitution. In March 1986, a 343-member constitutional commission was formed to draft this document. The commission had its origins in the Institute for the Study of Ethiopian Nationalities, which had been established in 1983 specifically to find solutions to political and social tensions that grew from Ethiopia's extreme ethnic diversity and inequalities. In a speech on May 1, 1984, President Mengistu Haile Mariam asserted:

> The National Democratic Revolution programme explicitly provides for the recognition of the rights of Ethiopian nationalities and the respect for and observance of their history, language and culture, in the spirit of socialism and the pursuit of a new life in complete equality, co-operation, brotherhood and understanding. In this regard, the resolution adopted by the Second Commission for Organizing the Party of the Working People of Ethiopia (COPWE)[33] Congress in order to ensure a solid basis for the democratic rights of the working people in this country and the establishment of the Institute for Nationalities is of great importance.[34]

After about three months of deliberations, the commission issued a 120-article draft document. A million copies of this draft were printed and distributed throughout the country. Between July and August, the draft was discussed at about 25,000 locations. According to official reports, more than a half million people suggested revisions. In August, the drafting committee reconvened for the purpose of considering some proposed amendments. In the end, the commission agreed to ninety-five amendments to the original draft, but for the most part, the changes were superficial.[35]

The People's Democratic Republic of Ethiopia (PDRE) was officially proclaimed on February 22, 1987, thus becoming only the sixth Afro-Marxist regime in Africa.[36] The constitution resembled a hybrid of the Soviet and Romanian constitutions. Although a council of state (an executive body of twenty-four) was tasked with the primary responsibility of running the state's day-to-day operations, a strong presidency was also needed. Interestingly, the authors of the new constitution chose not to endorse a direct approach to dealing with self-determination. The rights of nationality groups were deemed not as important as those of citizens belonging to mass organizations (e.g., workers and peasants associations, women's associations, student associations, etc.). In other words, individuals were expected to grant primary loyalty to these types of mass organizations, rather than to their ethnic kin.

The constitution created and detailed the structure and operations of the 835-member National Shengo, the supreme organ of state power. Those elected to office had first to be nominated by local cells of the WPE, mass organizations, military units, and selected other bodies. The National Shengo was responsible for electing the president and vice president of the country, and the vice presidents of the council of state. The prime minister, deputy prime ministers, other members of the council of ministers, and other officers in standing commissions were to be elected on recommendation from the president by the National Shengo. The president of the PDRE was granted sweeping powers. Like the emperor, he could appoint and dismiss governmental officers at any level, govern by decree, and in effect—despite the separation of power into executive, legislative, and judicial branches—operate above the law. Rather than operating as an autonomous legislature, the Shengo often found itself merely ratifying decisions that had already been made by the president.

The new government and constitution were officially inaugurated on September 10, 1987. Within a week, the PDRE turned its attention to burning issues related to group rights and self-determination, which it managed by issuing a proclamation calling for the administrative reorganization of the country, creating twenty-four administrative regions and five "autonomous regions."[37] This fiat was an obvious attempt to diffuse widespread discontent among various nationality groups, particularly in Eritrea, Tigray, the Ogaden, and some areas inhabited by the Oromo. Rather than forthrightly addressing its ethnic or nationality problems, the regime was clearly attempting to repartition the country so as to minimize the importance of large and relatively homogeneous regions, and to strengthen its ability to control politics and the economy. The regime granted autonomous status to the port city of Assab, in the province of Eritrea, and to the regional commercial center Dire Dawa, in the Ogaden, for example, thus retaining the economic cores of those respective provinces.

Reforms called for the creation of popularly elected provincial legislative assemblies and executive officers. Regional governments were to have at least partial control over policies and programs in such sectors as culture, health, education, taxation, and local economic development. Although the administrative reorganization of the country was intended to lend legitimacy to the

Marxist regime and its programs, this effort did not stem the tide of opposition. The reaction of the armed opposition nationalist movements was swift and negative.[38] Groups such as the OLF, TPLF, EPLF, and the Afar Liberation Front saw nothing new in the reforms and, in fact, stepped up their criticism and resistance against the regime. By the end of 1987, administrative reforms were a reality only on paper. The beginning of 1988 saw the TPLF and EPLF achieve significant battlefield victories against the Ethiopian forces. This was demonstrated by the fact that the TPLF and EPLF were now able to capture and hold territory that had been under the control of the Ethiopian government.

These negative developments had a profound effect on the morale of the Ethiopian military. In May 1989, an abortive coup was launched against the regime—at the same time that the Soviets had declared their intention to end their military and economic support of the Ethiopian government. The Ethiopian army had expanded to more than 600,000 at the time, and began to implode following the failed coup, as whole units of troops defected, taking their arms and weapons with them and joining opposition forces. Over the next two years, the TPLF and its recently created umbrella organization, the Ethiopian Peoples' Revolutionary Democratic Front (EPRDF), was able to capture all of Tigray Province, and large segments of Wollo, Gondar, and Shoa provinces. In Eritrea, the EPLF gained control of all of the territory except for the urban centers of Asmara, Massawa, and Assab. By late 1990, the entire country was in turmoil, and on May 21, 1991, the Marxist regime finally fell to the forces of the EPRDF; its leadership was either captured or went into exile.

Regime Change and Ethnic Federalism for Nation Building

When it came to power in 1991, the EPRDF government made a conscious decision not to suppress the national aspirations of ethnicities that made up Ethiopia. For example, in 1995 a government spokesman, citing the historic failure of the imperial and Marxist regimes to address the issues of ethnic tensions, mistrust, and conflict, stated, "We must find a solution which is beneficial to the Ethiopian people today, therefore, history will not provide the answer."[39] The Transitional Charter asserted that all of Ethiopia's nationalities had the right to self-determination and the right to govern their own affairs.

Within two years of coming to power, the new government announced its decision to reorganize the country administratively, creating states based on the principle of *ethnic federalism*. This approach was seen as the best way to demonstrate that the new regime was committed to social equity and democracy. The policy of ethnic federalism initially began to unfold through a series of proclamations, and eventually the right to self-determination was enshrined in the constitution of 1994.[40] Article #39 of the constitution, "The Rights of Nations, Nationalities and Peoples," spells out the procedure that nations and nationalities must follow to separate themselves from the federal state. It also establishes the rights of all states to write their own constitutions, and to write, speak, promote, and develop their own languages.[41]

Significantly, the right to self-determination accorded to every nationality group includes the right to secede from the federal state of Ethiopia. The constitution allows this action to be taken when at least two-thirds of the legislature of the nation, nationality, or peoples concerned vote to do so; after a three-year period, during which the vote is reviewed by the Constitutional Court and the Council of the Federation, the decision must be ratified in a state-wide referendum.

How has Ethiopia's novel experiment with ethnic federalism worked in practice? Clearly this policy has not resulted in widespread consensus that it effectively manages the challenges of extreme cultural diversity in the country. In fact, many members of the public see the policy as fatally flawed. Some even believe that this policy will ultimately result in the breakup of historic Ethiopia.[42]

On many occasions, government representatives have reasserted that their primary goal is to promote social justice for all of Ethiopia's constituent nationality groups. In 2002, for example, the then–prime minister Meles Zinawe stated that his regime was "resolved to empower and promote democratic principles giving affirmative actions [*sic*] to historically disadvantaged groups and relatively backward states."[43]

In the process of "putting together" this federal system, the EPRDF regime has created a devolved system of administration.[44] Alfred Stepan argues that this form of federalism is imposed from the center, rather than being arrived at through elite bargaining among all relevant elites (e.g., the former Soviet Union, the former Yugoslavia, and Nigeria following the military coup of 1966). Ethiopia's version of ethnic federalism claims to seek a closer relationship between the government and the people, and to create circumstances that facilitate popular empowerment. However, this policy clearly has real limitations, as the central government has maintained a good deal of power and influence at the federal level. For instance, most of government's taxing powers rest with the federal government, which has the responsibility to collect most taxes, including import and export taxes, set national economic and social policies, and establish national standards in such areas as commerce and trade, finance, and transportation. Also, the federal government has exclusive responsibility in foreign policy, national defense, monetary policy, and interstate transportation and commerce.[45] Whatever powers not assigned to the federal government are under the purview of regional state governments.

Important facts to take into account when attempting to evaluate ethnic federalism in Ethiopia are the country's large population size (over 80 million people), poorly developed and maintained transportation and communications infrastructure, general economic underdevelopment, and the abject poverty of large segments of the population both at the communal and regional levels. Additionally, the governmental capacity required of a complex federal system is limited in most parts of the country and particularly limited in poor regions. Certain states are barely able to independently finance a small fraction of their public works expenditures (e.g., Beneshengul-Gamuz, Gambella, Harari, Somali, Afar). In general, needed technical, administrative, and material resources are in short supply and are spread even more thinly as one proceeds down the administrative hierarchy.

Theoretically, the governments of regional states have the authority and power to identify policy preferences and to formulate their own development plans. These rights include setting their own budgets and making independent decisions about capital and recurrent expenditures. Moreover, central administrators have considerable influence on priority setting and expenditure strategies followed by the states. The lack of administrative capacities of some states, particularly the poorest ones, has a profound negative effect on ethnic federalism's ability to show progress in socioeconomic development, and thereby to elicit popular support for the regime and its policies.

Most importantly, administrative shortcomings at the state and district levels have handicapped official efforts to create a government that is closer to the people and that involves the populace more in determining how development goals are set at the grassroots level and how public funds are spent for development purposes. In most regions, basic public services such as the provision of adequate potable water and sanitation services, education, public health, food security, police and judicial services, and public works are generally available only on a limited basis. This reality has noticeable effects on how people feel about their personal and group situations in terms of basic citizenship rights. I addressed this issue in fieldwork I conducted in 2002–2003.[46] One goal of this exercise was to gauge the opinions of selected ethnic groups about the regime's efforts to promote and protect the citizenship rights of Ethiopians in general and their own nationality group in particular. The respondents were asked whether they felt that the right to self-determination of nationality groups was more important than the government's nation-building project.

The results of this survey suggested that the EPRDF is making some progress in engendering a sense of Ethiopian national identity that either transcends or coexists with a clear sense of ethnic identity among the country's desperate nationality groups. A major finding was that most Ethiopians, no matter what nationality group they belong to, do not reject the notion of the self-determination of nationality groups—only that this should not preclude equal citizenship rights at both the national and subnational levels. In other words, there is a widespread sense that various nationality groups should be allowed to govern their own affairs with regard to local and cultural issues, but at the same time maintain an affinity with and loyalty to the national community.

Throughout its modern history, Ethiopia has confronted the need to promote a common sense of national citizenship among its disparate nationality groups. Beginning with the rule of Emperor Haile Selassie I, the central government attempted either to suppress or assimilate groups that were joined to the empire as a result of conquest. In the process, he advanced the idea that all the people in his realm (excluding slaves), despite linguistic and cultural differences, were one family. He attempted to modernize Ethiopia from a feudalistic foundation, but various social contradictions undermined this process, which led to the imperial system's demise in 1974.

The regime that succeeded Haile Selassie began as a militant nationalist regime, but quickly turned to a "scientific socialist" approach to both national development and national political integration. Initially, the idea was to downplay ethnic differences in the interest of totally leveling society based on social and economic categories rather than on ethnic identity. Nevertheless, failure to resolve the "national question" plagued the Marxist-Leninist regime throughout its existence, leading to its collapse in 1991.

Building on most of the new institutions created by its Marxist-Leninist predecessor, including the Institute for the Study of Ethiopian Nationalities, the regime of the EPRDF attempted to elevate ethnic and cultural diversity among its nationality groups rather than to ignore it or suppress it. Thus was born a nation-state based on ethnic federalism, with the hope that power would devolve to ethnically based states, which would satisfy both the elites and the masses they comprised. Clearly, a large segment of the population supports political and administrative devolution, but widespread disagreement exists about ethnic federalism. At a very fundamental level, this issue creates and highlights the tension between national citizenship and an exclusive form of *state citizenship* rights. Unless this tension is resolved, Ethiopia's political instability will be an ever-present possibility, if not a reality.

6

Côte d'Ivoire

Ivorité *and* Citizenship

"We need a war because we need our identity cards. Without an identity card you are nothing in this country."
—Fighter for the *Forces Nouvelles,* quoted in Bronwen Manby,
   Struggles for Citizenship

The ending of the Cold War, the onset of multiparty elections, and the second wave of democratization served as catalysts for a debate over citizenship in Côte d'Ivoire.[1] Under French colonialism, beginning in 1895, Côte d'Ivoire had been one of eight colonial territories included in the French West African Federation;[2] it achieved its independence from France in 1960. Its first president was a physician and wealthy planter named Felix Houphouët-Boigny from the Baoulé ethnic group, which had settled in the south-central part of the territory in about the mid-1800s. Houphouët-Boigny had been active in regional politics in Francophone West Africa as early as the immediate pre–World War Two era, and had even served in the French National Assembly in Paris.

Once he assumed the presidency, Houphouët-Boigny set the country on a course for political stability and economic development. From the early 1900s, the economy was built around the production and export of coffee and cocoa. Timber production was also important. By the time of independence in 1960, Houphouët-Boigny had formed a dominant political party, the Parti Démocratique de la Côte d'Ivoire, popularly known as the PDCI. Although other parties were not legally prohibited, the PDCI was unchallenged in its rule over what became a de facto single-party state. The PDCI was a patronage party that consciously attempted to co-opt ethnic elite opponents of Houphouët-Boigny, both inside and outside his own group, the Baoulé.[3]

In the early 1990s, after years of political peace and stability—made possible largely by the skillful political leadership of Houphouët-Boigny and a vibrant economy—the Cote d'Ivoire began to unravel. Several precipitating factors deepened the crisis and eventually led to open violent social conflict. The country was simultaneously racked by economic crisis and consumed by ethno-regional tensions rooted in issues of identity and citizenship. To understand this dramatic shift, one must trace the evolution of the Ivorian state and nation back to the colonial period and link that moment to the formidable period of postindependence political and economic development: 1960–1983.

The Political Economy of Development during the Colonial Era

The formal French colonial presence in Côte d'Ivoire lasted less than two generations, from 1893 to 1960. When colonialists arrived in the area, they encountered less than a handful of societies that had had traditions of centralized authority—in the southeast and parts of the north. For the most part, some sixty distinct ethno-linguistic groups were organized into very small, segmented societies. No apparent unifying culture bound these disparate groups. In part, this diffusion made it easier for colonialists to impose their system of direct rule—at least in theory. In reality, depending on local situations, colonialists ruled directly or employed a mixed approach—direct and indirect—to governance. The colony that evolved was based on an agglomeration of distinct ethnic groups that had migrated to the region from neighboring areas. The south had groups that originated around present-day Ghana and belonged to the Akan ethno-linguistic cluster (e.g., Baoulé, Bété, and Kru). In the north, different groups could be roughly grouped as having originated in the Upper Niger Circle or the Sahel (e.g., Sénoufo, Mandé, Malenké, Bambara, and Dioula).[4] The French organized their system of colonial governance along the lines of the French prefect system as the basic administrative unit, with little regard for cultural differences of the people who inhabited these different units. The colonialists appointed, according to their own design, local chiefs, through whom they ruled over subject peoples and, in the process, treated the land occupied by these groups as subject to their own discretion rather than according to existing traditions. Indigenous agents were expected to implement and enforce rules, regulations, and policies.

During the colonial period, the places of origin of African subjects were noted merely for administrative purposes rather than for designating citizenship rights, and were based upon being so-called "sons of the soil." For example, after the creation of the Francophone West African Federation (1904) until the immediate postwar period, authorities could force Africans from any of the constituent colonies to relocate to another colony in the federation and yet still identify them as having originated from, and belonging to, certain locations in their colony of origin. Notably, however, the colonialists treated each colony in the federation as part of to the same regional administrative entity. In other words, nationality was held in common throughout the particular federations. In the process, the state superseded traditional authority in determining property rights, such as land ownership and land use.

The Emergence of the Cocoa and Coffee Economies

European planters introduced cocoa and coffee plantations to the southern part of Côte d'Ivoire colony in the late 1800s. African cultivators were encouraged to cultivate these crops for the market by the then–King of Sanwi.[5] However, these efforts were not as productive as had been hoped. Moreover, French plantation owners relied heavily upon the colonial administration to provide forced African laborers and other resources to keep their enterprises afloat.

Africans were also allowed to engage in coffee and cacao production for the market, and originally they, too, could rely on the colonial administration to supply forced laborers. Rather than engage in plantation production methods, at least initially, African producers were shareholders. African producers were not only from the southeast region, but were also migrants from other areas. In either case, they participated freely in the market. Between 1920 and 1960, these African farmers led the expansion in production that spread from the southeast to the southwest. In the process, they became settlers in the southwest, and because of the dominant role of the state in determining who had access to land, they ended up participating in the market alongside local entrepreneurs and immigrant planters from other regions of the colony. In some cases, these immigrants were sharecroppers; in others, they were independent producers. The indigenous people of the southwest soon regarded the major push from Baoulé entrepreneurs into their area in the 1950s as a veritable "invasion." Catherine Boone notes that by the end of the decade, the Dida and Gouro ethnic groups in the southwest had become minorities in their ancestral homelands.[6]

The southwest possessed virgin forests and other land that, in the interwar period, was ripe for cultivation; however, labor was in short supply.[7] Consequently, demand for immigrant labor in the coffee and cocoa industries grew. Before the end of the Second World War, this need was filled by migrant labor from not only Côte d'Ivoire but also neighboring colonies in the Federation. Most of these migrants came from Upper Volta, which bordered Côte d'Ivoire to the north. To facilitate the migration of potential laborers from Upper Volta, in 1932 the French fused Côte d'Ivoire and Upper Volta. For a time, amicable relations existed between African planters in need of cheap labor in the south and the leaders of the communities in the north, whence these laborers originated. However, when forced labor was abolished in French colonies in 1946, and a new more liberal government assumed office in Paris, Africans in all parts of the French community were granted a form of French citizenship and began to demand their rights to self-determination. Nowhere was this demand louder than in Upper Volta.

Although granted "citizenship," Africans in French colonies were not given "full citizenship." The only full citizens were the so-called *citoyens de droit français*.[8] These were the metropolitan French and Africans who had previously been granted such by virtue of having been the inhabitants of French communes in the region.[9] The second category of citizenship was for citizens of local status and former subjects. Notably, the primary identity of Africans continued to be based on their places of origin within the former colonial state. Thus, belonging to a particular community was locally based in tradition and custom.

After 1945 and the creation of the French Union to replace the old colonial structure, the subjects and then-citizens of the colonies were given expanded voting rights. However, universal suffrage was not granted until the French National Assembly passed the *Loi Cadre* in June 1956. This law granted *universal suffrage* for elections held after that date in all French African colonies. Immediately after the war, the colonies had been granted the right to vote for limited representation not only in regional representative institutions but also at the national level in Paris. With the creation of the French Union, in 1958, the colonies were granted a form of internal self-government.

The Independence Movement and National Political Competition

The ending of the Second World War and the worldwide trend away from imperialism seems to have triggered an escalation in political activism in all of

France's colonies. In Côte d'Ivoire, the leadership of the African nationalist movement consisted of individuals who had acquired the status of *évolué* during the latter part of the colonial period. That is, they had been formally educated and steeped in French culture, which was in keeping with the postwar ideology of assimilation that guided French policy in its colonies. Some *évolué* were valued as colonial administrators. In other cases, they became entrepreneurs and business leaders. Such was the case with Félix Houphouët-Boigny.

Initially, Houphouët-Boigny, in an effort to excel as a coffee and cocoa planter, actively recruited migrant laborers from the north. He and others like him lured this labor to the south by striking deals with indigenous "big men" from northern communities and promising the recruits that they would receive higher wages than were being paid by European farmers.[10] In 1944, along with seven other African planters from the south, Houphouët-Boigny formed the Syndicat Agricole Africain (SAA), and was chosen as the organization's president. African planters, by this time, were allowed to join the European planters' association, the Syndicat Agricole de la Côte d'Ivoire, but wanted to assert their independence economically and politically.[11] At the time, the primary demands of the SAA were restoring the same access to agricultural labor to African planters as were granted to non-African planters, and securing better prices for crops produced by Africans.

Houphouët-Boigny was a skilled organizer and almost immediately began to position the organization to assume a wider, more political role than its initial economistic orientation. In 1945, the SAA joined forces with an Abidjan-based voluntary organization to form the African Bloc. From this base, Houphouët-Boigny was able to garner enough support to be elected representative of Côte d'Ivoire and Upper Volta to the French Constituent Assembly in Paris, a consultative body that nevertheless had some legislative influence. In that role, he made some tactical alliances with progressive French political parties, including the Communist Party, and pushed for the adoption of measures important to his constituents in Côte d'Ivoire, such as ending forced labor and decoupling the union between the two colonies he represented.[12] In the process, Houphouët-Boigny created some political space that separated him from the pressures of elites in Upper Volta who, at the time, were competing with him for national leadership during the buildup to the independence struggle. Forced labor was abolished in 1946, the same year that Houphouët-Boigny was elected to France's top legislative body, the French National Assembly. A year later, the union between Côte d'Ivoire and Upper Volta was abolished.

The abolition of forced labor freed up African workers who now could start farms of their own. It also triggered a land rush that lasted a decade. Migrant farmers as well as immigrant labor flocked mostly to the southwest to take advantage of a booming market in cocoa and coffee. In the process, many European farmers decided to abandon attempts to become involved in the Ivorian market as producers. Emerging domination by African producers in markets of the 1950s has been described by Aristide Zolberg as the creation of a new class of planter bourgeoisie.[13] Chief among these new actors was Houphouët-Boigny, who systematically used his wealth and prestige to build his political party.

On the local scene, in 1945 Houphouët-Boigny formed a new political party, le Partí Démocratique de la Côte d'Ivoire (PDCI). Based on his experience as a trade union organizer in the northern part of the colony, he took advantage of his connections with northern immigrants when cultivating electoral support for the PDCI. Most importantly, he championed the rights of immigrants to vote, which proved to be a valuable resource when he became president of independent Côte d'Ivoire.[14] Significantly, most of the northern immigrants were Muslims and most of the southerners were Christians, though at the time this was not the cause of serious intergroup conflict. But as the issue of who could claim national citizenship grew in the late 1980s, the north–south division fused with a division between Muslims and non-Muslims and gained in significance.

By 1946, the PDCI had become the dominant political party in Côte d'Ivoire. From the very beginning, Houphouët-Boigny saw the PDCI as a patronage party. Through patronage, he was able to co-opt whatever opposition interests surfaced as a potential challenge. Moreover, the PDCI used strangers from the north to build its base in the southwest. For example, migrant planters used resources such as cash and transport to generate electoral support for the PDCI. The party, as a result of efforts of its immigrant supporters, came to dominate politics in urban and rural areas of the southwest, marginalizing the indigenous populations there.[15]

A critical juncture in France's relations with its African colonies occurred in 1958, when the French constitution was revised and the French Community was created. Colonies were given the choice of voting for complete independence or for membership in the Community. Initially, Houphouët-Boigny was in favor of continued association between Côte d'Ivoire and France and the French Community. He went on to campaign for a "yes" vote when a referendum was called on the matter in September 1958. In that referendum, only Guinea chose to separate; Côte d'Ivoire voted to remain. It had become a self-governing republic, but was still dependent on France for developmental assistance. In fact, one of the reasons Houphouët-Boigny pushed for a "yes" vote was that he expected French financial and technical support to increase once the Community was up and running. However, he faced growing popular demands for complete independence, and indicated to Paris that he now favored complete independence for Côte d'Ivoire.[16] On August 7, 1960, Côte d'Ivoire was granted its full independence, with Houphouët-Boigny as president.

The Rise and Fall of the Ivorian Miracle

The centerpiece of Houphouët-Boigny's economic strategy from the time of independence until the mid-1980s was what came to be known as "the Ivorian Miracle," which emphasized coffee and cocoa production for the world market. At the height of his rule in the 1970s, Côte d'Ivoire became the leading producer of cocoa in the world.

The country witnessed three phases of economic development. The first phase was from 1965–1975, when the gross domestic product grew at a rate of almost 8 percent per year and had the spillover effect of stimulating the growth of tertiary and industrial sectors. At the time, the country appeared to be becoming a model for showing how a developing country in Africa could implement a successful economic strategy based on the production of primary products at the same time that it diversified its economy. The second phase was brief, 1976–1980. This was a period of dramatic crisis and change in the world economic system as a whole, and the circumstances had a profound effect on the Ivorian economy. Over the first two years, the national GDP declined to about just under 8 percent per year; but in 1978 it rose rapidly to almost 12 percent. Feeling that the worst was over and that it was safe to dramatically increase public investment, the government gambled. However, it was bitterly disappointed when, a year later, the market dipped again, and Côte d'Ivoire was forced to borrow heavily to sustain growth.

The third phase of economic development was from 1981 to 1987. During this period, the economy as a whole collapsed, most notably the markets for cocoa and coffee. The overall terms of trade also rapidly declined, and the Côte d'Ivoire growth rate plummeted to around 5 percent. The government was forced to default on its payments to lenders and to request that the debts be rescheduled. Also, the World Bank and the International Monetary Fund required the country to submit to structural adjustment programs and to privatize many of its public investments.[17] For all intents and purposes, by the late 1980s the "Ivorian Miracle" had collapsed. By 1990, the country's real growth rate was less than 1 percent. By 2002, when the first civil war began, it was just under 2 percent.

Although President Houphouët-Boigny died in office in 1993, the economic crisis of the late 1980s had revealed signs that he was already losing his ability to control the country at both the elite and mass level. Economic crisis inspired popular protests over rising unemployment and commodity prices particularly in urban areas. There was dissent over land pressures and general issues relating to discrimination and citizenship. Young people who had come to the cities to take advantage of economic opportunities had to abandon their quests and return to their villages. Le vieux (the old man), Houphouët-Boigny, was now being roundly criticized—at least privately among southern elites— for favoring *allochthons* (strangers) over southern *authochthons* (indigenes).[18]

The Emergence of Tension between National Citizenship and Autochthony

As indicated, French colonialists categorized the various peoples who inhabited the eight colonies of Francophone West Africa on the basis of their autochthony, depending on their ethnicity, language, and region of residence. During the existence of the French West Africa Federation, inhabitants were considered French subjects rather than citizens of the Federation. When the Federation gave way to the French Community, these people became a special category of French citizens, which applied only to the colonies of their residence. They did not acquire national citizenship in the countries they were deemed to be affiliated with until those countries gained independence.

Until recently, the Ivorian constitution did not directly address the issue of citizenship. During the rule of Houphouët-Boigny, immigrants could vote and even own property in Côte d'Ivoire without anything but a de facto claim to citizenship rights.[19] One analyst described this state of affairs as "fuzzy citizenship policies."[20] In such cases, administrative practice and informal understanding among the authorities were more important than any formal law in determining citizenship. At the same time, Houphouët-Boigny treated northern immigrants as though they had full citizenship rights, allowing them to vote and own property.

Theoretically, one's citizenship was still popularly understood—particularly in areas of the south—to be based on autochthony; in practice, autochthony was not often a politically salient factor in the early stages of independence. Circumstances began to change in the mid- to late 1980s, when the

Ivorian economy entered into crisis and pressures emerged from within and outside the political system to open up and allow for multiparty democracy. In part these pressures were inspired by the increasing shortage of land in the south and the desire on the part of southern elites to eliminate the competition of immigrants.[21] The pressures were partly related to competition among southern elites for power as Houphouët-Boigny aged. These two factors were tied to each other, as northerners who were not recognized by southerners as autochthons became more politically active as both voters and political aspirants.[22]

The economic boom in coffee and cocoa was built on the labor of immigrants from within West Africa, particularly the former French colonies. At one point, an estimated one-quarter to one-third of the Ivorian population was foreign born.[23] At independence, most of the African immigrants came from Burkina Faso (formerly Upper Volta) and Mali. There were also French nationals and Lebanese immigrants. The most recent census indicates that the immigrant population of Côte d'Ivoire numbers about 4 million or 26 percent of the total. The Berkinabes account for about two million, or half; Malians 20 percent; and Guineans, 6 percent. The remainder is mainly Lebanese (as many as 60,000) and French (about 10,000).[24]

Most recent conflicts over citizenship and identity emerged out of the context of economic failure, pressures for multiparty democracy, growing scarcity of arable land, elite competition for economic as well as political power, and questions of citizenship. Conflicts over citizenship and identity were associated with the elevation of autochthony to a level unseen before in Côte d'Ivoire. Pierre Englebert notes that during Houphouët-Boigny's thirty-three years of rule, non-Ivorians could fairly easily obtain certificates of residence that gave them the right to access to land and other benefits of citizenship. However, circumstances began to change around the time of his death. Opposition politicians seeking to displace the old regime came to see identity certificate holders with citizenship rights as providing a distinct advantage for the PDCI. Ethnic entrepreneurs seeking to challenge the old order led the charge to designate autochthony as a determinant of voting and other citizenship rights, including running for the presidency of the country.[25] Not to be outmaneuvered, the PDCI leadership also picked up the mantle of autochthony, adopting the ideology of Ivorité.

Although tracing the exact origins of the ideology of Ivorité is difficult, some identify its first clear articulation in 1993, when Houphouët-Boigny's successor, Henri Konan Bédié, used it to deny his main opponent, Alassane Ouattara, the right to run for the presidency. Although he had served in several important national political offices, Ouattara was a Muslim from the north, whose parents were said to have been born in Burkina Faso. Because of his parents' nationality, he was not considered an autochthon. This lineage had not been a problem for Ouattara in the past, as Houphouët-Boigny had allowed immigrants to have citizenship rights. However, the autochthony movement was calling for a more precise definition of who was, and who was not, a citizen.[26] Under these new definitions, individuals first had to prove their Ivorian nationality; then they had to establish the location of their ancestral village within the country.

In 1994, Bédié, through the PDCI-dominated parliament, orchestrated the passage of a law requiring any candidate for the presidency to prove Ivorian heritage. Local authorities were now required to rule on requests by individuals to legitimate both their ancestral membership in a particular community within present-day Côte d'Ivoire and their parents' native birth. Ruth Marshall-Fratani provides evidence that this change had a profound effect on the reinforcement of territorial autochthony as the basis for determining who was Ivorian.[27] In addition to establishing their ancestral village, individuals were required to possess a certificate of identity stating their nationality.

The notion of national autochthony was further expanded in 1998 with the passage of a new land law. Whereas under Houphouët-Boigny even immigrants could own land, the law now limited land ownership to citizens. In the process, those, especially in the south, who could not prove that they were autochthonous were deemed ineligible to own rural land. Consequently, local traditional authorities played a significant role in confiscating land claimed by immigrants and redistributing it according to their own interpretation of customary law.[28] This practice further marginalized migrants from the north who could not show that they had ancestry in present-day Côte d'Ivoire.

The definition of who was and who was not a citizen of Côte d'Ivoire came to mean having one's origins in the southern part of the country. The question became: Among those deemed to be autochthonous to the south, who among southerners is the most autochthonous? Bédié's answer was, "*Ivorians de souche (of the original root)*," more specifically, the Baoulé.[29] These people were what Bambi Ceuppens and Peter Geschiere have termed "super-autochthons," because they historically had had experience in state formation and were thus distinguished from southern groups such as the Bété, who traditionally belonged to nonstate, segmented societies. In other words, the Baoulé were thought to be more purely Ivorian and to have proven leadership qualities. By this definition, Bédié distinguished the Baoulé not only from northerners but also from other southern ethnic groups. This classification was important because it allowed other Akan groups,[30] which includes the Baoulé and the Bété, to claim autochthony in reference to non-Akan groups. But the Baoulé claim to be the purest autochthonous group in the country. Thus, the Bété might rightfully claim to be among the first Ivorians, but not to have preceded the Baoulé.

Multiparty Politics and Conflicts over Citizenship

The reformulation and growing importance of autochthony occurred at the same time as increasing multiparty activity. Although several parties opposed the PDCI at the time of Houphouët-Boigny's death in 1993—most notably the Ivorian Popular Front (IPF), founded in 1982,[31] and the Alliance for a New Côte d'Ivoire—the Rally of the Republicans (RDR) founded by Ouattara in 1994 posed the most serious challenge to Bédié's designs on the presidency. By the early 1990s, the IPF experienced resurgence under the leadership of a Bété politician, Laurent Gbagbo. Both Ouattara and Gbagbo declared their intention to run for the presidency in the national elections in 1995.

After the death of Houphouët Boigny, a brief power struggle involving Bédié and Ouattara took place. At the time, the Ivorian constitution stated that in the event of an incumbent president's death, the office would temporarily go not to the prime minister but to the president of the national assembly, who at the time was Bédié.[32] Ouattara felt that as prime minister, he should assume the presidency, but Bédié exercised his constitutional right to fill the vacancy temporarily until a formal election could be held. Once he was at least temporarily in power, Bédié began a systematic attempt to remove Ouattara as a viable opponent, and to fend off his primary southern opponent, Gbagbo. In the process, he vigorously invoked his brand of Ivorité ideology. These events must be considered in the context of the period's growing popular unrest, particularly among university students.

The courts barred Ouattara from running in the 1995 elections, upholding the claim that he was not a true Ivorian, as his father had been born in what is now Burkina Faso.[33] Citing election manipulations by the PDCI, opposition parties, including the IPF, sat out the election, and Bédié was elected unopposed.

Between the 1995 and 2000 elections, Bédié and his supporters stepped up pressure on those who were considered nonautochthons, harassing them politically and driving them from land they occupied in the south. Ouattara re-doubled his efforts to be able to run for the presidency, and the IPF leader, Lau-rent Gbagbo, stepped up his own efforts to unseat Bédié.

As elections approached in 2000, the country was in deep economic and political crisis, thus setting the stage for a military coup mostly involving northern and non-Akan officers on Christmas Eve of 1999. A former chief of staff of the armed forces, General Robert Guei, a member of the marginalized Yakouba ethnic group, assumed power. Shortly thereafter, both Gbagbo and Ouattara returned from exile and began to prepare to run for the presidency once the way was set for a return to civilian rule.

On assuming office, Guei immediately declared his disdain for the notion of Ivorité and announced that his goal was to end official corruption. Initially, there were signs that he would only pave the way for a return of civilian rule, but in a very short period he reversed this position and declared his intention to stand for the presidency in 2000. Furthermore, in July of that year, he spon-sored a referendum to change the constitution to state that both parents, not just the father, of presidential candidates had to have been born in the country. Also, any candidate for the presidency had to have never had any nationality other than Ivorian, thus excluding naturalized citizens. Three months later, the Supreme Court, members of which Guei himself had appointed, declared that neither Ouattara nor Bédié was eligible to run for the presidency. This decision left the IPF candidate, Gbagbo, his only major political opponent and, in ef-fect, neutralized the Baoulé base of Bédié while keeping Ouattara from being a challenger. Guei's calculation seems to have been that Gbagbo, a Bété, would not be able to muster enough votes to defeat him.

The elections went forward, but when early vote returns showed Gbagbo leading, Guei halted the vote, claiming fraud. He then declared himself the winner. An immediate response came from Gbagbo's supporters, who took to the streets and attacked the presidential palace. Police and soldiers joined the protest, forcing Guei to flee. Gbagbo was then installed as the new president. However, the unrest continued, as supporters of the Rally of the Republicans (RDR) Party and Ouattara rioted, calling for an annulment of the elections and new elections in which Ouattara could compete. Gbagbo supporters re-sponded by attacking Ouattara supporters. Chaos reigned.

Before the end of the year, relative calm returned to the country after a tentative peace agreement was implemented. Gbagbo created a "government of national unity" that included representatives of the RDR. However, underlying tensions continued to smolder. Baoulé politicians flamed these tensions by claiming that Gbagbo was not an authentic Ivorian.

The First Civil War

Throughout this tumultuous period, and despite opposition from many quarters, Gbagbo returned to politics, supporting Ivorité as a governing principle. Once in office, he pushed the concept of Ivorité even further than Bédié had, creating the Office of National Identification, and emphasizing the necessity of asserting the national identity of legitimate citizens of the country.[34] Village committees were to certify whether individuals could claim autochthony in that community. Both Ouattara and his supporters perceived this gesture as an all-out attempt to deny their citizenship rights. Ouattara's support was mainly from the north among Muslims, who came to see themselves directly at odds with the Christian-dominated regime of Gbagbo. In the process, the first of two civil wars began in 2002 between northerners, most of whom were Muslims, and the southern Christian-dominated regime.

This insurgency can be clearly linked to Gbagbo's introduction of a formal process for determining Ivorian citizenship. The war had begun with a popular uprising in the north involving university students and petty officers from the area who felt excluded from legitimately claiming their Ivorian citizenship. Thus was born a movement that came to be known as the *Forces Nouvelles* (New Forces; FN),[35] comprised of soldiers, students, and politicians, all claiming to be fighting for their citizenship rights. The Forces Nouvelles considered themselves Ivorians and felt discriminated against by the rules governing Ivorité. Brownwyn Manby quotes one opposition combatant as saying, "We need a war because we need our identity cards. Without an identity card you are nothing in this country."[36]

The war virtually partitioned the country in two. Gbagbo initially blamed the uprising on foreign intervention and turned to France for military aid. French soldiers were dispatched to support Gbagbo, arriving in September 2002, but their charge was mainly to protect civilians. As the fighting dragged on, the Economic Community of West African States Monitoring Group (ECOMOG) also sent in peacekeepers. By 2003, this peacekeeping force numbered almost 6,000, including 1,500 from ECOMOG and 4,000 French peacekeepers. Together, these forces maintained dividing lines between the east and west and a so-called Zone of Confidence that divided the north and south.[37]

In January 2003, the Gbagbo government reached an accord brokered by the French with the Forces Nouvelles and the major political parties. This agreement was termed the Linas-Marcoussis Accord (LMA). Among its key provisions was the creation of a government of national reconciliation that included the FN. In addition, signatories to the accord agreed to work together to establish new rules relating to national identity, citizenship, and land rights. A UN monitoring committee was to oversee the implementation of this agreement. Nevertheless, in less than two years the agreement had broken down, and sporadic fighting resumed.

A second attempt was made to permanently settle the unrest. In the summer of 2004, talks held in Accra, Ghana, reaffirmed the principles of LMA, and stipulated that deadlines and benchmarks would be set for the total disarmament of combatants. However, these deadlines were never met, and fighting intensified. In the summer of 2005, yet another agreement was reached that lay out a new timetable for disarmament, national elections, and the enactment of legislation relating to citizenship and land rights. Following this step, direct talks began involving commanders of the UN peacekeepers and leaders of the warring forces. Until this time, the issues of citizenship and land rights remained unresolved. National elections were supposed to be held in September 2005, but were postponed. Not until May 2006 was a plan for the disarmament of combatants and national elections clearly articulated.

Finally, an African-brokered breakthrough agreement was reached in Ouagadougou, Burkina Faso, in March 2007. This was significant because, unlike previous agreements, it was spearheaded by Ivorians and directly addressed the citizenship issue for the first time. Rebel demands included rescinding the certificate of identification law, creating a path to naturalization for long-term immigrants, and repealing the 1998 Land Law.[38] The Ouagadougou Agreement called for establishing a reliable identification system and providing Ivorian credentials to all who did not have proper documents; creating mobile courts presided over by independent judges that would provide appropriate documents for individuals who had been born in Côte d'Ivoire but had never properly registered; and formulating new forgery-proof identification documents for both Ivorians and foreigners.

Despite this progress, no clear determination was made to state who was and was not a citizen. The Gbagbo government continued to assert that some northerners were fraudulently claiming citizenship. The opposition claimed that the government was acting in a malicious manner so as to continue to deny northerners their citizenship rights. The citizenship stalemate ended with the agreement on all sides that mobile courts could accept verbal testimony and incomplete documentation to determine an individual's citizenship. Petitioners could bring two witnesses to speak on their behalf, attesting to their place of birth or the citizenship of either one of their parents. Also, petitioners no longer had to go to their ancestral villages to have their cases heard. Instead, they could file petitions at their place of birth. Moreover, people who could show that they were born in the country to unknown parents could also qualify for an identity certificate.

The Ouagadougou Agreement did not resolve the dispute over the 1998 Rural Land Law, whose intent was to recognize and formalize customary land rights by setting out procedures and conditions for how customary rights would to be transformed into title deeds. However, it also stipulated that only Ivorian citizens could be considered for property ownership, which removed the possibility of migrants having legal claim to land even if they had resided on the land and cultivated it over an extended period of time. The law does allow Ivorian migrants from other regions of the country the possibility of obtaining titles outside their home regions. However, especially in the southwest, this practice would likely be met with stiff opposition. Original inhabitants generally continue to resent all migrants, domestic or foreign. The agreement only partially addressed this issue with its changes in citizenship laws.

The Ouagadougou Agreement included a provision for the demobilization of rebel forces and their incorporation into the regular Ivorian army. In the process of restructuring the armed forces, northerners and southerners were to be equitably distributed in the ranks of the officer corps and the ranks of nonofficers in the army.

Continuing Crisis, Elections, and the Second Civil War

Because of the first civil war, national elections were postponed several times between 2005 and 2010. In the elections that ensued, Ouattara emerged victorious after two rounds of voting. International observers hailed both rounds as largely free and fair.[39] However, the Constitutional Council refused to certify Ouattara and declared Gbagbo the winner. Both candidates, claiming victory, had the oath of office administered to them. Nonetheless, the international community, including the United Nations, considered Ouattara the winner. The supporters of each candidate immediately resumed fighting.

As fighting between opposing forces continued, the United Nations dispatched a peacekeeping force dominated by French troops to Côte d' Ivoire.[40] Gbagbo, who continued to occupy the office of the president in December 2010, demanded that the peacekeepers leave. The UN Security Council refused this order and extended the mandate of its peacekeepers to June 2011. Their mandate was to protect their own troops as well as civilians. When Ouattara forces decided to assault the main city of Abidjan in March 2011, very intense conflict—even involving the French forces—ensued. This flare-up ended just over a month later with the arrest of Gbagbo.

Violence throughout the country continued even as Ouattara was sworn in. In the cities, the struggle was largely between the two political factions, although some ethnic issues were also apparent. In the countryside, the conflict was mainly between those who considered themselves autochthons and those who were considered *allogene* (non-indigenous).[41]

In October 2011, the International Criminal Court began to investigate the charge that the Gbagbo regime had been involved in crimes against humanity during the conflict following the 2010 elections. It formally issued an arrest warrant for him. He was charged with four counts of crimes against humanity: murder, rape and other forms of sexual violence, persecution and "other inhuman acts," allegedly committed between December 16, 2010, and April 12, 2011. Gbagbo became the first former head of state to be tried by the ICC.

The Ivorian opposition was not intent on overthrowing the Ivorian state or on partitioning the country, only on clarifying and making the country's citizenship laws more just. The legal foundations of citizenship were not clearly established in the first thirty-plus years of independence; a traditional understanding of belonging held sway. As long as Houphouët-Boigny was able to maintain political control via the country's single-party system, and as long as the economy was prospering and not in crisis, conflicts over citizenship were not serious issues. However, the crises of the late 1980s undermined the regime's control, and the issue of autochthony assumed more importance than ever before. Discrimination involving those claiming to be autochthones and those whom they view as allochthons occurred in both the formal political arena and in society at large. The result was two civil wars over issues relating to citizenship and citizenship rights. Even though the legal basis for establishing citizenship and citizenship rights has been addressed, armed opposition by groups questioning the legitimacy of President Ouattara to claim Ivorian citizenship continue in the form of popular discontent within the country and within armed elements operating against his regime from border zones, particularly along the Liberian border.

7

Kenya

Citizenship, Land, and Ethnic Cleansing

"My property has been taken by the so-called indigenous people"
—Joseph Wanjama, BBC, interview transcript from Karen Allen,
  "Peace at any Price 2" (2008)

Kenya secured independence from British rule on December 12, 1963. The colonial era had lasted less than one hundred years. A notable aspect of colonialism in Kenya was that European settlers displaced indigenous African peoples to make way for exploiting the territory agriculturally. But it was not long before the colony came to be valued for much more than its potential for export agriculture. Large areas are blessed with a lush green, picturesque environment, teeming wildlife in the interior, and a long scenic coastline bordering the Indian Ocean. The Europeans regarded the colony's ecology as akin to that of the British countryside. Elspeth Huxley, the famous British writer, described Kenya at that time as "White Man's Country."[1] However, even as it was being constructed, this white "paradise" was constantly confronting discontent and even resistance among the indigenous populations over what they perceived to be the theft of their ancestral lands by European aliens. The land issue has continued to be a major issue of contention over the six-plus decades since the country gained its independence.

Enduring tensions over land and land rights were evident in the aftermath of national elections in 2007, when the country erupted into widespread ethnic and regional violence in large measure fueled by these issues. To some extent, this crisis was the result of the ethnic entrepreneurs and cultural brokers-cum-politicians who incited ordinary people in an effort to challenge or defend the outcome of the elections. But the root causes were deeper, involving as they did long-standing grievances held by some ethnic groups about being denied their citizenship rights, particularly regarding land and immigration. In Africa, land—and ancestral land in particular—tends to be symbolic of citizenship and, as such, often carries more weight than any legal definitions of citizenship.[2]

In this chapter, I trace the roots of ethnic grievances over land rights to the colonial period, with the settlement of Kenya's "White Highlands" and the Rift Valley, the displacement of the indigenous people, and the alienation of their traditional landholdings. White settlers in the central part of the colony created land pressures for the groups living there, particularly the Kikuyu. These pressures led to the so-called Mau Mau Rebellion (1952–1957). The alienation of Kikuyu land in the central part of the region must also be a part of the discussion on postindependence land disputes. As a part of the independence agreement, Africans were allowed to settle in previously white-controlled areas. Significantly, however, settlement schemes in the Rift Valley were, in part, intended to alleviate the land pressures affecting such groups as the Kikuyu, Kisii, and Maragoli Luhyia, but they totally ignored any prior land claims by the indigenous people among the minority so-called Kalenjin (Elgeyo, Endorois, Kipsigis, Kuria, Nandi, Pokot, Sabaot, Sebei, Marakwet, Terik, and Tugen) and Maasai.

This chapter concentrates on the postindependence conflict over land in the Rift Valley. It is there that we can most clearly identify the relationship between grievances over land rights and citizenship claims. We begin by discussing how the Rift Valley was opened up to and settled by whites; we examine the implications for the people already living there. The politics of land is traced from the beginning of European settlement to the independence period, with a particular emphasis on postindependence land and immigration policies. This process set the stage for low-intensity violence involving indigenous people and those whom they considered strangers, particularly after the return to multiparty democracy.

Settlement of the White Highlands and the Alienation of Indigenous Land Rights

Kenya became a part of the British East Africa Protectorate in 1895, and soon after was opened up for European settlement. As a part of establishing its presence in the African colonies that they claimed, colonial powers had to demonstrate effective administrative control over their respective areas. In the case of Kenya, displays of control were largely accomplished through military expeditions to bring indigenous peoples under control. For the most part, the occupation of Kenya was made possible through violence and by forcing African leaders to sign treaties submitting their people to British "protection."

By 1903, about one hundred white settlers were in the Kenya Highlands; by 1953, this population had grown to more than four thousand.[3] The land in the colony was now defined as Crown Land, and white settlers could purchase it at a nominal price. Many of the settlers had been loyal military or other civil servants. The idea was to open up the Highlands for commercial agriculture that was almost the exclusive right of white settlers. Africans were rendered as no more than cheap available labor. Almost immediately, Africans were forced through various forms of taxation (e.g., head taxes, hut taxes) to seek wage employment—however meager the remuneration was—mostly on European farms. By the end of the first two decades of the twentieth century, more than half the men of working age among the Kikuyu and Luo—the two largest ethnic groups in the colony—were employed on European farms.

The crown did hold some land under the rubric of the Doctrine of Public Trust, whereby land was administered for the people of Kenya. Trust Land was held by local governments on behalf of the local communities, groups, families, and individuals in accordance with whatever African Customary Law was relevant in those communities. These officials, however, had the authority to convert such lands into private land.[4] Once conversion was complete, the land was titled and became the sole property of those who had purchased it. Indigenous communities came to expect that their rights to land would be protected as Trust Land, but after independence this prospect was not certain.

Africans in the central region of Kenya were grouped into so-called "native reserves" in different parts of the colony.[5] This decree created land hunger among the people, particularly in the central part of the colony bordering on the White Highlands. This area was reserved for the Kikuyu, Embu, and Meru people, who could eke out a subsistence living as small-scale farmers and peasants.[6] However, their most important function during this period was to serve as a reservoir of cheap labor for European farms. No matter who the colonial power was, this pattern characterized other colonies with European settlers (e.g., Algeria, Côte d'Ivoire, South Africa, Southern Rhodesia). As elsewhere, also, African came to pay the bulk of the taxation but benefited little from the public policies and social services of the colonial regime. By the 1950s, although they made up less than 1 percent of the population of the colony, Europeans occupied privileged positions in both the political and economic spheres.[7]

In 1915, the colonial administration implemented laws prohibiting Africans from owning land in the Rift Valley, effectively displacing most of the pastoral communities living there. Moreover, pastoralists were considered less desirable as agricultural laborers, and the colonialists began to tap cheap labor from the areas undergoing population and land pressures, such as the Central, Nyanza, and Western provinces. Rather than having land rights of their own in these provinces, immigrants became either squatters on the outskirts of white farms or sharecroppers. In some cases, immigrants were purposely settled by the colonial administration in areas targeted for mixed farming by Europeans. For example, in 1939 the colonial administration settled more than four thousand Kikuyu in what is now Nakuru Province—an area some Maasai claim as ancestral homelands.

Prior to the Second World War, white settlers, and later Indian immigrants, had a voice in local governance. African governance was confined to their own ethnic localities and mainly in facilitation of colonial rule. In some cases, the colonialists appointed chiefs of their own to replace uncooperative traditional leaders. However, during the course of the war, Great Britain came to rely much more on the colonies to sustain its rule both at home and in the wider empire. In this context, Africans began to make inroads in areas such as local government and military service. Also, some limited political organization among the African was allowed; for example, in 1947 the Kenya African Union (KAU) was formed and, at the time, was headed by Kenya's future first president, Jomo Kenyatta. The purpose of KAU was to articulate an African voice of protest over population pressures, land shortages, environmental degradation, unemployment, and the rise in white power at the expense of Kenya's indigenous people.

African political development in the colony proceeded simultaneously with the economic discontent of groups such as squatters and residents of the reserves. The interwar period saw two significant developments in African political activism. First, formal education for Africans became more readily available, mostly through mission schools, and some young men were conscripted into the British army. Once the Second World War was over, these factors fueled a potent mix of discontent that gave rise to various social movements. At first, Africans demanded reform of the colonial system, but by the beginning of the 1950s they were demanding more and more political and economic rights. In large part, rising demands were part of the "Winds of Change" that were reaching gale force throughout the colonized world. Another factor was the leadership coming out of the burgeoning African intellectual class. With such influences, continued domination by the white minority was being vigorously called into question.

Eventually, in 1952, protest exploded into a full-scale uprising that came to be known as the Mau Mau Rebellion.[8] The majority of the Africans who joined it on the side of the rebels were from the Kikuyu, who were squatters or unemployed in the capital city, Nairobi. However, various elements of other ethnic groups—particularly those from the central part of the colony and the urban unemployed—also joined the rebels. Between 1952 and 1954, the colonial regime declared a state of emergency, banning African political organizations such as KAU, jailing leaders such as Kenyatta, proceeding to purge the urban areas and the reserves of able-bodied Africans, including former military conscripts, who might join the Mau Mau, and driving many others into the forests and mountains of central Kenya.

Rather than developing into a formal military organization, the Mau Mau operated like social bandits, living among the general population in rural areas and relying upon them for support.[9] Intense open conflict between Mau Mau warriors and the colonial forces came to an end in 1954. By that time, many Africans, mostly males, had been incarcerated in concentration camps, and a generalized fear was gripping the colony over the "black peril." Throughout the entire period of the rebellion, more than twelve thousand rebels were killed and over two thousand loyalists met the same fate. Europeans, the designated enemy, suffered comparatively fewer casualties. Only thirty-two Europeans were killed.

Although it did not lead to immediate independence, the struggle lay the foundation for what was to follow. By the mid-1950s, it was clear that, if protracted, African unrest could seriously destabilize the Kenyan economy. This prospect caused European industrial and commercial entrepreneurs who were just beginning to establish themselves in the colony, as well as many large-scale farmers, to reassess their position on independence. In 1959, an organization called the New Kenya Group emerged and was committed to a policy of multiracial politics. The entrepreneurs and rich farmers saw themselves as a progressive element among the white settlers, and came to support the idea of a transition to independence without any radical change in the economic and social structure of society. In the process, whites could keep their wealth and access to wealth, while Africans were given rights to universal suffrage on a common electoral roll.[10]

By this time, the colonial administration was convinced that a transition to African rule was necessary, as was transferring some land in the White High- lands to Africans. The question was *how*? This process was eventually ham- mered out in three phases at a Lancaster House Conference in England.[11] The two dominant African political organizations were the Kenya African National Union (KANU), headed by Jomo Kenyatta, and comprised mainly of support- ers from Kenya's largest ethnic groups, the Kikuyu and the Luo; and the Ke- nya African Democratic Union (KADU), headed by a politician from the coast, Ronald Ngala, and made up mainly of minority ethnic groups from all parts of the country. While KANU advocated a form of liberal citizenship, KADU was concerned with protecting indigenous rights, and therefore advocated a form of federalism that came to be known as *majimboism*—a Swahili term that re- fers to a devolution of power.

The Independence Movement and the Lancaster House Agreement on Kenya

The Lancaster discussions took place between 1960 and 1963. The purpose of the meetings was to devise a constitution that would lead to internal self-gov- ernment for the colony and, eventually, to complete independence. The main negotiators included the British Government, KANU, KADU, and initially the New Kenya Group. The first meeting was held in 1960, just following the end of the state of emergency. The issues turned not only on the structure of gov- ernance for an independent Kenya, but also on individual and collective prop- erty rights. African people had been stripped of their claims to land ownership and hoped to regain those rights upon becoming independent. No agreement was reached at the first conference, and an interim constitution went into ef- fect in April 1961.

The next full meeting at Lancaster House did not take place until the fol- lowing year. In the period between Lancaster House I and Lancaster House II, independence fever in Kenya escalated and so did discussions of federalism and land rights. By the time Lancaster II began in February 1962, majimboism had assumed center stage as it was being pushed vigorously by KADU and its supporters, as well as by some elements of the white settler population. Con- cern arose over the possibility of Kenya being run by an African government that favored a unitary political structure.

The British government publically proclaimed its commitment to protecting the interests of Kenya's Africans, but in reality its primary concern seemed to be protecting settler interests. Although bent on negotiating a settlement leading to independence, the British government clearly wanted to dictate the terms. For a time, the majimboists had some support in government circles, but as time went by they came to feel that settler interests could be best protected under a KANU-led government. In general, Lancaster House II could be considered a failure, though it led to agreement on a constitution for the colony's internal self-government.

The internal self-government constitution did not go into effect until June 1963. However, almost from the end of Lancaster House II, further negotiations were held under the rubric of Lancaster House III. The terms of the prior agreement remained in place, but details of the transition were worked out in private sessions involving Prime Minister Jomo Kenyatta and representatives of the British government. The internal self-government constitution, which went into effect in March 1963, among other things, called for a bicameral legislature, with a senate and a lower house. Legislative constituencies were to be determined by the population density of districts, and the parliament would choose a prime minister from the leadership of the party with the most representation. The prime minister was head of government, and the queen of England was the head of state.[12] Within less than a year, Kenyatta—citing the African tradition of strong centralized executive leadership—got the votes he needed in parliament to abolish the majimbo constitution and create the Republic of Kenya. This new arrangement, which removed the British monarchy as head of state and created a strong presidency, was the beginning of what came to be popularly known as Kenya's Imperial Presidency.[13]

By this time, the KANU leadership felt it was better to accept a federal constitution (majimboism), with the expectation that because of its looming legislative majority it could—in short order—change the constitution, replacing a parliamentary form of government and majimboism with a unitary republican form. KADU realized that the British were now calling the shots, and went along with the new constitutions. The terms of the prior agreement remained in place but the details of the transition were worked out in private sessions involving Prime Minister Jomo Kenyatta and representatives of the British government. In the end, the British government imposed the majimbo constitution on Kenya, though it sensed that this new governmental structure would be difficult to implement. Over the next year, the predicted challenges proved to be the case. The British were less interested in creating a democratic state in independent Kenya than in protecting their own interests.[14] Those interests dictated the development of good relations with the new independent African government of Kenya. In the process, although political independence was achieved for the African population of Kenya, a form of neocolonialism simply replaced the colonial system.[15]

Kenya became an independent state on December 1, 1963, and within months, parliament voted to abandon the majimbo constitution and to declare the Republic of Kenya. However, this move was not the death knell for majimboism. In fact, majimbo continued to be a part of everyday conversation. Kenyatta continued to delegate governmental functions to local administration, but overlay this practice with a strong provincial administration that was responsible only to the office of the presidency.[16] He also engaged in a form of "ethnic arithmetic," appointing certain ethnic leaders to key posts.[17] This strategy was meant as a gesture toward the minority elites, if not the minority populations. These elites came to assume privileged access to development resources, some of which they passed on to their constituents, but they tended to be primarily concerned with their own self-aggrandizement. Initially, this system worked well, but eventually it came to form the basis for tension and conflict between the majimboists and their opponents.

Land Hunger, Immigration, and Party Politics

At independence, the Kenyatta regime's objective was to create a political system based on the principles of liberal democracy. Rather than pushing to establish indigenous land rights in the ancestral areas of communal groups, it chose to adhere to the principles of British common law as related to land and property rights. Under that system, the British monarch had the authority to alienate and allocate land in Kenya. These powers were simply transferred to the chief executive at independence.[18]

Kenyatta's land policy adopted a liberal orientation, dictating that all citizens were free to live and work wherever they wished throughout the country, no matter their ethnic or regional origins.[19] Although minority elites agreed to this policy, they also seem to have assumed that they would be able to exercise power and control over their own ethnic and regional communities.[20] In fact, such management was, for the most part, the case during Kenyatta's rule. Kenyatta practiced a form of ethnic patronage in order to maintain the loyalty of elite supporters not only from among his own Kikuyu ethnic group but also from other ethnic groups, including the Kalenjin.

The independence settlement had made it possible for Africans to pur-chase farms formerly occupied by European settlers on the basis of "willing buyer–willing settler" agreements.[21] European farmers were given the option of retaining the land they had purchased during the colonial era or of selling the land to African buyers who could afford to purchase it. Large tracks of rich farmland were allowed to remain in the hands of European farmers who had been settlers. To make African land purchases possible, the new Kenyan gov-ernment and the departing British colonialists established a settlement pro-gram that provided loans. Land could be purchased either by individuals or by groups, such as cooperative societies or land investment companies. Some of the cooperatives and individuals buying land even involved Kalenjin elites. Many of the Kikuyu who had been squatters in the Rift Valley and at the coast took advantage of this system and purchased land where they were already settled. Others migrated from the overcrowded Central Province to take ad-vantage of the "land rush" in the 1960s and 1970s.[22] Between 1962 and 1966, approximately 20 percent of the land in the White Highlands was purchased through government-sponsored settlement schemes and transfer programs. In the 1970s, more European-owned farms were redistributed in this way. The ma-jority of people that took advantage of this program were Kikuyu; but some Maragoli Luhyia were also included.

As early as the middle of the 1960s, available land was becoming scarce, and competition for it became extremely intense. Notably, the president's of-fice, no matter what the situation, had enormous discretionary powers to alien-ate and allocate land, as could be clearly seen in the way President Kenyatta, as well as President Moi, used these powers. They both doled out title deeds not on the basis of demonstrated need but as patronage to their ethnic cronies and to other non-co-ethnic elites, who were among their most loyal supporters.

In the Rift Valley, Kalenjin elites found it difficult to compete with more capitalized businesses and ethnic elites from other parts of the country, par-ticularly with Kikuyu elites. At this point, the first signs of interethnic conflict over land in the independence period in the Rift Valley began to surface. For the most part, the first two decades of independence had been characterized by relative peace and consistent economic growth.

President Kenyatta worked hard to maintain the loyalty of minority elites, appointing them to key government positions and controlling them with pa-tronage.[23] In 1967, he appointed Daniel arap Moi, one of the most influential Kalenjin politicians at the time, to the position of vice-president. Despite continuous rumblings from some minority politicians who wanted a return to the majimbo (federal) constitution, Kenyatta was able to keep his multiethnic coalition together until he died in 1978. Even before Kenyatta's death, some segments of the Kikuyu elite began plotting to change the constitution so that the Kalenjin could not assume the presidency on the event of Kenyatta's death. Moi, a skilled politician, was able to beat back this challenge and, by 1982, he moved Kenya from being a de facto one-party state to a de jure one-party state, headed by the Kenya African National Union.[24] This same year saw an abortive military coup.[25]

Despite opposition to the development of a de jure one-party system, Moi forged ahead. He attempted to create what some called a cult of personality based upon the concept of *Nyayo,* a Swahili term meaning "footsteps."[26] Moi pledged to follow in the footsteps of Kenyatta, and even attempted to make Nyayo a national motto just as Kenyatta had used *Harambee!!* (Let us all pull together!!) as a rallying call for collective efforts of national development. However, Moi utilized this concept to signal the critical importance of religiously supporting his regime as a pathway to genuine development.[27] Some of his most loyal supporters took their loyalty to the extreme, regularly intimidating nonsupporters. At the same time, Moi structured politics in a similar way to the classic African authoritarian regime characterized by kleptocracy (rampant official corruption), and arbitrary, capricious, absolutist rule. Rather than engendering widespread support for himself, as Moi had intended, this brand of rule led to festering popular discontent and pushes, although at times gentle, by large segments of the population for constitutional reform and curbing presidential power.

Throughout the 1980s, civil society pushed back and raised critical issues relating to corruption and autocratic rule. Much of the corruption had to do with illegal transfers of land. Though the efforts of civil society were halting, they were aided by the worldwide trend toward democratizing authoritarian regimes.[28]

Before discussing the watershed moment in Kenya's political transition between 1990 and 2002, I will place this change into the context of long-standing political issues relating to land and access to land. This issue is very complex, and its several dimensions often conflate once triggered by electoral tensions and violence. The issue has two analytically distinct dimensions. One dimension relates to the view long held by Maasai and Kalenjin that their ancestral lands should be returned to them as a group, and even be legitimately occupied only by members of their group. Immigrants from other parts of Kenya were not only to have no land rights in these areas, but also were to return to their own ancestral homelands. The other dimension has to do with land-related graft and corruption going back to the emergence and strengthening of the "imperial presidency" under both Kenyatta and Moi. These two dimensions came together in dramatic fashion in the violence just after the decision to abandon the one-party system in 1991, and immediately preceding and following the National Elections of 2007.[29] Kenya's general population was determined to attack the problem of corruption relating to land by drastically reducing the powers of the presidency, and they wanted constitutional reform to accomplish this objective. At the same time, some indigenous groups—particularly in the Rift Valley and at the Kenya Coast—pushed for a return to majimboism as a way to control their own affairs, including land rights. In the Rift Valley, as long as Moi, a Kalenjin, was president, his group and other indigenous groups there felt that their interests would be protected. However with the introduction of multipartyism, this protection seemed less certain.

I will deal with each of these dimensions serially below. However, in the discussion of citizenship and land, I will only address this issue as it relates to the Rift Valley, not the Kenya coast. The impact of the political transitions that coincided with the transition to a multiparty system in the late 1980s and 1990s was profound. It is useful to divide Kenya's postindependence political history into two phases, particularly as these segments relate to the legal foundations of property rights. Phase I occurred from 1963 to 1990; Phase II was from 1991 to 2000.[30] In Phase I, institutions in place worked reasonably well to insure that the rule of law was efficiently, effectively, and fairly applied. However, significant changes that occurred in Phase II were a prelude to the breakdown of the rule of law and the beginning of a deep, pervasive, and pernicious culture of corruption. The change was particularly noticeable in the area of property rights.

Ato KwAmena Onoma has cogently analyzed this change, describing Phase I as a period in which the state created and reinforced institutions that facilitated a national land policy. In the process, Kenyans could be given or purchase land and be reasonably certain that their property rights would be upheld. Further, Ato KwAmena Onoma presents evidence that in Phase II, instead of upholding these laws and institutions, elites in the ruling party, KANU, systematically subverted them.[31] Rather than the president having to authorize all land transfers, after this time district commissioners and other divisional functionaries could also allocate land. In the process, the Department of Land Adjudication and Settlement (DLAS) and various land control boards saw their authority severely undercut by the resulting unpredictability of land adjudication practices.

During this period, having multiple titles issued to different people for the same piece of land was not uncommon, but such practices had implications for recordkeeping in the agencies designed to legitimize and protect land tenure rights. Multiple maps of the same areas also existed. All of this confusion set the stage for widespread corruption and escalating land disputes. Well-connected politicians, and especially government officials, often interfered with the way institutions charged with managing land rights operated on the ground. Citizen claims of property rights were enforced on a selective basis, often favoring corrupt politicians and other elites. These individuals came to see land not only as a way to engage in productive economic activities based exclusively on what the land would yield as agricultural or ranching ventures, but also for its ability to generate rents from investments (e.g., farming and tourism) and for the financial gain once it was sold or leased. Onoma notes that during this period many leading politicians, including President Moi himself and his cabinet ministers, fraudulently acquired large tracts of farmland, condominium complexes, shopping malls, hotels, and office blocks. In some cases, individuals acquired land just for the sake of acquiring it, with no other intention in mind. In other cases, they used land as a mechanism for gaining the support of individuals and groups during election campaigns. In large measure, these machinations were made possible in Phase II by the growing centralization of power in the office of the chief executive and the subsequent weakening of institutions initially meant to protect individual and group land rights.

Corruption and Land Rights

Corruption in land allocation had been an ever-present reality from the time of the Kenyatta regime; however, it escalated during the reign of President Moi—particularly before and after national elections.[32] A 2003 commission, popularly known as the Ndungu Commission, comprised of twenty prominent citizens, lawyers, and civil servants, appointed by then–President Mwai Kibaki, found that "Land was no longer allocated for development purposes but as political reward and for speculation purposes. *Land grabbing* became part and parcel of official grand corruption. . . ."[33] The commission was charged with inquiring into the allegation that, for a number of years, land was being allocated illegally. It was asked to make recommendations for a resolution. The commission found that between 1962 and 2002, close to two thousand illegal land titles had been issued, with a dramatic escalation between 1986 and 2002. The categories of land included public land such as forests, settlement schemes designated specifically for the settlement of the landless poor, national parks and game reserves, government administrative property, wetlands, research farms and even roads and land designated for road development.[34] In some cases, title deeds were even issued for nonexistent property!

The report went on to identify incidents in which individuals were granted title deeds to land and, without even occupying the land, transferred it to individuals or corporations purely for material gain. It found that land grabbing was pervasive and involved both public and trust land. The president's office had the authority to convert even trust land to private land if this move was deemed in the public interest.[35] The report was submitted to the president in July 2004. It was made public, and the government pledged to implement its recommendations—including prosecuting those found to have purchased and/or redistributed land illegally. A few high-profile blocks of land were recovered, and some people who were found guilty voluntarily surrendered land back to the government. But, for the most part, the recommendations were never specifically followed. The violence surrounding the 2007 national elections finally spurred the government into action, compelling it to issue the first-ever national land policy in 2010. This policy is enshrined in the 2010 constitution and has been hailed as its most progressive set of articles.[36] However, Kenya elites, especially in the Rift Valley, have been generally unwilling to endorse the policy.[37]

Most significantly, the Ndungu Report clearly revealed some of the most glaring signs of official corruption in the government and the economic sector—just the type of corruption that civil society had been clamoring to root out. The report also provided clear evidence of the unbridled power being wielded by the office of the president. The findings of the Ndungu Report were further confirmed with the election of the National Alliance Rainbow Coalition (NARC) government in 2002. At that time the public fully expected that the new government would move to curb the powers of the national executive, and eradicate the model of the strong presidency with a license for impunity. However, a new draft constitution issued in 2005 offered little change from the already existing system. As we shall see, this adherence to the status quo led to an escalation in popular discontent, which manifested during the buildup to the 2007 national elections and in the violence surrounding these elections. On the one hand, larger civil society was tired of corruption and bad governance;

on the other hand, indigenous groups, particularly in the Rift Valley, came to fear the further erosion of their claims for redress of the indigenous land issue.

Citizenship and Land Rights

As indicated, Kenya's land disputes date back to the colonial period. At the time, the indigenous residents of the colony were divided into provinces and districts based on language and culture. In all, there are just over forty distinct ethno-linguistic groups in Kenya. The British had brutally subjugated Africans and appropriated their land, paying lip service to caring for the interests of the African people, but nevertheless arbitrarily seizing the land and opening it up to European settlement. Africans were relegated to native reserves and to tribal trust lands. Moreover, they could not engage in economic activities that competed with settler interests. In large measure, the Mau Mau Rebellion was fueled by this situation, as were sporadic African uprisings in the Rift Valley.

Following the Second World War and the rise of the African independence movement, various indigenous groups began to demand the return of their customary rights to land—or, in the case of those communities most heavily affected by land and population pressure (e.g., the Kikuyu, Luhyia, and Kisii)—rights to resettle in other parts of Kenya. This demand gave rise to the majimbo movement, which was aimed at defending the rights of indigenous minorities and pushing for a regionalist solution for independent Kenya. This issue dominated the Lancaster House conference between 1960 and 1963. Drafters of the constitution finally agreed to call for a form of federalism (majimboism), but this structure was almost immediately abandoned after independence and replaced by a unitary form of government. Moreover, the only viable opposition party, KADU, voluntarily dissolved itself and folded into KANU, the dominant party at the time. The new president, Jomo Kenyatta, developed a strategy based upon the co-optation of ethnic elites, and rewarded them with high public office, access to development funds with which they could redistribute land, and other material benefits.

Immediately after independence, Kenya's economy was booming, and the coffers of the central government were full. In addition, the new government was the beneficiary of a strong system of provincial administration in which administrators at the subnational level were beholden to the president himself.[38] Kenyatta used the patronage at his disposal to build support among ethnic kin, but also among a diverse group of ethnic elites from other groups. Among the elites at the time of Kenyatta's death in 1978 was Daniel arap Moi, the powerful Kalenjin politician who, at one time, had been involved in the KADU leadership. Despite intrigue among Kikuyu politicians, who were leery of a minority from the Rift Valley assuming the presidency, Moi prevailed. Recognizing the source of his opposition among ethnic organizations such as the Gikuyu, Embu, and Meru Association (GEMA) and the Luo Union, Moi banned such organizations and began laying the groundwork for establishing a de jure one-party system. This aim was accomplished in 1982. Almost simultaneously, Moi began to strengthen his base among the major ethnic groups in the Rift Valley, the Maasai and Kalenjin.[39]

Originally the party of the largest ethnic groups in Kenya, the Kikuyu, Kamba, and Luos, KANU became the champion of ethnic minorities, particularly the Maasai and the Kalenjin. KANU no longer included groups such as the Kisii and the Luhyia, as they were seen as competitors for Rift Valley land. Although tensions over land had existed throughout the independence period, they were heightened during the rule of Moi, particularly after he agreed to abandon the single-party system and introduce multiparty democracy in 1991. As the move towards multiparty government intensified, Rift Valley politicians who saw their groups as indigenous to the region called for a return to federalism or *majimboism*.[40] Many indigenous people in the Rift Valley thought that such a move would involve the expulsion of "settlers," "foreigners," and "aliens" from the area in a veritable ethnic cleansing pogrom. However, many of the affected communities had been there for decades, its inhabitants having arrived as laborers on white farms, or as squatters, and later as new land and business owners. Proponents of this effort saw only groups like the Kalenjin, Maasai, Turkana, and Samburu (KAMATUSA) as "original inhabitants" of the land.[41]

Civil Society, Multiparty Democracy, and the Trigger of Post-Election Violence in Rural Areas of the Rift Valley

Throughout the 1980s, Kenyan civil society pressured for not only a retreat from the one-party state but also a return to multiparty democracy. By the end of that decade, the international spread of the newest wave of democratization contributed to a democratic breakthrough in Kenya. Between 1988 and 1992, constitutional changes were made, and Kenya's first multiparty election since independence occurred in 1992.

Moi was determined to remain in power, but was not without opposition. In 1991, the first opposition party in the multiparty era, the Forum for the Restoration of Democracy (FORD), was launched. FORD was headed by a Kikuyu businessman, Kenneth Matiba, and the old-line Luo politician Oginga Odinga. This party formed when international donors were placing increasing pressure on the Moi government for its official corruption and closed political system. At the time, several international donors either cancelled or suspended their aid packages to Kenya. The World Bank and the International Monetary Fund also announced they would not make new development aid available to Kenya unless its human rights record improved and it curbed corruption.[42] These reversals of fortune contributed directly to the introduction of the new multiparty system.

Although they were forming, opposition parties were far from being a united block. In fact, by the time of the election FORD had split into two, and there were in total six opposition parties. In 1992, Moi benefited from his incumbent position and the newness of the idea of multiparty elections. The government used its agents to disrupt opposition efforts through both intimidation and violence. For example, KANU and the government controlled the electoral commission that was responsible for the review and reform of electoral laws. Moreover, it used its executive and legislative powers to redraw the line for electoral districts and thereby to dilute the votes of opposition parties.[43] Also, the rules governing requirements for electoral victory were changed by the national legislature. To form a government, for example, candidates for the presidency had to secure 25 percent of the vote in five of eight provinces, in addition to a plurality of the votes. Should a candidate fail to get the proper distribution and number of votes, a runoff would take place. At the time of the elections, opposition parties were forbidden from campaigning in areas affected by ethnic disturbances. Elsewhere, violence and intimidation—often perpetrated by provincial administrators and elements of the security services—were rife.[44]

Between 1991 and 1997, more than 1,500 lives were lost as a result of ethnic clashes; scores more were internally displaced.[45] Beginning in 1997, violence and political intimidation became a regular feature of elections and relations between the ruling party and opposition parties. Most significant was the ethnic basis for these conflicts.

In 1998, President Moi appointed the Akinwumi Commission to study the causes of the ethnic clashes that had taken place between 1991 and 1998. The report was finally released in 2002. Among its findings was that prominent KANU politicians had fueled multiple incidents of ethnic clashes, mostly in the Rift Valley. For example, the report quoted MP William ole Ntimama, a Maasai politician, as saying, "We have now burned the FORD, multi-party politics and the National Democratic Party. All the ministers and KANU leaders you see here have resolved to fight together and follow President Moi together [sic]."[46]

In addition to such inflammatory remarks, groups of so-called "Kalenjin Warriors" systematically targeted Kikuyus and other nonindigenous groups with violence, often setting their homes ablaze, chasing them away, and even killing some. Leaflets were passed out telling the "foreigners" to leave the valley.[47] Under the pretext of presenting grievances over land, one objective of the KANU-sponsored violence was to depopulate these areas of any nonsupporters of KANU. The report further claimed that the problem was "tribal land" and that the Kalenjin did not want other people to live there while they were themselves landless. In that light, majimboism was meant to counter the advance of multipartyism; some would openly assert that they wanted majimbo so as to send non-Kalenjin back to their ancestral homes.[48] Barasa Kundu Nyukuri quotes one prominent Kalenjin politician as saying the Kalenjin would not succumb to threats and harassment from any quarter and would fight for their equal rights with other Kenyans. He went on to say, "The Kikuyu are playing the camel in the tent game whereby they now want to dominate the same people who had welcomed them to the Rift Valley."[49]

Even though this report came out after Mwai Kibaki had assumed office as president and was the leader of the opposition party, NARC, those identified as having been guilty of crimes over the period studied by the commission were never prosecuted. This negligence reinforced the idea that government officials continued to operate with impunity. Notably, in the aftermath of the return to the multiparty system, Kenyan civil society experienced resurgence. As in places such as Zambia and Zimbabwe, civil society sought out alliances with organized political parties. Dr. Willy Mutunga has effectively described how these events unfolded.[50] Civil society organizations under the leadership of lawyers and leaders of other professional organizations, church organization, trade unions, women's and youth groups, teamed up with opposition politicians in NARC to oust Moi and KANU, pushing for a constant public discussion of political issues and for constitutional reform. Rather than being confrontational, this movement was peaceful and constructive, which proved very effective in that Moi was not moved to use the full force of his office to clamp down on either the formal opposition or civil society.

At this time, NARC anchored its campaign in the promise to eliminate corruption and to recover all public land that had been illegally allocated under the Moi government. NARC voiced no clear position on addressing the demands of the indigenous people of the Rift Valley. Civil society saw itself as primarily involved in a constitution-making project, and organized itself under an initiative it labeled "the 4Cs" (The Citizens' Coalition for Constitutional

Change). The 4Cs cultivated an alliance with political parties and politicians because of their potential as mass mobilizers. Although this united front succeeded in displacing KANU in 2002—and should be credited for laying the foundation for constitutional change—transformation did not occur immediately.

By 2002, KANU had lost its cohesion, and opposition forces had come tenuously together in several new parties. The most cohesive of these was the National Rainbow Coalition, headed by former vice-president Mwai Kibaki with the support of prominent Luo politician Raila Odinga. It was generally assumed that, as president, Kibaki would work toward creating the position of prime minister, a post that would go to Odinga. However, this assumption was not realized, and the two severed ties, mainly over the terms of a new constitution that was supported by Kibaki. This draft did not allow for the creation of a power-sharing arrangement between president and prime minister.[51]

In 2005, a referendum on the proper division of powers at the executive level took place. Voters rejected the draft constitution by a tally of 58 to 42 percent. Raila Odinga took the results of this referendum—and Kibaki's unwillingness to support a more powerful position for the prime minister—as a signal to form his own party, the Orange Democratic Movement (ODM).[52] In the 2007 elections, Odinga ran for the presidency under the banner of the ODM, and Kibaki formed a new coalition, the Party National Unity (PNU). Six viable political parties contested the presidential elections, including the ODM, PNU, and KANU. Before the elections, ODM split into two, and KANU threw its lot in with PNU. In the Rift Valley, the Kalenjin and Maasai voters switched their allegiances from KANU over to the ODM. They tended to see the PNU as a Kikuyu party opposed to supporting their indigenous rights to land.

The results of the elections released by the National Elections Commission showed Kibaki as the winner by a margin of 47 to 44 percent. Significantly, 9 percent of the vote went toward the ODM-K, a splinter party headed by the Kamba politician Kalonzo Musyoka. Odinga and other opposition elites cried foul, and encouraged their followers to protest the elections. The tipping point came around December 30th, when Kibaki had himself sworn in as president even as votes were being recounted. This flagrant act ushered in several months of violent interethnic conflicts, which did not cease until former UN Secretary General Kofi Annan and other international actors negotiated peace.[53]

During the electoral campaign, Raila Odinga and ODM had led the Kalenjin and Maasai to expect that he would support a new version of majimboism under the rubric of "devolution." This plan clearly meant that he would devolve more political authority to local communities, but Kalenjin politicians who supported him suggested to their supporters that Odinga was in favor of expelling "aliens" and restoring land to the indigenous people of the Rift Valley.[54]

These developments relate to an exclusionary form of citizenship, but must be considered against the backdrop of long-standing ethnically based disputes over rights to land ownership. In the Rift Valley of Kenya, the national government does not recognize claims to land based on customary law. However, as has been argued above, during the regime of President Moi—particularly toward the end of his rule—the government tended to ignore the rule of law as it related to the land issue in the Rift Valley. The tendency became for Moi and his Kalenjin and Massai supporters to look upon title deeds issued during the Kenyatta era as "mere pieces of paper."[55] This perspective was particularly relevant in considering the trend toward purging the Rift Valley of "aliens."

For its part, the Moi regime had relied heavily on the judiciary to fight its critics as well as to help supporters of majimboism to evade legal sanctions on issues relating to land.[56] The Kibaki regime, however, did not follow this practice. In the 2007 electoral period, neither Kibaki nor Raila Odinga ever focused specifically on the claims of the Kalenjin and Maasai, but their issues continued to be a part of the discussion in the crescendo of calls for majimboism there, as could clearly be seen in the violence that accompanied the buildup and follow-up to the 2007 elections.

The Scope and Intensity of Ethnically Based Violence in the 2007 Elections

By the 2007 elections, ethnically based violence had become a regular part of the political process. However, ethnic politicians and their supporters rather than the government committed these incidents, often in the course of normal party activities. Even before the elections, ethnic instability existed in the Rift Valley around Mt. Elgon and in rural areas of Nakuru Province. In some cases, violence spilled over to neighboring areas. As in the past, violence was used to intimidate many non-Kalenjin living in the Rift Valley to sell or abandon their property and leave the area.

Tensions in the Rift Valley over land and belonging have never been resolved, and were in large measure a compounding factor in the interethnic violence of 2007–2008. Kalenjin politicians continue to conjure images of their people being denied equal rights with regard to land and other issues.[57] Moreover, they tend to blame the non-Kalenjin for these problems. For more than two decades, violence associated with everyday politics during the course of national elections had become commonplace, but the violence that followed the 2007 elections was unprecedented in terms of scope and intensity.[58] Although some disagreement exists over just how many people were killed, injured, or internally displaced, Anderson states that more than 1,000 people died and more than 300,000 were internally displaced.[59] In contrast, Keith Sommerville puts these figures at between 1,500 and 2,100 dead and more than 660,000 internally displaced.[60] The Commission of Inquiry into Post-Election Violence placed the number of dead at 1,133.[61]

Violence occurred in both urban and rural areas. In some places it was spontaneous; in others, it was planned; in still others, it was both. Here we are mainly concerned with rural violence related to land disputes in the Rift Valley. The most intense violence involving loss of life and internal displacement took place in Nakuru Province, around Narok, Eldoret, Uasin Gishu, and Trans Nzoia.

Evidence suggests that, as in the past, ethnic entrepreneurs and political brokers played a significant role in instigating violence.[62] In most cases, early-phase violence was directed toward those assumed to be Kikuyu, Luo, and Luhyia and Kisii immigrants. Urban areas assumed that ethnicity was indicative of support for one party or the other. However, in rural areas support did not matter as much as victims' assumed ethnic affiliation. When they addressed political rallies, politicians or their representatives did so in the vernacular of the area and, in many cases, used idioms familiar to the audience. For instance, in Kalenjin areas, the Kikuyu might be referred to as "mongooses" or interlopers, and the indigenous might be referred to as the "people of the milk."[63]

David Anderson quotes one Kalenjin elder, Jackson Kibor near Eldoret as saying, "We will fight. This is war. . . . We will start the War . . . We will divide Kenya."[64] Some perpetrators of violence viewed their efforts as a systematic attempt to drive "aliens" out of the Rift Valley. In some cases, this effort was centered on the assumed need to recover lost land for the indigenous people. In others, the aim was to purge particular areas of foreigners who were now so numerous that they marginalized the indigenous people and were coming to dominate them politically. By making the Rift Valley "ungovernable," indigenous people would be able to protect their culture and their traditions.

Whereas in the violence of the 1990s, Kalenjin Warriors had terrorized those considered "aliens," in 2008, Kalenjin force was met by vigilante groups sponsored by Kikuyu politicians, mostly made up of elements of a group known as Mungiki. In late January 2008, Mungiki gangs allegedly carried out systematic attacks against the non-Kikuyu population, believing they were supporters of the Orange Democratic Movement. Most of those attacked were from among the Luo, the Luhyia, and the Kalenjin ethnic groups around Nakuru. Vigilantes were said to have received guns and aid from state security forces. Also, some claimed that the Mungiki terrorists were supported by Uhuru Kenyatta, the Kikuyu leader in KANU.[65]

Another difference from the violence of the 1990s was manifested in the spread of ethnic tensions via public media. For example, between 2002 and 2007, a dramatic expansion of privately owned FM radio stations in the country took place. As early as 2005, such media were thought to have contributed to the spread of ethnic violence. Some politicians, among them William Ruto (Kalenjin) and Uhuru Kenyatta, currently own or have control over certain stations.[66] These stations have call-in shows and provide platforms for those with messages they want to deliver to the local community. In some cases, the messages are highly politically charged and disparaging of rival ethnic groups. Although this scenario recalls the role of Radio-Télévision Libres des Milles Colones (RTLM) in the genocide in Rwanda, no evidence exists that the Kenyan FM medium has been used specifically in that way. Stations have partisan positions but are not used to systematically spread ethnic hatred.[67] Still, it was not unusual to hear, for example on the Kalenjin FM radio station in the valley, such veiled threats as, "The time has come for us to reclaim our ancestral land."[68]

In an effort to explain the causes of violence surrounding Kenya's 2007 national elections, critics have tended to focus on voter fraud and the instigation of violence and intimidation promoted by ethnic politicians. However, deeper analysis of this event reveals that flawed elections and the rhetoric surrounding them were only precipitants of violence that was, in fact, based on historic grievances relating to identity, citizenship, immigration, and rights to land.

Violence occurred in the major cities and in the hinterland. In the Rift Valley, long-standing grievances over immigration and land added to the chaos. Since independence, sometimes through government programs and sometimes through voluntary migration, ethnic groups such as the Kikuyu, Luhyia, and Kisii had settled in various parts of the Rift Valley. In some cases, these groups moved to urban areas, but in others they migrated to rural areas that buttressed what were claimed to be the ancestral homelands of the indigenous population of an area. In either case, the issue of expanding "alien" populations was viewed as a matter of urgent concern to the indigenous people, who felt that they would become marginalized or completely "exterminated."[69] Their fears were exacerbated by ethnic politicians who curried the electoral support of the indigenous population. For example, although William ole Ntimama had been one of President Kenyatta's and KANU's most loyal Maasai supporters, serving in high-level political positions and doing the party's bidding in his home area, upon the return to a multiparty state, he reverted to championing his Maasai ethnic kin. As minister of lands, Ntimama welcomed Kikuyu immigrants to settle on the edges of the Mau Forests. However, when the central government moved to reclaim land in his district to create a water catchment, Ntimama was one of the most vigorous voices for the forcible expulsion of Kikuyus and other groups from the area. He cited that his opinion was not based on ethnicity but rather upon the need to protect the environment. Kalenjin who had recently settled in the area saw this purge as directed pointedly at them.

Nyukuri notes that it is a common phenomenon for ethnic political leaders to support liberal democracy when addressing national audiences, but in practice they consistently support "ethnic democracy."[70] In such cases, civic republican conceptions of citizenship are viewed as more important than conceptions of liberal citizenship—yet another example of the limits of formal constitutions in certain instances in Africa. For them to work as they are designed, constitutions must be supported by the political will and commitment of responsible leaders. Constitutions may be representations of the rule of law, but they do not always guarantee that citizenship rights are understood and implemented in the same way in all cases.[71]

8

Rwanda

Exclusionary Nationalism, Democracy, and Genocide

"Let slavery, servitude and discord be finished forever!" . . . Long live the
[Hutu] republic! Down with the [Tutsi] monarchy! . . . No more feudalism!
No more Kalinga [the drum that symbolized the power of the ruler]!"
—Anonymous, Butare, Rwanda 1990, quoted in Alison des Forges,
Leave No One to Tell the Story: Genocide in Rwanda

The Rwandan genocide of 1994 and the events that led up to it present a clear
case of social conflict based in exclusionary nationalism and the consequent
denial of citizenship rights.[1] Even though the Tutsi and the Hutu, who together make up 99 percent of Rwanda's population, are from the same ethnic
group, the roughly eighty-year colonial era saw the construction of divisive
identities, in which the two peoples were categorized into different *races,* one
inherently superior (the Tutsi) and the other inferior (the Hutu).[2] The Hutu
make up 85 percent of the population and the Tutsi 14 percent. The Twa make
up the remainder of the population. Because of the perceived physical differences among these groups, the colonialists—including European missionaries—considered them to be of different racial stock.[3] However, for centuries
the Tutsi and the Hutu occupied the same territory, had the same traditions,
and spoke the same language (Kinyarwanda). During the colonial period, they
even came to share the same religion, Roman Catholicism. However, the Tutsi
were predominately cattle herders, giving them higher status in society; thus,
over time, a lord–vassal relationship developed between the Tutsi and Hutu.

At the top of the sociopolitical hierarchy was the Tutsi king, or *mwami*, who was assumed to be divine. Below the king were several layers of chiefs responsible for such roles as commanding the king's regional armies, managing royal grazing lands, and managing agricultural land.[4] Chiefs tended to be Tutsi, but some Hutu also assumed such roles. Scholars suggest that the differences between Tutsi and Hutu largely had to do with occupational roles. Owning a substantial number of cattle generally afforded the individual the appellation of "Tutsi," whereas being without cattle might earn one the status of "Hutu." Hence, even those considered Hutu in lineage could rise up and become a Tutsi. However, such transformations were not common.[5]

By the mid-1800s—even before the beginning of the colonial era—the lord–vassal relationship that had been mutually acceptable to the Tutsi and the Hutu began to break down. Tutsi royalty became increasingly oppressive of the Hutu. Naturally, when they arrived, the colonialists formed alliances with the Tutsi royalty, eventually indirectly ruling their colony through the Tutsi nobility.

The Transformation of Hutu–Tutsi Relations on the Eve of Colonialism

Prior to the arrival of the European colonialists, no distinct Hutu and Tutsi tribes or ethnic groups existed. Yet even though the two groups were culturally the same, the colonialists looked upon and treated them as separate groups.[6] When they first arrived in the Great Lakes region between the fifth and eleventh centuries, the Hutu encountered a population referred to today as the Twa. The Hutu were agriculturalists, and the Twa were forest-dwelling hunters and gatherers. As Hutu agricultural practices began to take hold, the Twa retreated into the nearby mountains. The Tutsi began to gradually migrate into the region in the fourteenth century. Interactions among the three groups were initially peaceful, and a common culture and language developed. These nationality groups had none of the characteristics of distinct tribes. In fact, in cultural terms, the Hutu and Tutsi looked more homogeneous than anything else.[7] They shared the same language, lived side by side without any historic "Hutuland" or "Tutsiland," and had even intermarried.

Cattle ownership was seen as a status symbol, and the Tutsi used their possession of cattle to claim dominance in the social hierarchy as the Hutu and Tutsi cultures merged. On the eve of the nineteenth century, the social system was based on what has been described as patron-clientelism.[8] Tutsi nobility were a class unto themselves; but Tutsi who were not of royal lineage but who possessed cattle could have Hutu vassals. A Hutu could come to own cattle, but usually these were earned as a reward for service to a Tutsi patron. Thus developed a veritable caste system in which Hutus could rarely rise to a noble rank.

Colonialism and the Transformation of Social Identity

German colonialists arrived in the region in 1897, during the period known as the European Scramble for Africa. They were impressed with what they saw as the obvious noble qualities of the Tutsis. In short order, a myth based in the era's pseudoscientific racism emerged, suggesting that the racial differences among the groups were manifest in the typical physical features of the groups.[9]

The Twa, who are generally acknowledged to be the first inhabitants of Rwanda, are pygmies who traditionally lived as hunters and gatherers in the forests areas of the country, or were the servants of high-ranking local personalities. By contrast, the Hutu, who make up the vast majority of the population, were traditionally subsistence farmers. The archetypical Hutu, as first described by European anthropologists, was said to be round faced, with dark skin, a flat nose, thick lips, and a square jaw. The typical Tutsi was supposed to be tall, with a long face, light skin, a narrow nose, thin lips, and a narrow chin.

Some missionaries, anthropologists, and historians have claimed that the Tutsi migrated to the Great Lakes Region of Central Africa from northeast Africa, perhaps from southern Ethiopia. Others have suggested that the Tutsi were not originally from Africa, but from the East or Middle East. Some even considered the Tutsi descendants of the survivors of the lost continent of Atlantis.[10] Regardless of the Tutsi myth of origin, the colonialists saw them as a different race from the Hutu, a notion that was, until just after the Second World War, ingrained in all who lived in Rwanda.

Prior to the arrival of Europeans between 1860 and 1895, a Tutsi king, Mwami Kigeri Rwabugiri, carried out a series of military and political campaigns designed to centralize his authority and extend it throughout much of what we know as present-day Rwanda, except for the northwest. The first Europeans to enter the region were the Germans, who arrived in 1894—a decade after the Congress of Berlin had taken place. By 1897, in cooperation with Rwabugiri, the Germans established effective control. The Germans stayed until 1914, just at the beginning of the First World War. While the Germans were in the process of establishing effective control over Rwanda, Rwabugiri died, and an internal struggle to succeed him took place among the Tutsi nobility. The Germans did not understand the complicated local politics of the people of this area of the Great Lakes region of Africa, but they wanted to keep the monarchy intact so as to use it as an instrument of indirect rule. At the beginning of their rule, Germans numbered fewer than one hundred administrators in the colony.

Significantly, the colonial administration relied upon European missionaries to assist in the pacifying of the Rwandese. The most well-represented missionary group that came to operate in the region was the White Fathers, based in France. Leadership in this religious order was conservative and initially attempted to cultivate good relations with the Tutsi nobility. The primary objective of the White Fathers was general proselytization; but they felt that this effort would require the cooperation of the Tutsi nobility.

In the Germans, the Mwami and Tutsi chiefs had what came to be valued allies who helped them tighten their grip over their subjects, resorting to more ruthless practices than had ever been seen in Rwandese society. With the military backing of the Germans, the Tutsi nobility was able to step up the effort to drive the Hutu principalities out of existence and to completely subjugate the Hutu people.

Initially missionaries sent from Europe to proselytize came from conservative upper-class families. But following the First World War, they increasingly came from the working class. The liberal views of the younger priest assigned to Rwanda at this time contributed to the escalation of tensions between the conservative church leadership and the priests responsible for converting the general population to Catholicism. Even though the Germans lost control over the territory during the war, this event did not affect the work of the missionaries who had served as a support system for civilian administration.

Created in 1919, following the First World War, the League of Nations was dedicated to promoting world peace. One of its first diplomatic efforts was to determine the future status of the colonies of Germany and Italy in Africa. At the time, what is present-day Rwanda was comprised of two former German colonies, Ruanda and Urundi. The Belgians were given a mandate to administer this territory from 1922; this continued until the formation of the United Nations. In 1946, the two entities were separated into Rwanda and Burundi, and were administered by Belgium as a United Nations Trust Territory. This arrangement lasted until Rwanda achieved its independence in 1962.

The Church and the Construction of Social Domination

Until the 1920s, Christianity had spread very slowly in Rwanda, and most of the converts were poor or marginal people who looked to the church as a source of security in a transitional society. With the arrival of the Belgian administrative presence, the number of conversions in Rwanda increased dramatically. The Tutsi elite realized that the Belgians were firmly in control and that anybody who wanted to get ahead in the evolving society was going to have to meet with their approval; one way was to convert to Catholicism. For the most part, formal education was provided at mission schools, even for the Hutu. Elites realized that to break the cycle of poverty and underdevelopment, the Hutu would have to secure a formal education. However, Hutu access to formal education was at a rate dramatically below that of the Tutsi elite. On the whole, the Belgian reforms of 1926–1931 created a modern Rwanda that was centralized, efficient, neotraditional, and Catholic—but also very brutal. It was characterized by heavy taxation of the subject populations, and eventually required individuals to carry an identity card stating where they were born, where they lived, and the ethnic group to which they belonged. Belgian colonial practice reinforced the myth of a superior Tutsi race, a falsehood that had migrated from Ethiopia or elsewhere to the north into Rwanda. In the process, the Tutsi came to believe that they really were a superior race—whether they were rich or poor, chiefs or subjects.

The influence of European missionaries in the Great Lakes region of Africa continued to grow during the interwar period. In Rwanda, the White Fathers succeeded in winning over both Tutsi and Hutu converts, but continued to look upon the Tutsi as a favored group. Most of the African clergy leadership and priests were Tutsi. At the same time, the conservative leadership of the Catholic Church increasingly found itself at odds with younger European priests, who were often opposed to a close relationship with the Tutsi nobility and in favor of uplifting the downtrodden Hutu.[11] Out of this context a broad sense of Hutu identity and victimization began to emerge.

When they assumed control over the territory, the Belgians initially tried to integrate some Hutus into the structure of chieftaincy. However, by 1927 this approach had been abandoned, and from then on the Tutsis came to almost totally dominate such positions. By the end of Belgian colonial rule in 1959, forty-three out of forty-five chiefs were Tutsis, and out of 559 subchiefs, only ten were Hutus.

Notably, during Belgian rule the Catholic Church came to assume a major role in the creation and institutionalization of racial differences between various ethnic communities in Rwanda. The Tutsi were not *assumed* to be a superior race; indeed, this idea was enshrined in law with the complicity of the Catholic Church. Between 1927 and 1936, racial ideology was institutionalized in Rwanda, as evidenced by rules governing the differential access of Tutsi and Hutu in such spheres as education, state administration, and law.[12] Whereas in the past Hutu and Tutsi had had some fluidity in terms of identity and social mobility, after a 1933 census the categories became fixed. Hutu and Tutsi had no possibility of changing their identity no matter what changes occurred in their life circumstances.[13]

Although a sense of Hutu consciousness had existed throughout the colonial period, this ethnic identity among the group did not become widespread until after the Second World War. In large measure, one factor that contributed to this trend was the worldwide movement to end colonialism and to grant former subject people the right to self-determination. This conviction no doubt influenced the liberal ideas of young priests assigned to Rwanda who adhered to a form of liberation theology; and the increasing educational opportunities accorded for the Hutu.

The Rise of Hutu Nationalism

In 1957, the UN sent a trusteeship mission to Rwanda to assess the League of Nations mandate that had been given to Belgium in 1919, and to evaluate the possibility of moving the territory to independence. When the mission arrived in Rwanda, a group of nine Hutu intellectuals, including the future president of Rwanda, Grégoiré Kayibanda, presented it with a document that came to popularly be known as the Bahutu Manifesto.[14] The manifesto attempted to articulate the Hutu perception of what these Hutu elites called "the humiliation and socioeconomic inferiority" of the Hutu, and the political monopoly of the Tutsi "race" over Rwandese society. The document went on to claim that the Tutsi had invaded land that was historically occupied by the Hutu and the Twa. In other words, the Hutus claimed that the Tutsi were foreigners. The manifesto clearly pronounced that the Hutu people were being denied their inalienable rights as the indigenous inhabitants of Rwanda by an alien people, the Tutsi, and had been suffering under the oppressive rule of the Tutsi monarchy. As such, the Hutu demanded their independence not only from white European colonialists but also from the Tutsi monarchy, which held a political monopoly over Rwanda.[15] The most radical among the Hutu intelligentsia favored the creation of a "Hutu nation."

The Tutsi elite offered a counterposition to the Bahutu Manifesto, *Mise au Point* (The Statement of Views), a document that also viewed Rwanda's fundamental problem as "race." However, it called for an end to European colonialism and the surrender of Rwandan governance to the Tutsi nobility. The Statement of Views emphasized rapidly training the Tutsi to govern an independent Rwanda under the leadership of the reigning Tutsi elites. Although the political polarization between the Hutu and Tutsi had already begun, the statement completely ignored the potential of this division to become a problem.[16]

Political Parties and Revolution

Following the war, political parties rapidly formed in the country. The two dominant parties were the Rwanda Democratic Party/Party for the Movement and Emancipation of the Hutu (PARMEHUTU) and the Union Nationale Rwandaise (UNAR) or Rwandese National Union, which represented the Tutsi. The rapidity with which emerging African political movements called for independence caught the Belgians off guard, as it had at about the same time in their largest African colony, the Congo. In both cases, the Belgians had assumed that even with the UN mandate for movement toward independence, it would take many years before their African subjects were ready for self-rule. However, political unrest exploding in the Congo seemed to have somewhat of a contagious effect on two smaller Belgian Central African trusteeships, Rwanda and Burundi.

As inter-ethnic tensions intensified, a full-scale Hutu revolution broke out. The myth of Tutsi superiority/Hutu inferiority was compounded by growing economic inequalities and discrimination. This unrest forced the Belgians to realize that, as in the Belgian Congo, they were beginning to lose control of the situation; in late 1959, they hastily floated a plan for self-government in Rwanda. Nonetheless, the internal conflict intensified. The most serious area of conflict was in the northwest, where the Hutu principalities had made their last stand against the Belgian forces in the 1920s. Although the carnage was not as great as it would be in 1994, it was extremely bad, with Tutsi from the region being indiscriminately hunted down and killed. This chaos led to a massive exodus of Tutsis to the Belgian Congo, Burundi, Tanzania, and Uganda by 1963.

Even as the fighting continued, the Belgians organized local elections. Four main parties contested the election. The Hutu party, the Party of the

Hutu Emancipation Movement (PARMEHUTU), won the majority of just over three thousand local governmental positions and, in the process, the power of the chiefs was eliminated. On September 25, 1961, legislative elections were held. PARMEHUTU received 78 percent of the votes, the result of which was a total reversal of the social order. Rwanda had now come to be governed according to a nominal system of majoritarian democracy. The Hutus had ascended to power in accordance with their numbers, and the Tutsi had become a permanent minority. Politics was unmistakably along "racial" lines[17] and, as a result of the revolution and racial cleansing that accompanied and immediately followed it, more than 100,000 Tutsis were driven into exile in neighboring states (Burundi, Uganda, and the then–Belgian Congo). The stage was now set for rebuilding Rwandese society under Hutu rule. The question was whether Hutu elites could build a society in which the majority ruled and adhered to and protected the rights of minorities.

After the end of hostilities and the installation of a democratically elected government, a brief period passed during which the Hutu-dominated government headed by Grégoire Kayibanda attempted to reconcile with the Tutsis. Importantly, however, Tutsis were still seen as a separate, alien "race," and the only indigenous citizens of Rwanda were the numerically dominant Hutu and the minority Twa. The Rwandese constitution claimed the equality of all Rwandese citizens, but because they were foreigners, the Tutsi could not claim citizenship. They had been a privileged minority, and therefore were not seen as deserving beneficiaries of any "affirmative action" policies intended to right historic wrongs. Tutsi were allowed to live in Rwanda, but were targeted objects of Hutu violence. At the same time, Tutsi remained in the education system; they could engage in business; and they continued to play important roles in the Catholic Church. However, after 1964, quota systems limited their access to even ecclesiastical positions, and they were completely forbidden to engage in politics.[18]

Kayibanda was constantly under pressure from Hutu nationalists to completely eliminate the Tutsi from any opportunities and to transform Rwanda into a Hutu nation. Although Kayibanda's regime had systematically curbed the participation of Tutsis in society, this move did not satisfy Hutu hardliners. Between 1962 and 1973, Kayibanda used the everyday Hutu's fear of a return to the oppressive Tutsi monarchy to build support for continued vigilance against a counterinvasion. During his reign, Kayibanda not only painted a picture of the Tutsi menace, but also attempted to create a security system that guarded against attacks against him and his regime from regional opponents among his own Hutu people. Kayibanda was from the center of the country, and thus felt the need to protect his position from opponents from the south and the north. Between October 1972 and February 1973, Kayibanda set up vigilante committees, which he charged with rooting out enemies and potential threats to the regime. However, the general population did not share the president's paranoia, and no mass killings of Tutsis or Hutu enemies of Kayibanda took place. Only a few dozen people were killed during this campaign, but this slaughter was enough to stir fear in the psyche of many Tutsi, and led to another massive wave of Tutsi emigration. However, Kayibanda's strategy had the unintended consequence of creating a sense of threat and insecurity among Hutus in the north and the south; they believed that he was out to get them. With the emergence of sporadic conflicts in the north and south, a senior military officer named Major-General Juvénal Habyarimana, a Hutu from the northwest area of Gisenyi, decided to make his move and launched a bloodless coup on July 5, 1973. One of his first acts of office was to guarantee the security of the Tutsi, and to declare himself the protector of *all* "the children" of Rwanda, Tutsi as well as Hutu.[19] This move was greeted with a sigh of relief among the Tutsi, who were finding the sense of threat unbearable.

Catalysts and Context for Change

Habyarimana immediately made a significant departure from the policies of his predecessor, abandoning the assumption that Tutsi were of a separate race from the Hutu and the Twa. He now claimed them to be legitimate indigenous citizens of Rwanda. However, this rule applied only to those Tutsi who lived in Rwanda at the time, and not to those who had fled following the revolution. In fact, referring to the possibility of the right of return for Rwanda Tutsi in the diaspora, Habyarimana said the country was "full up," and that Tutsi in the diaspora should make their permanent homes elsewhere.[20]

By the time Habyarimana came to power, the damage had been done: the Tutsis had been politically marginalized. Throughout his entire tenure in office not a single Tutsi was elected to local government office, and only one Tutsi officer served in the whole army. Moreover, only two Tutsi were members of parliament, out of a total of seventy. There was even a quota system for admission to schools, with the Tutsi being guaranteed only 9 percent of school places. All in all, life was difficult for the Tutsi, who were victims of institutional discrimination. One positive factor was that no systematic pogroms or mass killing campaigns were launched against them.

Pledging to restore social peace when he came to power, Habyarimana outlawed all political parties except for the one he himself created, the National Revolutionary Movement for Development (MRND). He used this party as an instrument of personal rule. To get a government job, one had to belong to the party, and if one were a party member she or he had to adhere to strict principles of discipline and make sure that everyone with whom they came into contact did the same. More importantly, as his development priorities and political appointments made clear, Habyarimana favored the people of his home area, Gisenyi.[21] He expanded the quota systems left in place by his predecessor. Habyarimana spoke publically of national unity, but in practice was very much under the influence of Hutu hardliners from the northwest, the Akazu.[22]

Even though he had tightened his grip on politics, Habyarimana had no control over worldwide economic or political situations. In the mid-1980s, the world price for coffee, the country's main agricultural export, collapsed, as did the demand for Rwanda's main mineral export, tin. This market drop along with ever-present land pressures created a serious economic crisis for the country. Then the international donor community began to demand structural adjustments and reconceived their development aid and investment policies. By the end of the 1980s, economic pressure intersected with political pressures, as the donor community linked development assistance to commitment on the part of recipient countries to end corruption and democratize their political systems. At the same time, Habyarimana was challenged by the invasion in October 1990 by the Rwandese Patriotic Front (RPF), a force of Tutsi exiles from Uganda.[23] Even before this invasion, Habyarimana bowed to pressure and acknowledged that Tutsi, who had fled because of the violence of the revolution, would be allowed to return. Also, three days before the invasion of the RPF, the president made a speech before the Rwandan legislature announcing that Tutsi would be allowed to have passports and other travel documents.[24]

Between 1975 and 1990, France became Rwanda's chief provider of economic and military assistance. In keeping with a worldwide trend at the time, France hosted a Franco-African Summit in Paris in 1990 to discuss changes in its economic and political assistance to its African clients. This meeting's discussion made clear that France would link its donor assistance to a commitment from its clients to reform their political systems. Because Rwanda was so dependent on French aid, this stipulation had particular implications for the Habyarimana regime. As a direct result of pressure from France, Habyarimana announced that he was going to introduce a multiparty system in Rwanda. Even though most people felt that Habyarimana's commitment to multiparty democracy was shallow, various groups—including students and Hutu opponents of the president from the south—began to vigorously press for the introduction of a multiparty system. In this climate of unrest, Tutsi exiles based in Uganda decided to launch a war against the Habyarimana government.

The Tutsi Diaspora and the Need for Belonging

The Tutsi had previously made sporadic attempts at rebellion from inside and outside the country, but by the early 1970s many had fled to neighboring countries as refugees. Those Tutsi attempted to make the best of their situation and to integrate into their countries of exile; however, in the long run such assimilation proved impossible. For example, some in what is the present-day Democratic Republic of the Congo as well as in Uganda constantly pressured for naturalization if not complete acceptance as indigenous to the country.[25] However, those indigenous to their host countries saw them as nothing more than refugees, foreigners.

The bulk of the refugees in Uganda had left Rwanda in the early 1960s without knowing that they would remain in exile for almost thirty years. Many died, and many of their children were, in turn, born in exile.[26] The Rwandese refugees in Uganda created the Rwandese Refugee Welfare Foundation in 1979 to help victims of political repression during the reign of the dictator Idi Amin. The foundation was later renamed the Rwandese Alliance for National Unity.[27] Toward the end of his regime, Amin became extremely hostile toward Rwandan refugees, blaming them for Uganda's economic and political difficulties. From these origins, the RPF emerged.

When Milton Obote succeeded Amin, Uganda still did not a offer a positive environment for Rwandese refugees. They were stigmatized by the regime and harassed by indigenous Ugandans because they were thought to be "strangers" and "aliens." They were evicted from settlements outside refugee camps and told to move to the camps or return to Rwanda. After 1982, Rwandan refugees became regular victims of atrocities perpetrated either directly or indirectly by the Obote regime.[28] Conditions became so unbearable that some Rwandan refugees in Uganda were moved to join rebel movements aimed at toppling the Obote regime.

Most Tutsi refugees gravitated toward the National Resistance Movement (NRM), led by the present-day president of Uganda, Yoweri Museveni. Obote was overthrown in a military coup in 1985 and, after two successive military regimes, the government again changed hands in 1986 when the NRM seized power. Museveni is from an ethnic group called the Hima found in western

Uganda who are related to the Tutsi. With the aid of Rwandese Tutsi refugees, Museveni was able to take power in Uganda in January 1986. Some Tutsi, including the future Rwandan president Paul Kagame, were even formal military officers in the National Resistance Army.

When the NRM, the political wing, came to power, refugees who had been part of the NRA hoped their lot would improve. They had had hopes that once Museveni was in power, they would at least be considered for naturalization in Uganda. Helle-Valle found in a 1982 survey that most of the Rwandans she interviewed in Uganda hoped they would be able to make a life in Uganda. This aspiration was especially true among those not claiming land in Rwanda.[29] However, the internal politics of Uganda interfered. The issue of indigeneity, which had affected Asians during the reign of Idi Amin, surfaced once again, and the Tutsi refugees were left without a place to belong.[30] Though Rwandan refugees had contributed significantly to the success of the NRM in its assent to power, following the Ugandan civil war, they were harassed and discriminated against for being foreigners not only by Ugandans living in the west, but also by their former military colleagues. Some refugees who had lived and farmed on land and grazed cattle in the west outside of the refugee camps there were even expelled for not being indigenous with traditional rights. Ugandan herders and squatters were united in pressing the government to assert that Rwandese refugees had no citizenship entitlements in Uganda. This defensive posture was accompanied by intense debate and even violent clashes involving indigenous Ugandans and Rwandese refugees. In the end, Rwandan Tutsi were relegated to the status of nonindigene. By 1982, some forty thousand Rwandan refugees had been evicted from Uganda, many of them fleeing to Rwanda.[31]

The evictions in the early 1980s caught the Habyarimana regime off guard, and in the process undermined its policy of refusing the right of return to the Rwandese diaspora. The president felt compelled to close the Rwanda-Uganda border and to confine the returnees to isolated and heavily securitized camps. Ogenga Otunnu has noted: "The unwillingness of the two governments to recognize their displaced citizens, left the refugees without asylum and without a state to call their own."[32] At the same time, hostilities between the refugees in Uganda and the indigenous population escalated.

This fighting led refugees to abandon their push for naturalization in Uganda and to commit their efforts to returning to Rwanda. It was clear, however, that such a return would have to be accomplished through armed struggle. Habyarimana was still not clearly in support of the right of return for the Tutsi diaspora. Some members of the RPF who had been incorporated as units in the NRA left to join the invading RPF forces, and other Tutsi refugees also joined the force.[33] As justification for the 1990 invasion of Rwanda, the RPF claimed a desire to end to the tyranny and exclusion visited upon the Tutsi in Rwanda. They wanted their full Rwandese citizenship restored.

The RPF invaded Rwanda on October 1, 1990, and over the next three years waged a war against the Rwandan National Army. At the time, the Habyarimana regime, under intense pressure from external and internal sources, was at its most vulnerable. Inside the country, the government was being pressured by opposition groups to open up the political system even as it was being pushed by hardliners among the Hutu in the northwest to defend Hutu rights against all forces, in particular against *Tutsi Power.* The return of the Tutsi was seen as inevitably leading to the renewed domination and subjugation of the Hutu by this foreign minority. In this context, Rwandan society was gripped by what came to be known as *Hutu Power,* an ideology inspired by a Hutu sense of pride in their culture and a passion to protect the purity of the Hutu nation.

Civil War and Genocide

The Habyarimana regime, encouraged by the Akazu and other Hutu conservatives, increasingly drummed up popular support for the ethnic cleansing of Tutsis. The president relied on these entities for support, and as war raged preparations were made for a "final solution" to the Tutsi problem. What began as a youth movement transformed into a Hutu militia, the *Interhamwe* ("those who work/fight together"), which was bent on exterminating the Tutsis from Rwanda. The Interhamwe took up arms and trained for the moment they would be called upon to begin their "work" (ethnic cleansing and genocide).[34] At this time, the regime of then–President Juvénal Habyarimana was being pressured to liberalize politics and move away from one-party rule.

As the war continued, civilian Tutsis were constantly harassed and even killed by agents of the state as well as by the Interhamwe. President Habyarimana promoted the development of both the Interhamwe militia and Hutu hate media. Around the time of the RPF invasion, the southern opposition began to publish a magazine called *Kanguka,* which literally means "Wake Up." *Kanguka* was dedicated to exposing the failings of President Habyarimana's government. Habyarimana countered by sponsoring the creation of a rival magazine called *Kangura,* or "Wake Them Up," a particularly hateful and extreme publication supported by the Akazu from the northwest.[35]

A potent example of *Kangura's* hate messages can be seen in its issue dated December 10, 1990, which spelled out the "Hutu Ten Commandments." Among other things, the "commandments" declared any Hutu woman who married a

Tutsi man, or any Hutu who did business with Tutsis, traitors. They also called for complete dominance by the Hutu in all aspects of society. Hutu who opposed Habyarimana were singled out for condemnation. *Kangura* was representative of the hate media's effort to portray Tutsi as an overwhelming threat to Hutu ideals and freedom.[36]

As war with the RPF intensified, the Akazu wanted to reach more Hutus, particularly the rural population; thus, in 1993, they sponsored the creation of Radio-Télévision Libres des Milles Colones (RTLM). On paper, RTLM was a private company, but it quickly became the primary vehicle for the beleaguered Habyarimana to mobilize Hutu in all parts of the country with a message of hate for the Tutsi. Through this medium, radical right-wing Hutu intellectuals were able to whip up fear and hatred in a large segment of Rwanda's Hutu population, thus paving the way for the genocide of 1994. RTLM's programs featured lively music and interactive, informal talk shows that allowed listeners to phone in and express personal views. Many themes were drawn from articles appearing in *Kangura* and *Kanguka*.[37]

Through the media, Hutu propagandists reminded the masses of the lessons they had learned in school: there was a difference between the Nilotic (Tutsi) and Bantu (Hutu) nations. The Tutsi royalty were portrayed historically as rulers who believed they had a divine right to lord over, dominate, and exploit the Hutu. This hierarchy was thought to be the natural order of things. The propagandists emphasized that their role was to awaken the national consciousness of the Hutu and to encourage them to fight to prevent the return of Tutsi oppressors.

By the end of 1992, President Habryimana was bowing to outside pressure that he negotiate with the RPF. He liberalized his cabinet by including some Tutsi notables. A few months later, his government entered into secret negotiations with the RPF in Uganda. Later, talks were held in Paris, but serious negotiation aimed at a power-sharing agreement finally moved to Arusha, Tanzania. In July 1992, a cease-fire agreement was signed. The accord called for ending the arming of both sides by foreign supporters. On the political side, protagonists agreed to adhere to the rule of law and to respect human rights, pluralism, and democracy. The cease-fire was to be monitored by an OAU military observer group as well as by representatives of the RPF and the Habyarimana government.

On August 3, 1993, Habyarimana signed the peace agreement with the RPF, officially bringing the war to an end. The Arusha Accords ensured a right of return for Rwanda's refugee diaspora, promised the integration of the two warring armies into a single national defense force, and established a blueprint for a broad-based transitional government, composed of representatives of all the national political parties, including the RPF. Habyarimana would remain president until elections could be held, but his powers would be basically cere-monial. The plan also called for a UN peacekeeping force to be deployed in Rwanda until the country appeared to be back to normal.[38]

Some specifics of the Arusha Accords included a power-sharing arrange-ment whereby the RPF would have a total of five cabinet seats out of a total of twenty-one, and eleven seats in the transitional national assembly out of a total of seventy—a number equal to that of the ruling party, the MNRD. Forty per-cent of the military and 50 percent of the officer corps would consist of RPF ele-ments. In addition, multiparty elections were to take place twenty-two months after the accords were signed. On the face of it, one might have surmised that these terms would not be acceptable to the Akazu, and that it was going to be up to Habyarimana to win them over.

As it turned out, the Arusha Accords amounted to a political suicide note for Habyarimana. The Akazu and Hutu Power leaders accused him of selling out—and then charged him with being an accomplice to the RPF. Four days after the signing of the accords, RTLM began broadcasting from the capital city of Kigali, transmitting to every corner of the country. As mentioned, pro-gramming at the radio station was a mixture of inflammatory oratory and popular Hutu music designed to make listeners feel that hating and killing the Tutsis was their sacred duty. Articles in Kangura (one going so far as to sug-gest the time-period in which Habyarimana would be assassinated) echoed this sentiment.

The Arusha Accords were never implemented; and, in fact, while Habyari-mana was returning from a round of talks on implantation that had been held in Tanzania, his plane was shot down as it approached Kigali Airport.[39] Who shot the plane down will never absolutely be known, but the Akazu, RTLM, and Kangura blamed the event on the RPF. But why would the RPF commit this act? Things were going their way. Others blamed the French intelligence service. A more likely culprit would seem to have been hard-line Hutus who were upset at the prospect of giving so much up when the Arusha Accords went into effect.

On April 3, 1994, RTLM announced: "In the next three days there will be a little something here in Kigali, and also on April 7 and 8 you will hear the sound of bullets or grenades exploding."[40] It appears that the assassination of Habyarimana was the signal to unleash the Interhamwe, which would drag along the rest of the Hutu population in the process. In a thirteen-week period following the assassination of Habyarimana, it is estimated that up to 75 percent of the Tutsi population, more than 700,000 people, were killed. As many as 75,000 to 150,000 people are estimated to have participated in these crimes against humanity. By any definition, this was genocide—a "systematic, sustained, state-sponsored effort to eliminate a whole ethnic or nationality group over a limited period of time."[41] Mamdani quotes Robert Kajuga, the president of the Interhamwe, as asserting: "It's war against the Tutsis because they want to take power, and the Hutus are more numerous. . . . We have to defend our country. The government authorizes us."[42] After 1989, the massacre of Tutsis by Hutus had become common, but not on the scale that this violence would assume by 1994. State-sponsored systematic mass killings and ethnic cleansing of Tutsi began in the spring of 1994.

Genocide and Justice

In the end, the RPF was able to defeat the National Army and install a Tutsi-dominated regime. Since then, many efforts have been made by the government to punish and rehabilitate the *genocidaires,* those accused of having committed the atrocities. This campaign has been accompanied by an effort on the part of the international community to bring the perpetrators of the genocide to account. Just three weeks after the start of the genocide, the UN Security Council committed itself to organizing the International Criminal Tribunal for Rwanda (ICTR). The ICTR was established in November 1994, with a mandate to address any genocide or violations of international humanitarian law between January 1, 1994 and December 31, 1994. These crimes could have been committed not only inside Rwanda, but also in neighboring countries. It was clear that Rwandan government officials and their supporters—including members of the church—had committed acts of genocide in the country, and that the RPF forces were also guilty of violations of international humanitarian law. It would have been preferable to set up the ICTR inside Rwanda, but for security reasons it was set up in neighboring Tanzania. However, the Rwandans also set up their own national tribunal. It is estimated that at the high point of the work of the tribunals more than 125,000 people were being held inside Rwanda on suspicion of having been involved in the 1994 genocide—including men, women, and children. The ICTR has primary jurisdiction in these cases. It can at least theoretically have accused perpetrators extradited to its court from anywhere in the world. Notably, in general Tutsi, particularly if they were members of the RPF, escaped prosecution.[43]

The national tribunal was overwhelmed with the cases before it—despite the fact that by 2008, the international community had spent more than $100 million on the promotion of justice in postgenocide Rwanda. It would clearly take hundreds of years to prosecute the 30,000 people formally accused of genocide. In 1996, it was estimated that more than 100,000 Hutus were crammed into Rwanda's prisons—to be held there indefinitely without formal charges. By 2011, an estimated 10,000 people had died in custody.

Because of Rwanda's poor judicial infrastructure, and the fact that many who had been victims of the genocide were judges and lawyers, moving the trials along was difficult. Thus, in 1996, the government of Rwanda set up a system to prioritize individuals for trial according to the severity of the crimes they were alleged to have committed.[44]

The Rwandan government chose to use the formal court system only to prosecute central figures in orchestrating the genocide. More than 1 million people accused of having participated in criminal activities during the 1994 genocide were tried by community or *gacaca* courts. More than 12,000 gacaca courts were set up and, by 2012, hundreds of thousands of cases had been decided. Sixty percent of those tried were found guilty. The first trials began in December 1996, and by the end of the year 322 people had been judged. Of this number, 111 were found guilty and sentenced to death. An additional 109 got life sentences, and 81 received shorter sentences. By mid-2006, the national courts had tried approximately 10,000 genocide suspects. In 2007, the Rwandan government abolished the death penalty, which had last been carried out in 1998 when 22 people convicted of genocide-related crimes were executed. This development removed a major obstacle to the transfer of genocide cases from the ICTR to the national courts.

Nation Building after Genocide?

An RPF-backed transitional regime took power in July 1994. Paul Kagame, a leading commander of the RPF, became vice president and minister of defense. He had been head of military intelligence in the NRA in Uganda and a close confidante of president Museveni. Kagame was primarily responsible, with the assistance of the Ugandan army, for leading the RPF army in the cross-border effort to beat back remnants of the Interhamwe and other Hutu opponents in eastern DRC. Eventually, he was elected president in a landslide in Rwanda's first multiparty election, in 2003. His margin of victory was 95 percent, with broad support among all of those who voted. His nearest opponent polled less than 4 percent of the vote. Kagame was reelected president by a margin of 93 percent in 2010.[45]

Notably, since it came to power, the RPF-dominated regime has been constantly concerned with the threat of the former Interhamwe and other opposition groups engaged in military activities against it from the DRC. Over the past decade and a half, in an effort to strengthen its control over the country and to keep the Hutu combatants operating out of DRC at bay, the RPF regime interjected itself into two civil wars in the DRC, in 1996–1997 and 1998–2003. In the first war, Rwanda participated in an effort on the part of DRC opposition forces to displace the regime of Mobutu Sese Seko; the second incursion was to more effectively confront the Hutu opposition operating out of that country and threatening the Rwandan regime. It supported proxy wars involving groups related to the Rwanda Tutsi against the Democratic Front for the Liberation of Rwanda (FDLR).[46] In the latter incident, Rwandan forces penetrated deep into the DRC. Critics suggest that the real aim of the Kagame regime was to gain access to valuable minerals in the Eastern Congo.[47]

In addition to engaging in policies ostensibly meant to bring about justice in postgenocide Rwanda, the new Tutsi-dominated regime has created a veneer of national unity in this multiethnic state. Critics forcefully argue that this effort amounts to nothing more than social engineering.[48] Rather than growing out of democratic dialogue and bargaining, this process is—in large measure—driven from the top down, thus reinforcing the idea that it is more of an exercise in social engineering than in nation building based on the voluntary involvement of all relevant groups and their leaders. The aim seems to be to ignore or deny conflictual intergroup relations in Rwandan history: to wipe the slate clean and begin from the beginning.

The regime does not deny that its goal is to reconstruct Rwandan identity, a central indication of which was a new constitution and "Organic Law" introduced in 2003. Among other things, the terms *Hutu, Tutsi,* and *Twa* are now banned from public discourse. There are now "speech crimes," and often critics accused of such crimes are claimed to be spewing "divisionism" and "ethnic ideologies," or demonstrating a "genocide mentality." Any public discussion or recounting of the genocide must be officially approved.[49] Moreover, the Rwandan government has introduced several institution-building measures that are said to be efforts to get the perpetrators and victims of the genocide to live side by side in peace. For example, the constitution now defines the various social groups in ethnic rather than racial terms and asserts that all of the country's citizens share equal rights. Antidiscrimination laws have been put in place. The primary institution charged with the task of nation building is the National Unity and Reconciliation Commission (NURC).[50] A primary accomplishment of the NURC has been the establishment of solidarity or *Ingando* camps, which are said to engage in peace education.[51] These camps have existed since 1999, and have involved more than 90,000 participants. Some critics claim that the camps amount to nothing more than indoctrination sites for the ideology of the RPF. They deal with the sources of ethnic division in the country and are designed to convey a Rwandan history that emphasizes unity among the disparate groups.

In 2007, the Kagame regime established *Itorero ry'Igihugu,* designed as an informal education system based on the tradition of group dialogue. The government claims that the objective is to instill proper values and to cultivate leaders that promote national unity. Representatives are chosen from every region of the country, then trained and dispatched to their communities to educate the masses. They are expected to lead discussions on issues of national and regional importance. Over a two-year period, 115,228 participants took part in the program. Other nation-building activities aimed at promoting reconciliation include national seminars and summits.

Further evidence of the RPF's top-down social engineering strategy can be seen in the tight control it places on national politics. The RPF operates as a vanguard party seeking to incorporate most of the population; independent media, competitive opposition parties, and a vibrant civil society are not allowed to exist. In national elections, it is common for parties in opposition to the RPF to be harassed and intimidated. The government publically proclaims its commitment to decentralization and to "multiplying the points of power" in administration down to the grassroots level.[52] And yet it carefully screens all administrative appointments so as to ensure that regional movements do not have the ingredients for developing into national opposition movements.[53]

Despite outward manifestations of political quiescence in Rwanda, no real political freedom exists. The regime has a veritable monopoly on political correctness; in fact, a culture of fear and self-censorship prevails. This climate is, in part, due to the approach the RPF regime has taken to dealing with uncovering the root causes of the genocide and prosecuting the perpetrators. Indeed, many people fled rather than submit to the gacaca or tribunals process. With Rwanda having returned to relative peace and steady economic recovery, one glaring problem remains: the repatriation of not only the Tutsi diaspora but also the Hutu wanting to return from camps in neighboring countries. For example, some were driven into refugee camps in Uganda and eastern DRC. In both cases, they encountered hostilities from the indigenous populations, usually based on access to and use of farmland. When the Hutu and Tutsi refugees returned to Rwanda, the Kagame regime was faced with incorporating them into the general population. Returnees are categorized as "early case" or "later case." Early-case refugees left in the 1960s or early 1970s, and overwhelmingly consist of Tutsi. Later-case returnees were more recent and were mostly Hutu. Was either group—the Tutsi diaspora or recent Hutu refugees—to have their traditional land rights restored? In many circumstances, restitution was not possible. Following the revolution, in 1962, the Kayibanda regime redistributed substantial amounts of land that had been abandoned by fleeing Tutsi. When the RPF displaced the Hutu-dominated regime in 1990, many Tutsi engaged in land grabbing, settling as squatters. In addition, the new government appropriated land in order to resettle some returnees, a practice that was especially notable in the Eastern Province.[54]

Kagame quickly gained the admiration of the international donor community as one of a handful of "new generation African leaders."[55] He was a no-nonsense leader and had progressive ideas of good governance and national reconciliation. The donor community supported Kagame's desire to develop a new land law and land policy based on the principles of social equity. Indeed, general support went to two land-related development strategies: villagization programs in the northwest and promulgating a new land law and land tenure policy.[56]

On the face of it, each of these programs was expected to play a key role in resolving the problems of land pressures, and in resettling both early- and late-case refugees. In the northwest, the strategy was to set up *imidugudu* settlements, collective, multiethnic villages that would be modern and more efficient than traditional villages. Farmers were supposed to voluntarily relocate from their original farming plots to these newly created villages. In some cases, they could continue to farm their old land, but would have to travel some distance to get there. However, entry into this scheme wasn't voluntary—it was coerced. Although these strategies were supposed to promote integration, in fact, because of the way they operated, they contributed to interethnic tensions. For example, Catherine Newbury notes that even in ethnically mixed communities, resources for residents were often distributed in a way that favored the

Tutsi.[57] Many of the Hutu residents came to feel discriminated against and suffered from insecurity and a diminished quality of life. The Kagame regime utilized these villages both as a way to tackle the land problem and to undercut the possibility of effective opposition movements developing in the area.

The passage of the 2005 Organic Land Law was another significant innovation related to land law and land tenure. When some of the Tutsi refugees streamed into Rwanda immediately after the genocide, initially many of them simply took possession of land that had been previously occupied by Hutu. These parcels were known as *kubohoza* ("to help liberate"). Much of this land had belonged to others before the genocide—rather than to those who were allowed to occupy it after the RPF takeover. Most of those settled at the time were returning RPA soldiers.

Once it took power, the RPF government was under pressure from the international community to deal with problems relating to resettlement and land. What happened in Eastern Province is illustrative of the RPF's handling of this issue. The new land law was based on three principles: (1) the mandatory registration of land; (2) the consolidation of land to improve its productivity; and (3) the introduction of modern agricultural practices.[58]

In 2007, the President's Commission on Land was created in Eastern Province with the goal of resolving land disputes in an equitable manner. As it operated, the commission was supposed to promote "land sharing," which was accomplished through uncompensated land expropriation. Just after the genocide, senior military officers of the RPF, politicians, local administrators, and politically connected individuals acquired large tracts of land. The commission was charged with confiscating such property and redistributing it to citizens without land of their own. However, the criteria for redistributing the land was unclear, allowing those in charge of decision making engage in favoritism and other forms of corruption. In other words, they were in a position to violate the rule of law, which is often precisely what happened.[59]

As a consequence of Rwanda's flawed land policy over the past two decades, the RPF regime has missed opportunities to genuinely rebuild the Rwandan nation. Ethnic tensions, despite the perception by some outside observers continue to fester.

The civil war that began in Rwanda in 1990 was fundamentally a clash over exclusionary and inclusionary citizenship rights. By the late 1980s, exiled Tutsi felt that they did not belong in neighboring countries, where they were living as refugees after having been driven out of Rwanda in several waves. Although successful in becoming naturalized citizens in Tanzania, Tutsi were denied such opportunities in both the DRC and Uganda. The invasion of Rwanda was the RPF's effort to reclaim citizenship rights for the Tutsi within that country.

Since it came to power, the RPF regime has created a façade of political stability and commitment to equal citizenship rights. International circles praise the Kagame regime for its highly successful economic policies and good governance; however, its policies have generally failed to create a common sense of national citizenship between the Hutu and Tutsi. Thus a lingering question remains: Without good governance and the rule of law, is such a goal, in fact, possible?

Summary and Conclusion

Identity, Citizenship, and Social Conflict

"If you steal, do not steal too much at a time. You may be arrested. Steal cleverly . . . little by little."
—President Mobutu Sese Seko, from George Ayittey, *Africa Betrayed* (1992).

Among the most common causes of intergroup conflict in Africa today are disputes over identity and citizenship. In some cases, the identification of groups or individuals with an entire national community is called into question, but in most instances the autochthony within a subnational community is most salient. Consequently, we are forced to reconsider the process of sociopolitical transformation that has been taking place in Africa.

Some fifty-plus years ago, modernization theorists assumed that the process of modernization would lead invariably to the breakdown and ultimate demise of customary communal social systems and values—and to their replacement by more Western-style institutions. However, this phenomenon did not happen. It was further assumed that traditional societies would be transformed in such ways as to follow the lead of Western societies based on principles of liberal individualism and democracy. It was thought that subnational, communally based social systems would be completely replaced by modern, multiethnic nation-states. Rather than rejecting traditional values and institutions, the trend has been toward nations seeking coexistence and overlap between modern, multiethnic trends and the traditional values and institutions. Nowhere is this hybrid truer than in Africa, where this relationship has increas-

ingly led to ethnically based tensions and even conflict involving various social groups, with each other, with the state, or with a combination of the two.

A primary contention of this book has been that, although we cannot attribute all incidents of civil conflict in modern Africa to any one particular
origin, in many cases, the issue of citizenship and of explicit and implicit rights
and obligations is a sharp point of contention. How, then, do we define who is
a citizen of a particular community and who is not? Does citizenship in a nation-state imply the same thing at all levels of society? Or, can individuals or
groups claim citizenship in national communities without necessarily giving
up other identities based on kinship, region, and class and religious affiliation?
Have modernization and democracy contributed to broadening and deepening
a widespread sense of national citizenship in most African countries, or have
these processes contributed to intergroup conflicts among subnational communities and, in some cases, to conflicts that involve the interjection of exclusionary nationalism at the level of the nation-state itself?

To answer these questions in this study, I have found it useful to engage
in an exercise of social process tracing that considers three key factors: the
context or political culture in which politics takes place, the relevant social
structures that characterize a particular society, and the relevant sociopolitical
agents. At the same time, for change to come about, catalyzing factors and precipitating events must determine the pattern and direction of change. Analysis
must trace the interactions of all of these factors over time in order to identify
the relationships that most directly have contributed to the process of change.
In such circumstances, one must be cognizant that change occurs along different trajectories, at different levels, and in different domains (e.g., class, gender, race, ethnicity, economics, politics). It should also be noted that in real life
circumstances these levels, trajectories, and domains interact and give rise to
transformative changes, which is why we must always bear in mind the context in which change is taking place.

The case studies highlighted in this study offer important examples of how
conflict can occur at all levels during the process of political change. In the case
of Côte d'Ivoire, from the beginning of the postcolonial period, conflicts over
citizenship relating to land rights in certain parts of the country eventually led
to a definition of citizenship based on autochthony or the ancestral birthplace
of the families of individuals. This ancestral locale–based definition of citizenship led to the exclusion of presidential candidates and involved questions of
whether a given village was located in the country's postcolonial boundaries.

Although the two major groups in Rwanda, the Tutsi (14 percent) and Hutu (84 percent) account for 99 percent of the population and historically belonged to the same ethnic group, colonial-era European rulers presumed identifiable racial distinctions between the two groups. During the struggle for independence, the Hutu simultaneously engaged in a revolution against the Tutsi monarchy and, through democratic elections, came to dominate politics in the country. In the aftermath of Hutu electoral victory, more than 100,000 Tutsi were driven from Rwanda. Those remaining were not accorded full citizenship rights. When the second wave of democratization began to spread all over Africa in the late 1980s and early 1990s, exiled Tutsi, now disenfranchised as refugees in Uganda, decided to fight their way back into Rwanda to reclaim their birthrights. The Rwandan civil war in the early 1990s was in large measure an attempt on the part of the Tutsi not only to return to their ancestral homeland but also to claim full citizenship rights. In the post-1994 period, when the legacies of genocide produced a discourse of politically correct homogenizing analyses—denying ethnic identities—understanding the interplay of citizenship and social conflict at various levels of the nation is critical.

In postindependence Nigeria, with the enactment of the Federal Principle, access to certain social services and citizenship rights are contingent on proof that an individual's ancestral village is located in the particular jurisdiction in which she or he formally claimed such rights and privileges. In some cases, the immigration of groups from one Nigerian state and subnational jurisdiction to another led to conflict over land and access to certain social services. Migrants in states that border the north and the south of the country are regularly seen as foreigners and aliens, and thus cannot claim citizenship rights in an area. Recently, the interjection of exclusionary nationalism in intercommunal relations has led to a conflation of religious and ethnic identity conflicts, as demonstrated in clashes between Christians and Muslims.

In Kenya, where interethnic conflicts erupted before, during, and after the 2007 national elections, long-standing grievances among different groups were exacerbated by electoral rigging. These precipitating events, however, were rooted in a political system whose corruption permeated the highest levels of government and penetrated down to the grassroots, giving rise to historic disputes over immigration and land and property rights. The conflicts themselves were fueled by cultural brokers and ethnic entrepreneurs who wanted to protect a vote-rigged victory for themselves, or who felt they had been the victims of vote rigging and other electoral violations in the 2007 national elections. These events occurred after more than a decade of pressure from both civil society and formal political parties to transform Kenya from a one-party system to a multiparty democracy. When conflict relating to the elections broke out, long-standing tensions over immigration and land rights, particularly in the Rift Valley, erupted. Yet again, immigrants were accused of being alien and thus fair game for ethnic cleansing by groups that claimed the Rift Valley as their ancestral home. In other cases, newcomers maintained that they were under threat from autochthonous groups even though they had national citizenship rights in any part of the country.

The violence that coincided with successive national elections beginning in 1992 had roots in a tactic whereby politicians couched their appeals in terms of ethnicity, which they in turn fused with party identification. Ethnic politicians tended to identify with either the ruling party or some opposition party and to equate support for their party with support for the citizenship rights of their supporters.

In part, Ivorian, Rwandan, and Kenyan examples of conflicts over citizenship and identity in Africa in general could be seen as having been exacerbated by the level of political development on a continent in which the rule of law is not always clearly and firmly established.[1] Moreover, the autocratic tendencies of political leaders with entrenched bad governance practices and neopatrimonialism regularly fail to apply laws relating to citizenship in an unbiased manner. In fact, leaders often misuse state institutions, such as the courts and security forces intended to protect citizenship rights, and appropriate legal institutions as instruments of personal rule. The causes of tensions over citizenship claims are not always obvious and, depending on the circumstances, can emerge and lead to serious and sometimes violent social conflict.

It seems reasonable to ask: Are such tensions and conflict inevitable in Africa? Or, are African societies moving toward more modern institutions and democratic practices that guarantee civic awareness of shared citizenship rights and the rule of law? In either case, what factors contribute to the enduring conflicts over identity in Africa? What does the balance sheet show? What are the prospects for the future?

The Balance Sheet and the Way Ahead

To address these questions, we must assess where African development is at this moment in history and how its realities all came about. We have already spoken about the brief transitional moment at the time of independence, when Western-style democratic institutions were first introduced to Africa. We also noted the rapid drift toward autocracy in the mid-1960s, accompanied by increasingly failed economic policies and subsequent stagnation, and in some cases, by the near or complete failure of African states by the late 1980s. At the heart of these trends was always the African state and its economic and social development as shaped by international donor assistance.[2] Although external actors were initially focused on promoting the institutionalization of liberal democracy in Africa, by the mid-1960s, their main political concern was promoting political stability, even under the auspices of authoritarian rulers.[3]

It is generally agreed by Africanists that Africa experienced a watershed moment by returning to multipartyism and market liberalism beginning in the late 1980s. How can the nature and timing of these changes be explained? In *Emerging Africa,* Steven Radelet argues that at least seventeen African countries, excluding oil exporters, can be considered emerging economies, which is cause for great hope.[4] Radelet further argues that fundamental political, social, and economic factors converged with strategic choices made by political and economic leaders to trigger changes in these countries. First were the reintroduction of multiparty politics and the rise of liberal democratic institutions and more accountable governments. This move occurred almost simultaneously with the introduction of "sensible" economic policies; the end of the stifling debt burden, which was an outgrowth of austerity measures including conditionalities imposed by providers of international development assistance (World Bank, IMF, and other multilateral institutions and bilateral governments); the spread of new technologies (i.e., the World Wide Web, cell phones); and the emergence of a new generation of progressive leaders in African public and private sectors.

While Radelet's argument for this "Great Transformation" in African development is generally well documented and convincing in statistical terms, the macro view he presents requires deeper contextual analysis. How do these changes look on the ground in those seventeen countries and others? What clues do they offer to indicate that Africa's poorest countries may charter similar paths? How critical was the juncture of late 1980s and early 1990s in the long view of African development? In other words, if we accept that these changes were critically important, does that mean that they are durable?

The importance of decisive moments in history is well documented. For example, in a highly acclaimed recent book, Daron Acemoglu and James Rob-

inson trace the importance of critical junctures in explaining how some societies embark on a path toward prosperity—and others, for various reasons,
end up choosing paths that lead them into deeper poverty.[5] The difference,
they argue, between societies that took off and prospered and those that did
not was the choices made by political leaders to use inclusive versus extractive institutions in governance and economics. First, leaders chose inclusive
political institutions, thus creating enabling environments for developing inclusive economic institutions.[6] This change did not happen all at once, but
over an extended period of time. The primary example used by Acemoglu and
Robinson is the Glorious Revolution in England in 1688, which resulted in the
abolition of royal absolutism and established the first parliamentary democracy. This event was followed by the Industrial Revolution, which began in 1750
and lasted one hundred years.[7] Significantly, these authors note, even as these
changes were occurring in England, African people were not able to benefit
from them, in part because the Industrial Revolution in England and in Europe generally saw Africa as a source of slave labor used to extract resources
not only from Africa itself but also from other colonies being established in
foreign lands. By the time they achieved independence, African colonies had
not experienced a political phase akin to the Glorious Revolution, nor had they
benefited from their own industrial revolutions. African colonies had missed
the critical juncture leading to self-sustained growth and prosperity, yet were
faced with popular demands that new leaders of independent Africa satisfy the
welfare expectations of their citizens. This conundrum offers but one example
of the challenges faced by independent African states as a result of the legacy
of European colonialism.

Implicit in the arguments made by Acemoglu and Robinson is the critical
importance of institutions that lay the foundation for liberal democracy and
laissez-faire economics. The weight of history and path dependency, then, are
important—but not decisive. Human agents in the form of political leaders
are required to make strategic choices. Although they suggest a causal link
between politically inclusive institutions and inclusive economic institutions,
Acemoglu and Robinson reference outlier situations in which extractive (autocratic) political institutions continue while inclusive economic institutions
are chosen by autocratic leaders, as occurred in the People's Republic of China
and South Korea. Thus, the unanswered question is whether African states can
bypass the sequence of phases experienced by England and other European
countries and successfully establish inclusionary political systems and liberal
economic institutions.

The well-developed general theory offered in *Why Nations Fail* seems like a useful framework for analyzing many countries and regions; however, because of its Eurocentric bias, based on liberal democracy and free market economics, the book falls short of capturing the essence of prosperity or poverty in places such as Africa. A more useful approach would not necessarily be based on a general theoretical foundation but on a relational perspective, as employed in this work, which attempts to understand how some counties succeed and others fail given their particular contexts and social structures, and the strategic choices made by political and economic leaders. This perspective should also be flexible enough to allow for differences in the patterns and sequences of creating inclusive economic and political institutions, as well as for the partial introduction of either of these types of institutions.

The theory offered by Acemogolu and Robinson is useful in that it identifies the centrality of the weight of history, path dependency, or other crucial factors explaining the direction and pattern of change from one society to the next. The argument and evidence offered by Radelet, on the other hand, appear superficial, as they neither consider the weight of history; path dependency from country to country; the strength of the state vis-à-vis other important actors; the commitment of its leaders to the long term, equitable promotion of the public good in their countries; nor the domestic and international structural factors outside the control of the leaders of the countries under study. For example, even though the risk of secessionism throughout the continent seems small, intrastate conflicts could continue to serve as hindrances to political and economic development. Some critics argue that rather than being deep and durable, the changes now taking place in several parts of Africa are fragile. They are not as penetrating and permanent as they need to be to achieve takeoff. For example, Jorge Arbache and John Page present evidence showing that the growth accelerators in most of Africa's economies are not generally associated with improvements in such important variables as investment and savings.[8]

In the foregoing pages, I have sought to situate African states within the context of their own history and to understand how that history interacts with the current political context and social structures, in turn creating environments in which political leaders must make choices about development and democracy. What is abundantly clear from the present analysis is that institutions matter—but they do not matter all of the time. Also obvious is that for political institutions to work the way they are designed to, commitment on the part of leaders, political opposition, and civil society must be strong.

Good Governance

What is governance and what, indeed, is "good governance"? The concept of governance has long been the subject of debate among academics and practitioners alike.[9] For our purposes here, we follow the lead of political comparativists, who view governance as the application of the rules of public management. As such, it involves human agents who are charged with controlling and distributing the resources of society, and with regulating relations between state and society and between and among different social groups. At the same time, governance involves more than traditional "public administration." The popularity of the concept emerged at the same time that international donors were attempting to evaluate the extent to which their development assistance was instilling values around efficient and effective public management in promoting the well-being of the citizens in countries receiving such aid. Multilateral institutions like the World Bank were careful not to get involved in the issue of regime types, and tended to emphasize the social and economic management of polities, not their political aspects.[10] Politics initially entered into this discussion insofar as they affect the protection of human and political rights of all citizens in recipient countries.

Goran Hyden, Julius Court, and Kenneth Mease identify three integral dimensions of governance in the context of development: economic, political, and administrative.[11] Economic governance involves decision making that affects a country's economy; political governance involves policymaking; and administrative governance involves policy implementation. International development agencies came to adopt this all-encompassing notion in their efforts to evaluate the performance of regimes receiving their support. Over the past two decades, the international development community has arguably become the most influential stakeholder in the field of governance. This authority is especially true in Africa, where states continue to rely upon the international donor community to provide many of the resources needed to develop society—including finance, expert advice, and political support.

In practice, the concept of governance has been narrowed to public management (mainly in fiscal matters and donor assistance in building democratic institutions), promoting social justice, and protecting human rights.[12] Hyden points to the importance of a meeting in Paris involving international donors that took place in 2005, culminating in the issuance of the Paris Declaration. At that time, donors made a decision to emphasize the policy priorities of recipient countries and to step back from their roles as primary agenda setters in African development. The idea was to enable recipient countries to take ownership in improving their own governance in the pursuit of development. Since then, the work of the African Union's Peer Review Mechanism has been heralded by donors as a concrete example of Africans taking responsibility in assessing their own development needs and the effectiveness of the strategies they choose to follow. Critics argue that, in practice, the donors continue to set the development agenda on the continent. Moreover, although this new approach is supposed to favor closer involvement of a recipient country's citizens in setting the local development agenda, some incumbent regimes continue to dominate agenda setting and decision making. Some donors would rather evaluate the *results* of this new strategy rather than the *performance* of recipient governments in such matters and popular participation and human rights.[13] Yet again, though the goal is good governance—a concept that implies the promotion of liberal democracy—African regimes tend not to be consistently evaluated on the basis of human rights and popular participation. A good example is Rwanda, where donors have rationalized working with an entrenched autocratic regime that regularly violates human rights and government is not always accountable and transparent.[14] The Rwandese Patriotic Front (RPF)-dominated regime has effectively managed its image and made strategic choices to increase the role of women and to establish select local political and economic organizations to interact with donor agencies. Although claiming to uphold the equality of its citizens under the law, the Tutsi-dominated government has systematically institutionalized discriminatory practices against Hutu citizens, despite claims that, in postgenocide Rwanda, ethnic identity does not matter.

Good governance is thus thought to mean democratic governance. Paul J. M. van Hoof has described it as a means of achieving the goals of human development as an end in itself—as "values, policies, and institutions that are governed by human rights principles, that is equality, nondiscrimination, participation, inclusiveness, accountability, and the rule of law."[15] What he found in a study of local governance assessment in Southern Africa was that knowing the right person was viewed as more important than knowing the laws and policies governing the distribution and redistribution of certain types of resources. In the process, well-designed policies intended to achieve the goals of good governance were not being properly applied. As in other parts of Africa, the public and private spheres in everyday South African life continue to overlap, and neopatrimonialism enduringly serves as an impediment to good governance. Personal connections rather than institutional rules seem more important for getting things done than strict adherence to the rules of good governance.

Merilee Grindle has coined the phrase "good enough governance" to refer to governance that fits the minimal conditions necessary to enable political and economic development to occur in a particular context.[16] This notion is reminiscent of ideas advanced by economist H. A. Simon that are based upon "satisficing" or achieving not the optimal results in making policy choices but results that meet an adequate level of acceptability.[17] This method would imply a value-free approach to governance.

The concept of satisficing might seem understandable given the realities of the social, economic, and political contexts found in Africa in that it seems to be devoid of some of the ethnocentric baggage normally associated with the idea of good governance. However, the present work does not subscribe to the idea that good governance need be equated with a well-formed liberal democracy. Instead, it contends that good governance should be evaluated on the basis of whether those who rule are respectful of universal human rights and the unbiased application of public policies. This system, however, is a work in progress. Neopatrimonialism continues to be a key factor in Africa and, oftentimes, produces corruption that, in turn, hinders progress toward development. Also, in an effort to evaluate the effectiveness of governance, one must consider the presence or absence of the political will of incumbent leaders to implement policies that are fair and that conform to the rule of law. This study did not have access to classified internal documents that informed the decision making of incumbent African leaders, but the policy choices that leaders made in the context of their respective country's history and social structures—and the consequences of these choices—allow us to identify patterns.

The remainder of this chapter is dedicated to assessing the roles of corruption, political will, and the rule of law in helping us understand the ongoing salience of citizenship identity and the social conflicts that are often rooted in those claims. The subsection on the rule of law will link the analysis to specific examples from the case studies as well as to other important examples.

Corruption

It is generally agreed that corruption serves as a drag on economic growth and development as well as on the political progress of transitional societies moving from autocracy toward political liberalism.[18] Corruption is particularly acute in societies undergoing profound institutional change. Samuel Huntington, writing on the prevalence of corruption in developing countries in the imme-diate post–World War Two period argues that it is likely to occur when socie-ties are experiencing changes in their basic value systems. As such, corruption is a manifestation of the absence of effective political institutionalization. New rules are not clearly defined, or the mechanisms for enforcing those new rules have not yet been firmly delineated.[19] Huntington further argues that the pas-sage of strict laws against corruption, in fact, multiply the opportunities for official and unofficial corruption.[20] Offenders frequently seek ways of circum-venting such new rules, as necessary institutions for enforcement take time to be established and become effective. During the *longue durée* (long term), societies must be content with incremental progress. In the meantime, rules and regulations are poorly applied, if applied at all. If elites in both the public and private sector are not willing to adhere to these new rules, the way is open for them to flout the law and bring along with them significant segments of the population at large. Moreover, new rules, social control, and enforcement mechanisms for both are often not yet widely known and accepted.

Contemporary Africa has particularly acute problems with corruption. Each year, corruption costs, at the very least, an estimated 25 percent of the continent's GDP.[21] It has many dimensions, ranging from high-level political graft involving millions of dollars to low-level bribes offered to low-level public officials, such as policemen and customs officers.[22] The largest amounts of graft (grand corruption) are, of course, the most detrimental to Africa's sustained economic growth. Petty corruption also has a noticeable effect on the ways in which public institutions—including the rule of law—operate. In the process, public trust of government is undermined.[23] A good example of this loss of faith can be seen at the lower levels of the state judiciary. Bribery of low-level court officials, such as magistrates and judges, has become a characteristic way for the average citizen to speed up adjudication of his or her legal matters.[24]

The present study is most concerned with three main categories of corrup-tion: political, administrative, and professional. Political corruption includes public officials using their offices to engage in favoritism, nepotism, prejudice, and unlawful and arbitrary imprisonment of individuals seen as a personal threat to the ruling group; violence; and manipulation of the law. As men-tioned, traditional societies may not distinguish between an executive political leader in a personal sense and a leader as a public official. Today, the role of public official is not coterminous with one's personal role in society. The public office is designed to place the public good ahead of an individual's efforts to maximize personal resources. Yet in Africa today, most autocratic rulers do not make this distinction, as confirmed in the work of Transparency International, whose *Corruption Perceptions Index* annually ranks countries based on the opinions of experts. This index, despite its wide use by those interested in measuring corruption around the world, is flawed, relying as it does on data from a wide range of sources often based upon subjectively derived findings and conclusions. Consequently, the *Corruption Perceptions Index* has difficulty identifying the absolute levels of corruption in each country. Nevertheless, it provides some clues to the scale of corruption by country, data that can be backed up through investigations conducted by independent forensic auditors. One such audit in Kenya in 2003 uncovered a decade-long scandal involving the illicit smuggling of gold mined in DRC/Zaire and sold by government officials at enormous profits on the international market. The scandal cost Kenya an estimated 10 percent of its annual GDP.[25]

In the 2011, the least corrupt African country out of 182 countries in the Transparency International report was Botswana, which ranked 32nd; Sudan was ranked number 177.[26] Even though Somalia was placed last on the list, this ranking was somewhat suspect because, in reality, there is no Somalia. The Somali Republic has been a failed state for more than two decades and its remnants have yet to cohere as one unified state.

Although it is generally considered a manifestation of bad governance, corruption is difficult to measure in any precise manner. Bad governance inevitably leads political leaders at all levels to establish regimes of personal rule, which opens the way for political, administrative, and economic corruption. Notably, in some cases, members of society come to accept or have ambivalent attitudes toward the corruption of their leaders.[27] The reasoning in such cases is often simply that this practice is what people do when they have the power. Moreover, they seem to feel that anyone who can get away with minor deception or fraud without being caught should not be condemned.

Administrative corruption involves individuals who occupy bureaucratic positions designed to uphold the public trust but who nonetheless violate that responsibility on a regular basis. The officials may include public managers in various bureaucratic roles, police, military officers, or judges. For example, a public official might engage in simple or grand theft; misuse her or his public office in the issuance of government licenses or contracts; accept bribes; demand money as a form of protection, or engage in extortion. Professional corruption refers to illegal acts that are detrimental to the development of society and are practiced by nongovernmental officials in their roles as professionals (e.g., business executives, teachers and academics, contracting agents).

Arvind Jain has noted that the most serious corruption takes place when public funds are diverted to spending sectors intended to provide for the general good of the society.[28] It is particularly difficult to identify and measure this type of corruption when significant segments of the population are, indeed, benefiting from a policy, or when claims can be made that, in the long run, benefits will accrue to some segments of society. For example, this line of reasoning was used to justify the regime of Daniel Arap Moi in the 1980s when land that had been the ancestral homeland of the Ogeik peoples in the Rift Valley's Mau Forest area was appropriated by the state to create an environmentally important water catchment area.[29] The Ogeik were displaced without consultation or compensation for the land they were forced to vacate.

Displaced Ogeik were resettled in the Rift Valley, but new groups of displaced people were also settled on land that had been set aside for that purpose. New nongazetted land was carved from the Mau Forest for a resettlement zone that would include the Ogeik as well as some other internally displaced ethnic communities that had fled the ethnic clashes in 1992 and 1997. However, corrupt government officials also illegally appropriated large tracks of Mau Forest land or made land available for their privately owned companies and individuals from their own ethnic communities.

In 2009, the area was targeted as a priority for the much-needed water catchment zone, and a decision was made to evict entire communities that had been resettled or recently settled in the area. The government further resolved to favor the resettled ethnic communities originally from the region, making them the last to be considered for eviction. Those who had bought or been given land illegally were to be the first evicted. This situation resulted in intense conflicts among the Ogeik community, other resettled communities, and other outside entrepreneurs, communities, and ethnic groups that had been authorized to purchase land and to acquire title deeds even though they did not fit the initial profile of those internally displaced communities who would be settled in the Mau Forest. Some individuals and groups who had purchased Mau Forest land legally or illegally protested, demanding compensation if they were evicted—whether or not they had legal title deeds.

The stated objective in establishing the catchment zone was to protect the environment for the entire nation, and indeed the entire East Africa region. However, political corruption over land in Kenya was once again exposed. Political, administrative, and economic fraud combined, leading to conflicts over land and citizenship rights. The most deleterious form of corruption in Africa today is perpetrated by high-level government and business officials, which in any case implies the complicity or failure of executive officials to uphold the rule of law and the equality of citizenship rights. In other words, well-placed human agents are crucial in any society.

Political Will

In making choices about governance strategies, executive leaders can work toward serving the collective public good in a noncorrupt, impartial way, even when the desire to meet personal incentives would dictate otherwise. In other words, political leadership is about choices. Leaders who are committed to good governance show that they have the political will to place the needs of their citizens ahead of their own. There may be some minor digressions from this rule, but in general the mark of a leader committed to good governance can be seen in the policy priorities she or he sets. Acemoglu and Robinson emphasize the strategic choices made by leaders and the connection between those choices and prosperity or poverty, progressive development or lack of progressive development. Robert Bates, employing a rational choice perspective, paints a picture of state leaders seeking to maintain equilibrium in relations between themselves and the communities they serve. He argues that state failure in Africa can be attributed to leaders who have valued their own personal wealth, power, and steady access to rents in the form of income either from the economic factor endowments of their countries, foreign aid and corruptly gained rents from foreign agents, or taxes paid by their citizens. When it widens, the gap between rents or the income of the leader can lead her or him to engage in predation to compensate.[30]

Good examples of leaders having the political will to put the people first might include Mwalimu Julius Nyerere, the late president of Tanzania, and Seretse Khama, the first president of independent Botswana. After independence, Nyerere embarked upon a policy of Ujamaa Socialism and restricted politicians from holding public offices that would provide opportunities for personal enrichment. He also tempered whatever expectations the population in general might have had that independence would enable them to freely accumulate personal wealth. Nyerere led by example, adhering to a frugal lifestyle and regularly emphasizing the goals of equality and social justice.[31]

In Botswana, the British colonial administrators designated the territory as a protectorate and left the traditional political institutions intact. This relationship had been negotiated with London by a delegation of Tswana chiefs. The Tswana political system was characterized by what might best be described as a federation of limited chieftainships, with a king as the chief executive. This system was characterized by rules governing the accountability of those who occupied executive leadership. It was a centralized system of rulership that left traditional authorities to make rules and policies in an autonomous, largely democratic fashion, relatively free from the interference of European colonialists. The Tswana leadership made the choice to seek complete independence and sovereignty and opted to engage in party politics rather than insist on strict conformity to the traditional political system. At the same time, rather than accept liberal democracy wholesale, they incorporated democratic elements into their traditional system of governance.[32]

At independence, Botswana came to be governed by the Botswana Democratic Party (BDP) headed by Seretse Khama, who was from a royal lineage. On the economic front, the country was at first involved in ranching and meat export. Even though the leaders of the country knew there was the possibility of extractive industries such as gold and diamond exploration, they did not pursue these opportunities because they felt that this would encourage European prospectors to become involved, thereby undermining Botswana independence.[33] Once they achieved their sovereignty, the leaders of Botswana chose to develop the mining industry on their own terms. Because of the inclusive democratic traditions that already existed, Khama and the BDP were insulated from the kinds of excessive demands by various elites and interest groups that plagued other African countries at the time. Strict regulations and controls were put in place so as to discourage corruption and exploitation of the country's mineral wealth. In the process, Botswana's new leaders prioritized utilizing the gains from their economic activities to develop the country and to provide opportunities and social services that benefited all of the people of Botswana instead of just a few.[34]

In sharp contrast to the positive political will demonstrated by Botswana's leaders at independence, the majority of postcolonial African leaders chose to satisfy the demands of powerful constituencies at the expense of society as a whole. For example, Kwame Nkuruma, who ruled Ghana at independence, and Kofi Busia who followed him are generally regarded as leaders who placed politics ahead of economic development, prioritizing the transfer of political resources to elites whose support they coveted, instead of addressing the welfare demands of the masses.[35] In Sierra Leone, successive regimes after independence put their desire for personal political and economic power ahead of the most basic of public services.[36] As time went on, leaders operated with impunity and increasingly restricted popular participation and human rights.

Notably, the dramatic shift from autocratic rule that occurred in many countries beginning just over two decades ago was not a signal that democracy had triumphed or that African leaders en masse had come to see the light and were prepared to place the public good first. What occurred was no more than the reintroduction of multiparty politics. Some governments adopted the outward signs of inclusionary politics rather than democracy in practice. Reformers such as Fredrick Chiluba in Zambia and Laurent Gbagbo in Côte d'Ivorie quickly resorted to some of the same excesses they had charged their predecessors with, causing deep political crises. In the political realm, these predicaments were—to a large extent—rooted in claims of discrimination based upon perceived citizenship status.

To be sure, some institutional changes took place, such as term limits and the requirement that parties with candidates competing for the position of chief executive (e.g., in Kenya, Nigeria) empirically demonstrate the support of a broad segment of the national population. However, it was just as common for incumbent leaders and their elite supporters to engage in fraud, violence, and intimidation to discourage any real shifts in the locus of power. Even when autocratic leaders moved from the scenes, they often tried to influence those who succeeded then, thereby keeping their bases of power intact.[37]

The neopatrimonial form of executive leadership that developed in Africa after independence has persisted—even as trends toward more democratic institutions have recently begun to take hold. The extent of this movement can be seen in the example of Kenya, where since independence, forty-five constitutional changes have been designed to strengthen the overwhelming power of the chief executive.[38]

Rule of Law

In Africa today, the principles of liberal democracy are everywhere aspired to, if not practiced. Central to this model is "the rule of law," which Peter Shivute has defined as the idea that the legitimacy and authority of the state and government are enshrined in a code of laws, usually a written constitution. The rule of law is supposed to guard against arbitrary and capricious rulers and to limit their powers based upon widely understood constitutional principles. The rule of law is said to be the bedrock of democracy. Shivute goes on to argue that the hallmarks of this concept include the separation of powers among the three branches of government (executive, legislative, and judiciary); a bill of rights guaranteeing the free expression of ideas, a free press, and free and fair elections for public office; and an independent judiciary and the equality of all citizens before the law.[39]

Although the rhetoric of "rule of law" is widespread, its application and the degree of respect it commands vary from country to country. Again, one of the most devastating effects of the drift toward and ultimate entrenchment of autocracy on the continent shortly after independence was the collapse of the rule of law everywhere. This breakdown was due to a common assumption that Africa needed to develop strong executive leadership in order to temper interethnic conflicts based on poverty and ethnic tensions.

Jennifer Widner traces the collapse of the rule of law in Africa back to this period. She singles out Uganda in the early 1970s as a place and time in which attacks on the judiciary were most intense. These assaults took place under the reign of the military dictator Idi Amin Dada. For example, when Chief Justice Benedicto Kiwanuka attempted to put constraints on the arbitrary exercise of power by the military regime, he was assassinated.[40] Another dramatic example of the breakdown of the rule of law during the period of the drift toward autocracy in Africa was the assassination of three high court judges in Ghana, who in the 1970s were targeted by anti-regime elements.[41]

Before the early 1990s, a number of politically motivated assassinations of jurists took place in Uganda, Ghana, and elsewhere on the continent. Lawyers were intimidated or otherwise forced into silence, and judges were removed from office by unconstitutional means. These acts accompanied a deepening of popular and official disrespect for the judiciary as an institution. In the process, the powers of the executive were broadened and became based less on the rule of law and more upon caprice. This trend continued well into the 1980s and has only recently begun to be reversed. In other parts of Africa, during the most autocratic period since independence, the role of the chief executive has became increasingly elevated, and the roles of the other two branches, the legislature and judiciary, have become less and less respected. During his rule, Mobutu sese Seko in Zaire (DRC) installed a patronage system that in effect incorporated all three branches of government in his own personality. This was a clear example of the trend toward the establishment of the ascendancy of the "integral state" in Africa.[42]

Everywhere in Africa between the mid-1960s and the late 1980s, judiciaries became less independently effective. Because legislators had access to development resources, legislative institutions were arguably more respected than judicial institutions. An indication of the low esteem of jurists during this period can clearly be seen in the views of one jurist in Tanzania. Quoting an officer of the Law Society of Tanganyika in the 1990s, Jennifer Widner uncovered the sentiment in the African legal profession that "Lawyers faced hard times after 1965. . . . No African president likes lawyers. We tell people what they can do and what they cannot do. No president likes that. Only in the late 1990s did the Law Society begin to play more of a role in public policy matters."[43]

The return to multiparty democracy in Africa has seen a trend toward constitution reform and toward reasserting the law as it relates to the separation of powers among the three branches of government; however, these provisions are often only adhered to in the rhetoric of political leaders—a duplicity clearly demonstrated in the case studies here. Evidence of this could be seen in reports over the past decade of the continued intimidation of not only lawyers and judges but also witnesses.[44] At the same time, some progress is being made. In many places, a press that is freer than ever has coupled with the resurgence of civil society. Yet, the general population is at the earliest stages of learning when it comes to their constitutions and constitutional rights.

Civic education is taking place in some countries, but is mainly carried out by international nongovernmental organizations through voter education and legislative training projects. There is some talk of the need for civic education through the schools, but this has not become common practice.[45] In part, this development could be an indication of the desire on the part of governments to avoid the pitfall of partisanship, as might occur in places such as Ethiopia, South Africa, and Rwanda, given their long histories of ethnic/race-based conflicts. Clear ways to educate the population about the rule of law and their rights according to those laws must be found.

In Ethiopia, establishing new principles of constitutionalism represents a particularly profound challenge, as liberal political institutions and rules according to a unitary national constitution are so new. At the lowest levels of the judiciary, judges often do not have high levels of formal education or appropriate training, and tend to be poorly compensated. Consequently, they might engage in petty corruption, accepting or demanding bribes for service. Moreover, they often do not have a good sense of the terms of the national constitution and how it applies to their own communities. This lack of education and proper training, along with inadequate infrastructural and administrative support for the judicial system, inhibits equal application of the rule of law.

In Rwanda, much of the country's judicial capacity was destroyed during the 1994 genocide. Jurists were either killed or fled the country. Needed judicial infrastructures were severely damaged. The country is only now beginning to reestablish its capacity to enforce the rule of law effectively. To the extent that there have been some strides in this direction, progress has mostly been in regard to attempts to render justice in the aftermath of the 1994 genocide.

Further difficulty in reestablishing the rule of law in Africa can be seen in the electoral arena. Even as African countries moved toward reestablishing a multiparty democracy, their attempts to develop and implement laws intended to prevent electorally based corruption have often been flouted. For example, the Kreigler Report found that both in the run-up and during the 2007 Kenyan national elections, political parties consistently and blatantly violated laws and regulations relating to the conduct of democratic election as well as the Electoral Code of Conduct. Charges might be filed against them with the high court, but these groups have never been brought to account. The executive branch, which is responsible for such prosecutions, has simply refused to do so. In some cases, political parties sponsored or engaged in ethnically based violence against citizens of other ethnic groups.[46] Violence growing out of such disputes also occurred in Tunisia, Egypt, Nigeria, and Côte d'Ivoire.

In addition to national constitutions dictating the rule of law, African states are signatories to international legal protocols, and their governments often claim to adhere to the standards set out in these agreements. For example, most African governments are members of the African Union and have signed on to adhere to the "African Union Convention on Preventing and Combating Corruption," as well as to the "African Union Peer Review Mechanism," the "Universal Declaration on Human Rights," and other agreements designed to commit countries to the principle of good governance and the rule of law.[47] In addition, most African countries have anticorruption agencies; however, these are controlled by the chief executive who, in many cases, denies them their independence and effectiveness. As long as the accountability of the executive branch is uncertain or unpredictable, the fight against corruption will be severely hampered. This is yet another example of the importance of the political will of the executive to commit to upholding the rule of law and to govern in a just manner. Effective political institutions must back up this commitment. Should this not be the case, the potential for conflicts rooted in identity and citizenship claims in Africa will simply continue.

Notes

1. Identity, Citizenship, and Nation Building in Africa

1. Weiner, "Political Integration and Political Development"; Rostow, *Stages of Economic Growth;* Leys, "Rise and Fall of Development Theory"; Enloe, *Ethnic Conflict and Political Development;* Azikwe, "From Tribe to Nation: The Case of Nigeria"; Dorman, Hammett, and Nugent, "Introduction: Citizenship and Its Casualties in Africa."

2. Emerson, *From Empire to Nation;* Young, *Politics of Cultural Pluralism;* Cook and Sarkin, "Who is Indigenous?"; Indian Society, "Module IV."

3. Apter, "Some Reflections."

4. Gellner, *Nations and Nationalism.*

5. Young, "Nation, Ethnicity and Citizenship," 252.

6. Calhoun, "Nationalism and Ethnicity."

7. Barber, "Jihad vs. McWorld."

8. Smith defines a nation as "a named and self-defining human community whose members cultivate shared memories, symbols, myths, traditions, and values, and inhabit and are attached to historic territories or homelands, create and disseminate a distinctive public culture and observe shared customs and standardized laws." Although many of the "new" African states exhibit these characteristics, they were not originally self-named and defined. Smith, *Ethno-Symbolism and Nationalism,* 29.

9. Oommen, "Introduction: Conceptualizing the Linkage."

10. Englebert, *Africa: Unity, Sovereignty and Sorrow.*

11. Ndegwa, "Citizenship and Ethnicity"; Joireman, Nationalism and Political Identity.

12. Enloe, *Ethnic Conflict;* Adejumobi, "Citizenship, Rights."

13. Englebert, *Africa,* 75–80.

14. Mamdani, "Beyond Settler."

15. Herbst, "Politics of Migration and Citizenship."

16. Young, "Nation, Ethnicity and Citizenship," 242; Adejumobi, "Citizen," 148–149; Neuberger, *National Self-Determination;* Mamdani, *Citizen and Subject.*

17. Geschiere, *Perils of Belonging,* 53.

18. Keller, "Secessionism in Africa"; Lake and Rothchild, eds., *International Spread of Ethnic Conflict;* Young, *Politics of Cultural Pluralism.* This situation is equally true of modern Ethiopia, which is the product of the construction of an empire based on internal conquest.

19. Bah, "Democracy and Civil War."

20. Bratton, Mattes, and Gyimah-Boadi, *Public Opinion;* Keller and Omwami, "Federalism, Citizenship"; *Afrobarometer,* "An African-Led Series."

21. Robinson, "National Versus Ethnic Identity."

22. Botswana, Lesotho, Malawi, Mali, Namibia, South Africa, Tanzania, Zambia, and Zimbabwe.

23. Ethiopia is governed by a system of ethnic federalism. It has nine states in which the dominant ethnic groups in the state constitute a nationality. In this study, respondents were classified according to their nationality group. See Keller and Omwami, "Federalism, Citizenship," 37–69.

24. Young, "Nation, Ethnicity and Citizenship," 255; Manby, *Struggles for Citizenship in Africa;* Herbst, "Politics of Migration and Citizenship"; Heater, *What Is Citizenship?*

25. Manby, *Struggles for Citizenship in Africa,* 1.

26. Keller, "Political Institutions."

27. Bates, *When Things Fell Apart.*

28. Ibid., 9–10, 132–134.

29. See Nkrumah, *Neocolonialism;* Amin, *Accumulation on a World Scale;* Rodney, *How Europe Underdeveloped Africa.*

30. See Young, ed., *Neocolonialism.*

31. See Jackson and Rosberg, "Personal Rule."

32. See Davies, "J-Curve."

33. See Acemoglu and Robinson, *Why Nations Fail.*

34. Lofchie, "Political Constraints on African Development." See also Wallerstein, "Range of Choice."

35. See Young, *Postcolonial State in Africa;* Chabal, *Political Domination in Africa;* Sklar, "Democracy in Africa."

36. Bates, *When Things Fell Apart,* 3–29.

37. See Lindberg, "It's Our Time to 'Chop.'"

38. Joseph, *Democracy and Prebendal Politics in Nigeria.*

39. See Ojo, *Problems and Prospects.*

40. Constitution of the Federal Democratic Republic of Ethiopia.

41. See Keller, *Revolutionary Ethiopia.*

42. Keller, "Making and Remaking State and Nation in Ethiopia."

43. Sklar, "Democracy in Africa."

2. Theoretical and Formal-Legal Dimensions of the Concept of Citizenship in Africa

1. Although this history is generally agreed upon, some, like J. M. Barbalet, claim that citizenship is "as old as settled human communities." See Barbalet, *Citizenship;* Marshall, *Class, Citizenship and Social Development;* Ndegwa, "Citizenship and Ethnicity"; and Sadiq, *Paper Citizens.*

2. Aristotle, Politics.

3. Brubaker, "French Revolution."

4. Ibid., 30.

5. Wallerstein, "Citizens All Citizens Some," 650–679.

6. Ibid.

7. Tilly, "Emergence of Citizenship."

8. Marshall, *Class, Citizenship and Social Development;* Adejumobi, "Citizenship, Rights."

9. Marshall, "Citizenship and Social Class"; Barbalet, *Citizenship.*

10. Manning, *Francophone Sub-Saharan Africa.*

11. Mamdani, *Citizen and Subject.*

12. Young, *African Colonial State in Comparative Perspective.*

13. Oyelaran and Adediran, "Colonialism, Citizenship."

14. Keller, "Constitutionalism," and "Transnational Ethnic Conflict in Africa."

15. Mamdani, "Beyond Settler."

16. Adejumobi, "Citizenship, Rights"; Dorman, Hammett, and Nugent, "Introduction: Citizenship and Its Casualties in Africa."

17. Englebert, *Africa: Unity, Sovereignty and Sorrow.*

18. Keller, "Secessionism in Africa"; Baker, "Separating the Sheep from the Goats"; Young, "Nation, Ethnicity and Citizenship."

19. Adejumobi, "Citizenship, Rights"; Dorman, Hammett, and Nugent, "Introduction: Citizenship and Its Casualties in Africa."

20. Kasfir, "Explaining Ethnic Political Participation"; Joireman, Nationalism and Political Identity.

21. Ndegwa, "Citizenship and Ethnicity"; Sklar, "Democracy in Africa"; Ekeh, "Colonialism and Two Publics in Africa."

22. Bayart, *Illusion of Cultural Identity,* 77.

23. Barbalet, "Citizenship in Max Weber."

24. Ndegwa, "Citizenship and Ethnicity," 602.

25. Mouffe, "Democratic Citizenship and Political Community"; Ndegwa, "Citizenship and Ethnicity," 602–603.

26. Lynch, "Wars of Who Belongs Where."

27. Bratton, Mattes, and Gyimah-Boadi, *Public Opinion;* Keller and Omwami, "Federalism"; *Afrobarometer,* "An African-Led Series."

28. Adejumobi, "Citizenship, Rights," 148–149; Keller and Omwami, "Federalism, Citizenship and National Identity in Ethiopia."

29. Although the term originated in colonial Francophone Africa, because of the character of some postcolonial claims and conflicts, some ethnic communities in Anglophone Africa have recently been described as being based on autochthony. For a good example, see an analysis of land conflict in Western Kenya by Lynch, "The Wars of Who Belongs Where," 391; Berman, "Ethnicity and Democracy in Africa."

30. Ceuppens and Geschiere, "Autochthony: Local or Global?"

31. Jackson, "Sons of Which Soil?"

32. Ibid., 113.

33. Geschiere, "Autochthony, Belonging and Exclusion," 46; Geschiere, *Perils of Belonging.*

34. Geschiere and Nyamnjoh, "Capitalism and Autochthony: The Seesaw of Mobility and Belonging."

35. Ceuppens and Geschiere, "Autochthony: Local or Global?," 190.

36. Mamdani, "Beyond Settler and Native," 659; Moore, "Africa's Continental Divide"; Boone, "Conflict over Property Rights," 5; Boone, *Political Topographies of the African State.*

37. Nzongola-Ntalaja, "Citizenship and Exclusion in Africa," 4.

38. Adams and Turner, "Legal Dualism and Land Policy," 6.

39. Lemarchand, *Rwanda and Burundi.*

40. Nzongola-Ntalaja, "Citizenship and Exclusion in Africa," 4.

41. It is important to note that this movement did not involve all of Francophone Africa, let alone Africa as a whole. However, where it took place, this process involved collections of

nationally significant interest groups. Places like Zaire had an emphasis on the representation of groups by region.

42. Robinson, "National Conference."

43. Whitaker, "Citizens and Foreigners" and "Blurring the Line"; Nyamnjoh, *Insiders and Outsiders* and "From Bounded to Flexible Citizenship."

44. Whitaker, "Citizens and Foreigners," 116.

45. Jackson, "Sons of Which Soil?," 104.

46. Ceuppens and Geschiere, "Autochthony: Local or Global?," 194.

47. Osaghae, "Colonialism and Civil Society in Africa."

48. MacLean, *Informal Institutions and Citizenship.*

49. Manby, *Struggles for Citizenship in Africa* and *Citizenship Law in Africa*; Herbst, "Politics of Migration and Citizenship"; Heater, *What Is Citizenship?*, 80; Sadiq, *Paper Citizens*, 16.

50. Heater, *What Is Citizenship?*, 84.

51. Heater, *What Is Citizenship?*, 96–97; Oommen, "Introduction," 44.

52. This point is an important one in Africa today, because some places trace descent back to the original village or neighborhood of birth; others relate ancestry to the colonial territory of residence as of a certain date (e.g., when the territory came under European rule or when the territory became an independent state). I shall return to this point.

53. Herbst, *States and Power,* 234–237; Oyelaran and Adediran, "Colonialism," 181.

54. Okuk, "GoSS Mission."

55. Manby, *Citizenship Law in Africa,* 32.

56. Ibid., 32; In places where matriarch is the rule, the birth country of the mother would obtain.

57. Ibid.

58. Englebert, *Africa,* 65–66.

59. Klein, "Mass Expulsion from Ethiopia."

60. Englebert, *Africa;* Hickey, "Caught at the Crossroads."

61. Adejumobi, "Citizenship, Rights," 103.

3. Toward an Analytical Framework of Identity and Citizenship in Africa

1. McAdam, Tarrow, and Tilly, *Dynamics of Contention.*

2. Process tracing is a fundamental tool of qualitative political analysis based upon diagnostic evidence. It is most useful in studies that involve within-case analysis. This particular study does not engage in a full-blown application of this approach, but lays the foundation for a much larger study that would need to be based on reinterpretive history and thick description. (Bennett, "Process Tracing and Causal Inference"; Collier, "Understanding Process Tracing.")

3. Brady, "Data Set Observations," 237–242.

4. Freedman, "On Types of Scientific Inquiry," 221.

5. Rogowski, "How Inference."

6. Bennett, "Process Tracing and Causal Inference," 208–209.

7. Since its independence in 1960, the country has gone through three name changes: Republic of Congo (1960–1965), Zaire (1965–1997), and the Democratic Republic of Congo (1997–present); here I will refer to the DRC throughout.

8. Nzongola-Ntalaja, *Congo: From Leopold to Kabila* and "Citizenship and Exclusion in Africa."

9. Ibid., 4.

10. Jackson, "Sons of Which Soil?"

11. Nzongola-Ntalaja, "Citizenship and Exclusion."

12. *Constitution of the Congo.*

13. Jackson, "Sons of Which Soil?," 104.

14. Ibid., 105.

15. By 2012, the United Nations was charging that this group was being sponsored by the governments of Rwanda and Uganda. The purpose of M-23 was said to be less to protect the human rights of Tutsi in DRC and more motivated by a desire to gain access to the vast mineral wealth of the eastern DRC.

16. Keller, "Political Institutions."

17. Przeworski, *Sustainable Democracy.*

18. Przeworski, "Some Problems in the Study of the Transition to Democracy," 48.

19. Sisk, *Democratization in South Africa.*

20. LeBas, *From Protest to Parties.*

21. Harbeson, Rothchild, and Chazan, eds., *Civil Society and the State in Africa.*

22. Bayart, "Civil Society in Africa."

23. Young, *African Colonial State,* 38.

24. Tarrow, *Power in Movement.*

25. See Scott, *Weapons of the Weak.*

26. Fearon and Laitin, "Violence and the Social Construction of Ethnic Identity."

27. Edelman, *Symbolic Uses of Politics,* 177.

28. Des Forges, *Leave No One to Tell the Story.*

29. Aluaigba, "Tiv-Jukun Ethnic Conflict," 6–8.

30. In 2013, Kenyatta and Ruto, while still being indicted by the ICC, were elected president and vice-president respectively of Kenya.

31. Nyukuri, "Impact of Past and Potential," 13.

4. Nigeria: Indigeneity and Citizenship

1. Suberu, *Public Policies and National Unity,* 8–9.

2. See Whitaker, *Politics of Tradition.*

3. Smock, *Ibo Politics,* 16; Young, *Politics of Cultural Pluralism,* 461.

4. Horowitz, *Ethnic Groups in Conflict.*

5. Smock, *Ibo Politics.*

6. Young, *Politics of Cultural Pluralism,* 466.

7. Ibid., 468–470.

8. Ignatius, *Broken Back Axel.*

9. In 1963, when the Mid-West region was created, that south central area was separated from the east. Large segments of the Ibo people live there.

10. Young, *Politics of Cultural Pluralism,* 472–473.

11. Horowitz, *Ethnic Groups in Conflict.*

12. Suberu, *Public Policies and National Unity,* 11.

13. Ibid., 17–19.

14. Ibid.

15. Suberu, *Federalism and Ethnic Conflict.*

16. Ibid., 34–35.

17. Mamdani, *Citizen and Subject;* Mamdani, "Beyond Settler and Native"; Geschiere, *Perils of Belonging;* Manby, *Citizenship Law in Africa.*

18. Whitaker, "Blurring the Line," 13; Englebert, *Africa*, 206.

19. Geschiere, *Perils of Belonging*.

20. Aminzade, "From Race to Citizenship," 43.

21. This is not to say that "xenophobia" does not exist in places such as South Africa or Kenya, which has recently seen a massive influx of refugees from neighboring countries. See Taylor, *Culture and Custom of Zambia*; Nyamnjoh, "From Bounded to Flexible Citizenship."

22. Akyeampong, "Race, Identity and Citizenship in Black Africa"; Nyamnjoh, "From Bounded to Flexible Citizenship."

23. Federal Republic of Nigeria, Chapter II, Sec. 25.

24. Many Nigerian communities use the distinction between indigenous and nonindigenous to determine who is eligible to hold chiefly titles in the community and to participate in traditional institutions of governance. Who is eligible to own land is also often governed by tradition. It is thus clear that tradition continues to have sway in local communities. See Human Rights Watch, "They Do Not Own This Place," 10; Krause, "A Deadly Cycle."

25. Suberu, *Public Policies and National Unity*, 49.

26. Federal Republic of Nigeria, Sub-section 14(3).

27. Federal Republic of Nigeria, Sub-section 14(4).

28. World Bank, "Implementing Affirmative Action."

29. Human Rights Watch, "They Do Not Own This Place," 1–2.This report claims that many states refuse to employ nonindigenous people in their state civil service and most, if not all, states refuse the right for nonindigenous students to compete for academic scholarships. Also, nonindigenous individuals must contend with a range of less formal discriminatory practices, such as barriers to political participation and access to basic services and infrastructure in the communities where they live. Critics argue that this practice amounts to no more than second-class citizenships for those who choose or must live outside of the areas in which they were born.

30. Human Rights Watch, "They Do Not Own This Place," 19.

31. Mamdani, *Citizen and Subject*, 660.

32. World Bank, "Implementing Affirmative Action," 10.

33. Adesoji and Alao, "Indigeneship and Citizenship in Nigeria," 1569.

34. Higazi, "Jos Crisis."

35. World Bank, "Implementing Affirmative Action," 13.

36. Albert, "Ife-Modakeke Crisis."

37. Best, Idyorough, and Shehu, "Communal Conflicts."

38. Ibid., 87–96.

39. Aluaigba, "Tiv-Jukun Ethnic Conflict."

40. Ibid., 1–2; Nnoli, "Ethnic Violence in Nigeria."

41. Best, Idyorough, and Shehu, "Communal Conflicts," 96–104.

42. Momoh, "Pathology of Citizenship in Nigeria"; Isa-Odidi, "Ethnic Conflict in Plateau State," 18.

43. Higazi, "Jos Crisis," 10; Krause, "A Deadly Cycle."

44. Johnson, "Boko Haram."

5. Ethiopia: The Politics of Late Nation Building and the National Question

1. See Levine, *Greater Ethiopia*; Parham, *Government of Ethiopia*.

2. See Keller, *Revolutionary Ethiopia*.

3. See Markakis, *Ethiopia*; Reid, *Frontiers of Violence*.

4. See Keller, "Ethiopia: The Revolutionary Transformation."

5. See Keller, "Ethiopia: Revolution, Class."

6. See Keller, *Revolutionary Ethiopia.*

7. Markakis, *Ethiopia,* 337; Keller, *Revolutionary Ethiopia,* 136.

8. Keller, *Revolutionary Ethiopia,* 139–141; Smith, *Making Citizens in Africa.*

9. See Marcus, *Life and Times of Menelik II;* Rubenson, *Survival of Ethiopian Independence;* Erlich, *Ethiopia and the Challenge.*

10. Jonas, *Battle of Adwa.*

11. Iyob, *Eritrean Struggle for Independence;* Keller, *Revolutionary Ethiopia,* 150–151.

12. See Sellassie, *Ancient and Medieval Ethiopian History.*

13. Keller, *Revolutionary Ethiopia,* 152.

14. Ibid., 153. On November 14, 1962, under duress, the National Assembly voted overwhelmingly to make Eritrea a province of Ethiopia.

15. See Johnson, "National Question."

16. See Reid, *Frontiers of Violence.*

17. See Laitin and Samatar, *Somalia.*

18. Keller, *Revolutionary Ethiopia,* 157.

19. *Ethiopian Observer,* "Emperor Haile Selassie's Speech."

20. Ibid.

21. Ethiopian Ministry of Foreign Affairs, "Ethiopian Government Aide Memoire."

22. See Gilkes, *Dying Lion,* 215–216.

23. Samatar, "Ethiopian Federalism"; Human Rights Watch, "Collective Punishment."

24. Baxter, "Ethiopia's Unacknowledged Problem"; Union of Oromo Students in North America, "A Brief History of Oromo."

25. Hassan, *Oromo of Ethiopia.*

26. See Keller, *Revolutionary Ethiopia,* 15–64.

27. Ibid., 160.

28. Baxter, "Ethiopia's Unacknowledged Problem," 288.

29. See Keller, *Revolutionary Ethiopia,* 160–161.

30. See Keller, "Ethno Genesis of the Oromo-Nation."

31. Ottaway, *Ethiopia: Empire in Revolution,* 91.

32. Keller, *Revolutionary Ethiopia,* 205.

33. In the Amharic language this is the acronym for The Commission for Organizing the Party of the Working People of Ethiopia.

34. Institute for the Study of Ethiopian Nationalities, "Documents on the Establishment," 19.

35. Ibid., 239–240.

36. At the time, there were only five other Sub-Saharan countries that could be labeled in this manner. See Keller and Rothchild, eds., *Afromarxist Regimes.*

37. See Preparatory Committee for the Founding of the People's Democratic Republic of Ethiopia, "Ensuring the Rights of Nationalities."

38. See Keller, "Remaking the Ethiopian State."

39. Quoted in Tronvoll and Aadland, "Process of Democratization in Ethiopia," 47.

40. Prime Minister of the Federal Democratic Republic of Ethiopia, *System of Regional Administration.*

41. All of the nine states have their own constitutions, which were established over the 1995–1998 period. Whereas the creation of a federal constitution involved an elaborate process of drafting by a special commission, deliberation by the public as well as by the Consti-

tutional Assembly, and finally adoption by the Constitutional Assembly, state constitutions, after being drafted by committees of the respective state legislatures, were simply adopted by the state legislatures. See Regassa, "State Constitutions in Federal Ethiopia."

42. See Aberra, "Tribalism Rules in Ethiopia," 20; Brietzke, "Ethiopia's 'Leap into the Dark'"; Gudina, *Ethiopia: Competing Ethnic Nationalisms;* Alemayehyu, "Ethnic Federalism in Ethiopia"; Serra-Horguelin, "Federal Experiment in Ethiopia."

43. *Ethiopian Herald,* "Forum Discusses Decentralization."

44. See Stepan, "Towards a New Comparative Politics," 320.

45. See Keller, "Ethnic Federalism and Democratization."

46. The fieldwork was, in part, designed to answer such questions as: How satisfied are various ethnic communities with the efforts of the federal government to uphold their equal rights as citizens? To what extent do respondents in this study have a sense of their *Ethiopian* identity? To what extend do they see their identity with their own identity group as more important than their identity with their national citizenship? To get at least partial answers to these questions, I administered a survey to 277 respondents in the regional states of Oromia, SNNPR (Southern Nations, Nationalities, and People's Regional State), Tigray, Amhara, Benishangul-Gumuz, and Ethiopia's capital city, Addis Ababa. The statistics were analyzed via cross-tabulation and regression analysis. Data collection was limited in some regions because of security concerns, but a targeted effort was made to include respondents from the three most populous regions of the country and in ethnically diverse or heterogeneous areas. See Keller and Omwami, "Federalism, Citizenship and National Identity."

6. Côte d'Ivoire: *Ivorité* and Citizenship

1. Englebert, *Africa;* Whitaker, "Blurring the Line"; Woods, "Tragedy of the Cocoa Pod."

2. The colonies in the federation were Mauritania, Senegal, French Sudan (now Mali), French Guinea, Côte d'Ivoire (Ivory Coast), Upper Volta (now Burkina Faso), Dahomey (now Benin), and Niger. Zolberg, *One Party Government.*

3. Ibid., 11–17.

4. Boone, *Political Topographies of the African State,* 184.

5. Ibid., 188–189.

6. Ibid, 185; Woods, "Tragedy of the Cocoa Pod."

7. Boone, *Political Topographies of the African State,* 185.

8. Zolberg, *One Party Government,* 81–82.

9. The French established four colonial towns in what is present-day Senegal in the mid-1800s (Saint-Louis, Dakar, Gorée, and Rufisque). Anyone living in those towns, including Africans, in 1848 was granted full French citizenship rights. This citizenship was still qualified in that it applied only in those communities. However, through higher education and being steeped in French language and culture, residents of the communes could rise to the level of being considered an *évolué* ("evolved"), which qualified them for rights of full French citizenship including the vote, and the ability to run for public office at the national level (France). Nonetheless, *évolué* still experienced discrimination in dealing with the French of the metropolis. See Johnson, *Emergence of Black Politics in Senegal;* Diouf, "French Colonial Policy."

10. Boone, *Political Topographies of the African State,* 196–197.

11. Ibid., 194–196.

12. McGovern, *Making War in Côte d'Ivoire,* 15–16.

13. Zolberg, *One-Party Government,* 26.

14. Mamdani, "Ivory Coast," 2.

15. Boone, *Political Topographies of the African State,* 198.

16. Zolberg, *One-Party Government,* 233–249.

17. Mongabay, "Ivory Coast—The Economy."

18. Ceuppens and Geschiere, "Autochthony: Local or Global?," 394.

19. Marshall-Fratani, "War of 'Who Is Who?'"; Woods, "Tragedy of the Cocoa Pod," 648; Englebert, *Africa,* 208.

20. Bah, "Democracy and Civil War," 610.

21. Houphouet Boigny had encouraged immigrants to push the "frontiers" of cocoa production further to the southwest. Local communities were encouraged to treat them as guests and to make land available for them to temporarily use. However, over time these land grants came to be seen by those that settled in the area as permanent. See Ceuppens and Geschiere, "Autochthony: Local or Global?," 393.

22. Chauveau suggests that the definition of autochthony shifted as the frontier of the cocoa zone changed. For example, in the 1960s, autochthony was mainly claimed by the indigenous people of the southwest against the Baoulé, whom they considered invading strangers. Since independence, the term *allogene* has come to be associated both with Baoulé and northerners in the southwest. Most recently, the term has been used by southerners almost exclusively in reference to northerners who, for whatever reason, are in the south. See Chauveau, "Question foncière et construction," 114.

23. Marshall-Fratani, "War of 'Who Is Who?'," 31.

24. McGovern, *Making War in Côte d'Ivoire,* 14.

25. Englebert, *Africa,* 208.

26. Ceuppens and Geschiere, "Autochthony," 394.

27. Marshall-Fratani, "War of 'Who Is Who?'," 46.

28. Englebert, *Africa,* 208.

29. This idea was promoted by the country's first anthropology professor, Niangoran-Bouah, who proposed a regrouping of Ivorian ancestors so that those related to the "trunk" would be determined to be the most autochthonous. Members of this group would be considered linked by a common myth of origin. Other southern groups would be considered less autochthonous because they were not connected to this myth. Moreover, it is claimed that those belonging to the "trunk" can trace the origins of the birth of the Côte d'Ivoire specifically to 1893. See Ceuppens and Geschiere, "Autochthony," 394.

30. This term refers to a cluster of people in southeastern Côte d'Ivoire and Ghana who speak the Twi language. The Baoulé, Mandé, and Bété are the main groups found in Côte d'Ivoire.

31. One of the founders of this party was a university professor named Laurent Gbagbo. At the time, opposition parties were illegal, and Gbagbo spent most of the 1980s in France, where he had the support of French socialist intellectuals.

32. McGovern, *Making War in Côte d'Ivoire,* 17.

33. Bah, "Democracy and Civil War," 601–602; Manby, *Struggles for Citizenship in Africa,* 10.

34. Englebert, *Africa,* 209.

35. The political base of the movement included elements of the Patriotic Movement of the Ivory Coast, the Ivorian Popular Movement of the Great West, and the Movement for Justice and Peace.

36. Manby, *Struggles for Citizenship in Africa,* 1.

37. Bah, "Democracy and Civil War."

38. Ibid., 611.

39. Bassett, "Winning Coalition, Sore Loser."

40. Banigas, "Post-Election Crisis in Côte d'Ivoire."

41. Straus, "'It's Sheer Horror Here.'"

7. Kenya: Citizenship, Land, and Ethnic Cleansing

1. See Huxley, *White Man's Country*; Jackson, "White Man's Country."

2. See Dorman, Hammett, and Nugent, "Introduction," 18; Nzongola-Ntalaja, "Citizenship and Exclusion in Africa," 4; Mamdani, "Beyond Settler and Native"; Moore, "Africa's Continental Divide"; Boone, "Conflict over Property," 5; Boone, *Political Topographies of the African State*.

3. Leys, *Underdevelopment in Kenya*, 29.

4. Southall, "Ndungu Report," 145.

5. See Bates, *Beyond the Miracle*, 18.

6. Native lands or trust land occupied by African subsistence farmers could not be titled. These African farmers had only the right to farm exclusively for subsistence. See Bates, *Beyond the Miracle*; Kabubo-Mariara, "Land Conservation in Kenya," 153.

7. Barnett and Njama, *Mau Mau from Within*, 24; Bates, *Beyond the Miracle*, 20.

8. Barnett and Njama, *Mau Mau from Within*.

9. Ibid.; Keller, "A Twentieth Century Model"; Hobsbawm, *Bandits*.

10. Leys, *Underdevelopment in Kenya*, 42–43.

11. See Maxon, *Kenya's Independence Constitution*.

12. Ibid., 105–106.

13. See Iqbal, "Kenya's New Constitution."

14. Ibid., 275.

15. Leys, *Underdevelopment in Kenya*.

16. Bienen, *Kenya*.

17. Keller, "State, Public Policy."

18. Ndungu, "Tackling Land."

19. See Southall, "Ndungu Report."

20. Leys, *Underdevelopment in Kenya*, 228–229.

21. Human Rights Watch, *Divide and Rule*, 16.

22. Ibid., 24.

23. Bienen, *Kenya*.

24. Widner, *Rise of a Party-State*.

25. Curry and Ray, "Pambana of August."

26. Moi, *Kenya African Nationalism*.

27. Ibid., In 1980, Moi had made all ethnically based organizations illegal.

28. See Mutunga, *Constitution-Making*; Rutten, Mazrui, and Grignon, *Out for the Count*.

29. In December 1991, KANU delegates meeting at Kasarani Stadium in Nairobi repealed Section 2A of the constitution, thereby making Kenya a multiparty state. At the same time, term limits on the office of president were enshrined in law.

30. See Onoma, *Politics of Property Rights*.

31. Ibid., 145.

32. See Ndungu, "Tackling Land," 144; Southall, "Ndungu Report," 147.

33. Republic of Kenya, *Report of the Commission*, 8.

34. Ibid., *passim*.

35. Harbeson, "Land and the Quest," 24–25.

36. Kenya Law Reports, *Constitution of Kenya*. Article 60 of the constitution declares that land access shall be equitable and Article 61 declares that all land belongs to the people . . . collectively as a nation, as communities and as individuals. Yet, the constitution does not get into the political thicket of communally held land rights. Among the provision of the law are: (1) the establishment of a national land commission; the prohibition of holding of freehold titles by foreigners; (3) conversion of all existing freehold titles and 999-year leases to 99-year leases; (4) the investigation of historic injustices and mechanisms for resolving post-1895 land claims; (5) repossession by the government of illegally acquired land titles; (6) repeal of the Trust Land Act and conversion of trust land to community land; return of illegally acquired trust land to communities; and (8) compulsory government acquisition of all land on which minerals are discovered with compensation to affected communities. See also, Kenya Law Reports, *Trust Land Act*. Revised edition 2010.

37. Dolan, "Kenya."

38. Bienen, *Kenya.*

39. Although the Kalenjin group had been categorized as such as early as the 1940s, with each group having its own distinct culture and social system, they now came to assume a larger identity as a political grouping.

40. Human Rights Watch, 16–17; Nyukuri, "Impact of Past and Potential," 12–13; Manby, *Struggles for Citizenship*, 15.

41. Joireman, *Where There*, 8.

42. Olsen, "Europe and the Promotion."

43. LeBas, *From Protest to Parties*, 231–232.

44. Ibid., 232–233.

45. See Boone, "Land Conflict and Distributive Politics in Kenya," 78.

46. See *Daily Nation,* "Special Report," 44; Human Rights Watch, "Kenya," 11.

47. See *Daily Nation,* "Special Report," 55–60.

48. Ibid., 1–6, 17; Nyukuri, "Impact of Past and Potential," 12–13.

49. Nyukuri, "Impact of Past and Potential," 13.

50. Mutunga, *Constitution-Making*, x.

51. MacArthur, "How the West Was Won," 228.

52. International Crisis Group, "Kenya in Crisis," 2; Cheeseman, "Kenyan Elections of 2007," 172–173.

53. International Crisis Group, "Kenya in Crisis," 21–26.

54. See Anderson and Lochery, "Violence and Exodus," 329–330; MacArthur, "How the West Was Won," 232. At no time did Odinga advocate expulsion of those alleged to be "aliens."

55. See *Weekly Review,* "Indigenous and the Natives."

56. Human Rights Watch, *Divide and Rule*, 68.

57. Nyukuri, "Impact of Past and Potential," 13.

58. See *Report of the Independent Review;* Commission of Inquiry into the Post-Election Violence (CIPEV), "Report of the Commission of Inquiry"; Human Rights Watch, "Kenya. Turning Pebbles." The chairman of the commission was Justice Philip Waki.

59. Anderson and Lochery, "Violence and Exodus," 328.

60. See Somerville, "Violence, Hate Speech," 82.

61. See Commission of Inquiry into the Post-Election Violence (CIPEV), "Report," 305.

62. See *Report of the Independent Review*, 95.

63. Somerville, "Violence, Hate Speech and Inflammatory Broadcasting in Kenya," 94.

64. Anderson and Lochery, "Violence and Exodus," 334.

65. Mueller, "Political Economy," 203.

66. Both have been indicted by the International Criminal Court for allegedly having sponsored and even indirectly participated in the violence that followed the 2007 elections. For example, they are said to have used their radio stations to threaten members of other ethnic groups living in certain areas. See Human Rights Watch, "Kenya: Turning Pebbles," 5–8.

67. Somerville, "Violence, Hate Speech and Inflammatory Broadcasting In Kenya," 92–97.

68. International Crisis Group, "Kenya in Crisis," 13.

69. Ibid.

70. Nyukuri, "Impact of Past and Potential," 24.

71. Keller, "Constitutionalism, Citizenship," 60.

8. Rwanda: Exclusionary Nationalism, Democracy, and Genocide

1. See Adejumobi, "Citizenship, Rights"; Mamdani, When Victims Become Killers; Englebert, Africa.

2. See Newbury, Cohesion of Repression; Prunier, Rwanda Crisis.

3. See Prunier, Rwanda Crisis, 5–8; Longman, Christianity and Genocide, 59–63.

4. Mamdani, When Victims Become Killers, 68.

5. Longman, Christianity and Genocide, 35.

6. On the colonial invention of African "tribes," see Hobsbawm and Ranger, eds., Invention of Tradition, 250.

7. The Twa are pigmoids.

8. Newbury, Cohesion of Repression, 73–147. Newbury argues that over time, the nature of this relationship changed. Originally, clientelism related to the cattle lineages, and was based on reciprocity, but by the nineteenth century, clientage became more arbitrary and came to refer to the requirement that the Hutu give cattle to a patron within the lineage. During the colonial period, clientage had come to mean that a patron could arbitrarily confiscate the personal property of those deemed his clients.

9. Mamdani, When Victims Become Killers, 44–46.

10. See Clark, "Rwanda: Tragic Land," 76; Mamdani, When Victims Become Killers, 79–87. In some cases, myth was based on the Biblical Hamitic Hypothesis that the Tutsi were actually the descendants of Ham, one of the sons of Noah. Because he saw Ham showing disrespect toward him, Noah cursed the descendants of Ham with black skin. The Hamitic races were viewed as a subset of the Caucasian race and thereby superior to the Negroid races found in Africa.

11. Longman, Christianity and Genocide, 51–56, 67.

12. See Lemarchand, Rwanda and Burundi, 75–76. This legal cover tended to reinforce Tutsi attitudes of racial superiority.

13. Mamdani, When Victims Become Killers, 88–93, 101.

14. See ibid., 116–117; Prunier, Rwanda Crisis, 45; Newbury, Cohesion of Repression, 191.

15. Mayersen, "A Political Monopoly."

16. Ibid., 172–173; Mamdani, When Victims Become Killers, 171–172.

17. Mamdani, When Victims Become Killers, 99. Mamdani notes that following the 1933–1934 national census, "there were no groups, only races"—a notion that became ingrained in Rwandese society and continued to hold sway at the time of the Rwanda Revolution and its immediate aftermath.

18. Mamdani, When Victims Become Killers, 134.

19. Ibid., 138.

20. Reed, "Exile, Reform," 482–483.

21. See Van der Meeren, "Three Decades in Exile," 257. The mythology of northwestern Rwanda Hutu holds that only those from Gisenyi and Ruhengeri areas are "pure," unadulterated Hutu.

22. See Prunier, *Rwanda Crisis*, 87–89.

23. Ibid.

24. See Mamdani, *When Victims Become Killers*, 153, 159.

25. See Watson, "Exile from Rwanda," 5; Nzongola-Ntalaja, "Citizenship and Exclusion." It is estimated that even before 1959, Banyarawanda had lived for centuries in Uganda, and constituted the sixth largest ethnic group there.

26. These were mainly Tutsi refugees; however, as early as the 1920s, some natives of Rwanda, mostly Hutu, had taken refuge in colonial Uganda, fleeing the harsh conditions imposed by Belgian colonialists and their Tutsi nobility supporters. Helle-Valle, "Banyarunda in Uganda."

27. See Prunier, *Rwanda Crisis*, 67.

28. Helle-Valle, "Banyarunda in Uganda," 164–200.

29. Ibid., 228.

30. Watson, "Exile from Rwanda," 9.

31. Otunnu, "Rwandese Refugees," 20.

32. Ibid., 22.

33. Straus, *Order of Genocide*, 192–193. Otunnu suggests that the reason many Banyarawanda had joined the NRA in the first place was to gain some training that would better prepare them for armed intervention in Rwanda. See Otunnu, "Rwandese Refugees."

34. Struas, *Order of Genocide*, 26–27.

35. Des Forges, *Leave No One*, 72–91.

36. Ibid., 83.

37. Ibid., 68–73.

38. Reed, "Exile, Reform," 492–494.

39. Golloba-Mutebi, "Who Killed Habariymana?"

40. Gourevitch, *We Wish to Inform*, 110.

41. United Nations, "Universal Declaration of Human Rights."

42. See Mamdani, *When Victims Become Killers*, 212.

43. See Sebarenzi, "Justice and Human Rights."

44. See Tiemessen, "After Arusha." The highest priority was given to those whose criminal acts placed them among the planners and organizers or leaders of the genocide or of a crime against humanity. This category included individuals accused of genocidal rape or sexual torture. The second category included persons whose criminal acts or acts of criminal participation placed them among the perpetrators or accomplices in homicide. The third, persons whose criminal acts or participation made them guilty of other serious assaults against a person or group of people; and finally, persons who committed offenses against property. Anyone placed in category 1 would be tried in the conventional courts, but those placed in categories 2–4 would be tried in the local *gacaca* courts. Gacaca, in Kinyarwanda, literally means "justice on the grass," and traditionally referred to the practice of community leaders sitting down outside to mete out justice on behalf of the community. The process spanned a decade beginning in 2002. But the gacaca courts have deposed almost two million cases and convicted some 37,000 of those charged. Despite the government's efforts to allay the fears of those who might appear before the gacaca courts, many Hutu remained fearful and, a good number of them went into exile rather than agreeing to be judged by them.

45. See Dagne, "Rwanda: Background." Critics, both internally and abroad, have complained that this election was accompanied by a significant suppression of freedom of expression, the disappearance of several voices of opposition, and the arrest and beating of opposition party leaders.

46. This is a Hutu-based group operating out of the Western DRC and engaged in fighting DRC and Rwandan forces inside the region and in a low-intensity war within Rwanda.

47. See Reyntjens, "Waging War Abroad"; Straus and Waldorf, "Seeing Like," 4.

48. Ibid.

49. See Hintjens, "Post-Genocide Identity," 9–10.

50. United Nations, "Outreach Programme."

51. See Mgbako, "Ingando Solidarity Camps," 201.

52. See Horowitz, *Ethnic Groups in Conflict.*

53. See Longman, "Limitations to Political Reform"; Gready, "You're Either with Us"; Ingelaere, "Ruler's Drum"; Sebarenzi, "Justice and Human Rights."

54. See Lischer, "Civil War, Genocide," 271.

55. See Ottaway, *Africa's New Leaders.*

56. See Newbury, "High Modernism"; Huggins, "Presidential Land Commission."

57. See ibid., 235.

58. See Huggins, "Presidential Land Commission," 7.

59. Ibid., 258–259.

Summary and Conclusion

1. This phenomenon is changing in some places, as constitutional challenges to even customary law is becoming gradually more common. See Joireman, *Where There Is No Government,* 52.

2. See Ake, *Development and Democracy;* Bratton and van de Walle, *Democratic Experiments in Africa.*

3. See for example, Huntington, *Political Order in Changing Societies.*

4. Radelet, *Emerging Africa,* 15–21.

5. Acemoglu and Robinson, *Why Nations Fail,* 91.

6. Whether political development must precede economic development for progress to occur has not been conclusively established. See, for example, Przeworski et al., *Democracy and Development;* Moyo, *Dead Aid.*

7. Acemoglu and Robinson, *Why Nations Fail,* 102–110.

8. Arbache and Page, "How Fragile."

9. See Hyden, Court, and Mease, *Making Sense of Governance.*

10. See Jaycox, *Challenges,* 72.

11. Hyden, Court, and Mease, *Making Sense of Governance,* 15.

12. See Hyden, "Making the State Responsive," 5.

13. Ibid., 14.

14. See Williams et al., "Joint Governance Assessment."

15. van Hoof, "Local Governance Assessment."

16. Grindle, "Good Enough."

17. See Simon, *Reason in Human Affairs.*

18. See, for example, Jain, "Corruption: A Review." Also, Mbaku, *Corruption in Africa.*

19. Huntington, *Political Order in Changing Societies,* 59–60.

20. Ibid., 62.

21. See Hope and Chikulo, eds., *Corruption and Development;* Ayittey, *Africa Betrayed;* Moyo, *Dead Aid;* Siegel, "Corruption and Sustainability."

22. Blundo and de Sardan, *Everyday Corruption.*

23. Grand corruption can be found in state-society relations, and in relations involving political and economic elites; petty corruption is sporadic and can be found in everyday interactions in the larger society.

24. See Alou, "Corruption," 147.

25. See Wallis and White, "Kenya: Officials"; Wrong, *It's Our Time to Eat,* 62–63.

26. See Transparency International, *Corruption Perception Index.*

27. See Smith, *A Culture of Corruption;* Wrong, *It's Our Turn to Eat;* Lindberg, "It's Our Time to 'Chop.'"

28. See Jain, "Corruption: A Review."

29. See Ogeik Peoples' Development Organization, "Dynamics of Conflict"; Ongugo et al., "Livelihoods"; Siringi, "Forest Conflict."

30. See Bates, *When Things Fell Apart.*

31. See Nyerere, *Freedom and Development;* Nyerere, *Freedom and Socialism.*

32. Samatar, *An African Miracle;* Holm and Molutsi, *Democracy in Botswana.*

33. Acemoglu and Robinson, *Why Nations Fail,* 413.

34. Although Botswana is comprised almost entirely of ethnic Tswana, there are a few minorities. However, the discontent of minorities has not emerged as a threat to the governance of the state.

35. See Owusu, *Uses and Abuses;* Acemoglu and Robinson, *Why Nations Fail,* 65–66.

36. See Kpundeh, *Politics and Corruption in Africa;* Acemoglu and Robinson, *Why Nations Fail,* 376–377.

37. See Keller, "State in Contemporary Africa"; Young, *Postcolonial State in Africa.*

38. See Hanson, "Corruption in Sub-Saharan Africa."

39. Shivute, "Rule of Law," 213; See also Widner, *Building,* 27.

40. See Widner, *Building,* 114–116.

41. Young, *The Postcolonial State,* 169.

42. Ibid., 19–23.

43. Widner, *Building,* 123–124.

44. See, Anaba, "Nigeria" (2004) and Jeffrey Moyo, "No Reforms in Zimbabwe" (2013).

45. See Smith, *Making Citizens in Africa.*

46. See *Report of the Independent,* 55.

47. See African Union, *African Union Convention.* Other relevant international human rights instruments, of which most African states are members, include the International Covenant on Economic, Social and Cultural Rights and the International Covenant on Civil and Political Rights.

References

Aberra, Worku. "Tribalism Rules in Ethiopia." *New African* (September 1993): 20.

Abioye, Funmilola Tolulope. "Rule of Law in English Speaking African Countries: The Case of Nigeria and South Africa." Ph.D. diss., University of Pretoria, 2011.

Acemoglu, Daron, and James Robinson. *Why Nations Fail: The Origins of Prosperity and Poverty.* New York: Random House, 2012.

Adams, Martin, and Stephen Turner. "Legal Dualism and Land Policy in Eastern and Southern Africa." In *Land Rights for African Development: From Knowledge to Action.* Consultative Group on International Agricultural Research, 2006. Accessed December 20, 2011. http://www.capri.cgiar.org/pdf/brief_land.pdf.

Adejumobi, Said. "Citizenship, Rights, and the Problem of Conflict and Civil Wars in Africa." *Human Rights Quarterly* 23, no. 1 (2001): 103–170.

Adesoji, Abimbola, and Akin Alao. "Indigeneship and Citizenship in Nigeria: Myth and Reality." *The Journal of Pan African Studies* 2, no. 9 (2009): 151–165.

African Union. *African Union Convention on Preventing and Combating Corruption.* (2002). Accessed November 1, 2012. http://www.africa-union.org/official_documents/ Treaties_%20Conventions_%20Protocols/Convention%20on%20Combating%20 Corruption.pdf.

African Union, New Partnership for Africa's Development. *African Peer Review Mechanism.* Midrand, South Africa: NEPAD Secretariat, 2011.

Afrobarometer. "An African-Led Series of National Public Attitude Surveys on Democracy and Governance in Africa" (1999–2001). Accessed February 9, 2012. http://www.afro barometer.org/index.php?option=com_content&view=article&id=14&Itemid=27.

Agence Nationale de la Recherche. "The Politics of Xenophobic Exclusion in Africa: Mobilisations, Local Order and Violence" (2009). Accessed July 1, 2011. www.ifas.org.za

Ake, Claude. *Development and Democracy in Africa.* Washington, D.C.: Brookings Institution, 1996.

———. *The Feasibility of Democracy in Africa.* Dakar, Senegal: Codesria, 2000.

Akyeampong, Emmanuel K. "Race, Identity and Citizenship in Black Africa: The Case of the Lebanese in Ghana." *Africa* 76, no. 3 (2006): 297–323. Accessed April 18, 2012. http:// www.docstoc.com/docs/55677674/Race-identity-and-citizenship-in-black-Africa-the-case-of-the-Lebanese-in-Ghana-(1).

Albert, Isaac O. "Ife-Modakeke Crisis." In *Community Conflicts in Nigeria: Management, Resolution and Transformation,* edited by Onigu Otite and Isaac Olawale Albert, 142–183. Ibadan: Spectrum Books, 1999.

Alemayehyu, Abate Nikodimos. "Ethnic Federalism in Ethiopia: Challenges and Opportunities." M.A. thesis, Faculty of Law, University of Lund, 2004.

Allen, Karen. "Bank Scam Threatens Kenya Economy." BBC News (July 11, 2006). Accessed November 1, 2012. http://news.bbc.co.uk/2/hi/africa/6123832.stm.

———. "Peace at Any Price 2." BBC News (January 2008). Accessed May 12, 2012. http://www.youtube.com/watch?v=mcMcRMqyV2A.

Alou, Mahaman Tidjani. "Corruption in the Legal System." In Everyday Corruption and the State in Africa: Citizens and Public Officials, edited by N. B. Afrifari and M. T. Alou, 137–176. London: Zed, 2006.

Aluaigba, Moses T. "The Tiv-Jukun Ethnic Conflict and the Citizenship Question in Nigeria." 2011. Accessed January 11, 2012. http://ebookbrowse.com/moses-t-aluaigba-the-tiv-jukun-ethnic-conflict-and-the-citizenship-question-in-nigeria-pdf-d51107157.

Amin, Samir. Accumulation on a World Scale: A Critique of the Theory of Underdevelopment. New York: Monthly Review Press, 1974.

Aminzade, Ronald. "From Race to Citizenship: The Indigenization Debate in Post-Socialist Tanzania." Studies in Comparative International Development 38, no.1 (2003): 43–63.

Anaba, Innocent, and Jennifer Diei. "Nigeria: Retiring Judge Decries Intimidation of Judges by Lawyers, Litigants." Vangard (February 24, 2004).

Anderson, David, and Emma Lochery. "Violence and Exodus in Kenya's Rift Valley, 2008: Predictable and Preventable?" Journal of Eastern African Studies 2, no. 2 (2008): 328–343.

Apter, David. "Some Reflections on the Role of Political Opposition in New Nations." In Comparative Studies in Society and History, edited by Andrew Shryock, 154–168. Cambridge: Cambridge University Press, 1962.

Araia, Berhane Berhe. "Citizenship, Constitutional Legitimacy and Identity in Post-Colonial African Nation-States." Ph.D. diss., University of North Carolina, 2006.

Arbache, Jorge Saba, and John Page. "How Fragile Is Africa's Recent Growth?" Journal of African Economies 19, no. 1 (2009): 1–24.

Aristotle. The Politics. Translated and with an introduction by Carnes Lord. Chicago: University of Chicago Press, 1984.

Arriola, Leonardo R. "Patronage and Political Stability in Africa." Comparative Political Studies 42, no. 10 (2009): 1339–1362.

Awolowo, Chief Obafemi. Path to Nigerian Freedom. London: Faber & Faber, 1947.

Ayittey, George B. N. Africa Betrayed. New York: St. Martin's Press, 1992.

Azikwe, Nnamdi. "From Tribe to Nation: The Case of Nigeria." Foreword to Themes in African Political and Social Thought, edited by Onigu Otite. Enugu, Nigeria: Fourth Dimension, 1975.

Bachmann, C., C. Staerklé, and W. Doise. Re-Inventing Citizenship in South Caucasus: Exploring the Dynamics and Contradictions between Formal Definitions and Popular Conceptions. Final Research Report, University of Geneva, 2003.

Bah, Abu Bakarr. "Democracy and Civil War: Citizenship and Peacemaking in Côte d'Ivoire." African Affairs 109/437 (2010): 597–615.

Baker, Bruce. "Separating the Sheep from the Goats among Africa's Separatist Movements." Terrorism and Political Violence 13, no. 1 (2001): 66–86.

Baldauf, Scott. "Special Report: As ICC Names Suspect Kenyan Leaders, Records Reveal Talk of More Ethnic Cleansing." Christian Science Monitor, December 14, 2010.

Balewa, Abubakar Tafawa. Mr. Prime Minister: A Selection of Speeches Made by Alhaji the Right Honourable Sir Abubakar Tafawa Balewa, K.B.E., M.P., Prime Minister of the Federal Republic of Nigeria. Apapa: Nigerian National Press, Ltd., 1964.

Banigas, Richard. "Post-Election Crisis in Côte d'Ivoire: The Gbonhi War." *African Affairs* 110/440 (2011): 457–468.

Barbalet, J. M. *Citizenship: Rights, Struggle and Class Inequality.* Milton Keynes, England: Oxford University Press, 1988.

Barbalet, Jack. "Citizenship in Max Weber." *Journal of Classical Sociology* 10, no. 3 (2010): 201–216.

Barber, Benjamin. "Jihad vs. McWorld." In *Braving the New World: Readings in Contemporary Politics,* edited by Thomas Michael Joseph Bateman and Roger Epp. Nelson Education Limited, 1995. Accessed June 6, 2011. http://www.trentu.ca/politics/documents/POST235-barbero001.pdf.

Barnett, Donald, and Karari Njama. *Mau Mau from Within: Autobiography and Analysis of Kenya's Peasant Revolt.* New York: Modern Reader, 1966.

Bassett, Thomas J. "Winning Coalition, Sore Loser: Côte d'Ivoire 2010 Presidential Elections." *African Affairs* 110/440 (2011): 409–479.

Bates, Robert. *Beyond the Miracle of the Market: The Political Economy of Agricultural Development in Kenya.* Cambridge: Cambridge University Press, 2005.

———. *When Things Fell Apart: State Failure in Late Century Africa.* Cambridge: Cambridge University Press, 2008.

Baxter, P. T. W. "Ethiopia's Unacknowledged Problem: The Oromo." *African Affairs* 77, no. 308 (1978): 283–296.

Bayart, Jean-François. "Civil Society in Africa." In *Political Domination in Africa,* edited by Patrick Chabal, 109–125. Cambridge: Cambridge University Press, 1986.

———. *The Illusion of Cultural Identity.* Chicago: The University of Chicago Press, 2005.

Bekoe, Dorina. "Kenya: Setting the Stage for Durable Peace?" United States Institute of Peace, 2008. Accessed July 24, 2012. http://www.usip.org.

Bennett, Andrew. "Process Tracing and Causal Inference." In *Rethinking Social Inquiry: Diverse Tools, Shared Standards,* edited by Henry E. Brady and David Collier, 207–219. Lanham, Md.: Rowman and Littlefield Publishers, 2010.

Berman, Bruce J. "Ethnicity and Democracy in Africa." Japan International Cooperation Agency Research Institute, 2010.

Best, S. B., Aliamijeabee E. Idyorough, and Zainab Bayero Shehu. "Communal Conflicts and the Possibility of Conflict Resolution in Nigeria: A Case Study of the Tiv-Junkun Conflicts in Wukari Local Government Area, Tabara State." In *Community Conflicts in Nigeria: Management, Resolution and Transformation,* edited by Onigu Otite and Isaac Olawale Albert, 82–117. Ibadan: Spectrum Books, 1999.

Bienen, Henry. *Kenya: The Politics of Participation and Control.* Princeton, N.J.: Princeton University Press, 1974.

Blundo, G., and J. P. Olivier de Sardan, eds. *Everyday Corruption and the State in Africa: Citizens and Public Officials,* with N. B. Afrifari and M. T. Alou, 3–15. London: Zed, 2006.

Bøås, Morten. "'New' Nationalism and Autochthony: Tales of Origin as Political Cleavage." *Africa Spectrum* 1 (2009): 19–38.

Boone, Catherine. "Conflict over Property Rights in Africa's Liberalized Political Economies." Unpublished paper presented at the 2009 Annual Meeting of the African Studies Association.

———. "Land Conflict and Distributive Politics in Kenya." *African Studies Review* 55, no.1 (2012): 75–103.

———. *Political Topographies of the African State: Territorial Authority and Institutional Choice.* Cambridge: Cambridge University Press, 2003.

Brady, Henry. "Data Set Observations versus Causal Process Observations: The 2000 U.S. Presidential Election." In *Rethinking Social Inquiry: Diverse Tools, Shared Standards,* edited by Henry Brady and David Collier, 15–31. Lanham, Md.: Rowman and Littlefield, 2010.

Bratton, Michael, and Nicholas van de Walle. *Democratic Experiments in Africa: Regime Transitions in Comparative Perspective.* New York: Cambridge University Press, 1997.

Bratton, Michael, Robert Mattes, and E. Gyimah-Boadi. *Public Opinion, Democracy, and Market Reform in Africa.* Cambridge: Cambridge University Press, 2005.

Brietzke, Paul. "Ethiopia's 'Leap into the Dark': Federalism and Self-Determination in the New Constitution." *Journal of African Law* 40 (1995): 19–38.

Brinton, Jasper Yeates. *The Constitution of the Congo (Promulgated August 1, 1964).* American Society of International Law, 1965. Accessed July 1, 2011. http://books.google.com/ books?id=vK1BAAAAIAAJ&q=inauthor:%22Congo+(Democratic+Republic)%22&dq =inauthor:%22Congo+(Democratic+Republic)%22&hl=en&sa=X&ei=K7GyT-7AOOe piQLrtr2mBA&ved=0CEsQ6AEwAA.

Brown, Stephen. "Quiet Diplomacy and Recurring 'Ethnic Clashes' in Kenya." In *From Promise to Practice: Strengthening Capacities for the Prevention of Violent Conflict,* edited by Chandra Sriram and Karin Wermester, 69–100. Boulder, Colo.: Lynne Rienner Publishers, 2003.

Brubaker, Rogers. "The French Revolution and the Invention of Citizenship." *French Politics and Society* 7, no. 3 (1989): 30–49.

Calhoun, Craig. "Nationalism and Ethnicity." *Annual Review of Sociology* 19 (1993): 211–239.

Ceuppens, Bambi, and Peter Geschiere. "Autochthony: Local or Global? New Modes in the Struggle over Citizenship and Belonging in Africa and Europe." *Annual Review of Anthropology* 34 (2005): 385–407. Accessed December 4, 2011. http://anthro.annualreviews .org/errata.shtml.

Chabal, Patrick. *Political Domination in Africa: Reflections on the Limits of Power.* Cambridge: Cambridge University Press, 1986.

Chauveau, J. P. "Question foncière et construction nationale en Côte d'Ivoire." *Politique Africaine* 78 (2000): 77–125.

Cheeseman, Nic. "The Kenyan Elections of 2007: An Introduction." *Journal of Eastern African Studies* 2, no. 2 (July 2008): 166–184.

Clark, John R. "Rwanda: Tragic Land of Dual Nationalisms." In *After Independence: Making and Protecting the Nation in Post-Colonial and Post-Communist States,* edited by Lowell Barrington, 71–106. Ann Arbor: University of Michigan Press, 2006.

Collier, David. "Understanding Process Tracing." *PS: Political Science and Politics* 44, no. 4 (2011): 823–830.

Commission of Inquiry into the Post-Election Violence (CIPEV). "Report of the Commission of Inquiry into the Post-Election Violence" (October 16, 2008). Accessed August 1, 2012. http://www.communication.go.ke/Documents/CIPEV_FINAL_REPORT.pdf.

Connor, Walker. *Ethnonationalism: The Quest for Understanding.* Princeton, N.J.: Princeton University Press, 1994.

Constitution of the Federal Democratic Republic of Ethiopia. December 8, 1994. Accessed July 19, 2012. http://unpan1.un.org/intradoc/groups/public/documents/cafrad/ unpan004722.pdf.

Cook, Amelia, and Jeremy Sarkin. "Who Is Indigenous? Indigenous Rights Globally in Africa, and among the San in Botswana." *Tulane Journal of International and Comparative Law* 18 (2008): 93–130.

Curry, Kate, and Larry Ray. "The Pambana of August—Kenya's Abortive Coup." *The Political Quarterly* 57, no. 1 (1986): 47–59. Accessed September 15, 2012. http://onlinelibrary .wiley.com/doi/10.1111/j.1467–923X.1986.tb00700.x/abstract;jsessionid=DF7C0116577 EC89E4DB5B65600328FE0.d03t01.

Dagne, Ted. "Rwanda: Background and Current Developments." *Congressional Research Service* (June 1, 2011). Accessed August, 28, 2012. http://www.fas.org/sgp/crs/row/R40115 .pdf

Daily Nation. "Special Report: Report of the Judicial Commission Appointed to Inquire into Tribal Clashes in Kenya-Rift Valley" (2002). Accessed July 24, 2012. http://www.hrw .org/sites/default/files/related_material/Akiwumi.Rift%20Valley.pdf.

Davies, J. C. "The J-Curve of Rising and Declining Satisfactions as a Cause of Some Great Revolutions and a Contained Rebellion." In *The History of Violence in America: Historical and Comparative Perspectives,* edited by Hugh Davis Graham and Ted Robert Gurr, 671–709. New York: F. A. Praeger, 1969.

Des Forges, Alison. *Leave No One to Tell the Story: Genocide in Rwanda.* New York: Human Rights Watch, 1999.

Diamond, Jared. *Collapse: How Societies Choose to Fail or Succeed.* New York: Penguin, 2005.

Diamond, Larry. "Foreword," xi–xxi, in Rotimi T. Suberu, *Federalism and Ethnic Conflict in Nigeria,* Washington, DC: US Institute of Peace, 2001.

———. "The Rule of Law versus the Big Man." *Journal of Democracy* 19, no. 2 (2008): 138–149.

Diouf, Mamadou, "The French Colonial Policy of Assimilation and the Civility of the *Originaires* of the Four Communes (Senegal): A Nineteenth Century Globalization Project," *Development and Change* 29, no. 4 (December 2002): 671–696.

Dolan, Gabriel. "Kenya: New Voices Needed in Kalenjin Land." *Daily Nation* (May 6, 2011). Accessed January 28, 2012. http://allafrica.com/stories/printable/201101310104.html.

Dorman, Sara, Daniel Hammett, and Paul Nugent, eds. "Introduction: Citizenship and Its Casualties in Africa." In *Making Nations, Creating Strangers,* 3–26. Leiden, Netherlands: Brill, 2007.

Dorsch, Hauke. Review of *The Perils of Belonging: Autochthony, Citizenship, and Exclusion in Africa and Europe,* by Peter Geschiere. *Anthropological Quarterly* 82, no. 2 (2009): 301–305.

Edelman, Murray. *The Symbolic Uses of Politics.* Chicago: University of Illinois Press, 1964.

Ekeh, Peter. "Colonialism and Two Publics in Africa: A Theoretical Statement." *Comparative Studies in Society and History* 17, no. 19 (1975): 81–112.

Embassy of the United States, Nairobi. "Cable: Kenya Electoral Crisis: Explaining Rift Valley Violence" (2008). Accessed December 7, 2011. http://wikileaks.org/ cable/2008/01/08NAIROBI310.html.

Emerson, Rupert. *From Empire to Nation: The Rise to Self-Assertion of Asian and African Peoples.* Cambridge, Mass.: Harvard University Press, 1960.

Englebert, Pierre. *Africa: Unity, Sovereignty and Sorrow.* Boulder, Colo.: Lynne Rienner Publishers, 2009.

Enloe, Cynthia. *Ethnic Conflict and Political Development.* Boston: Little, Brown, 1972, 1985.

Erlich, Haggai. *Ethiopia and the Challenge of Independence.* Boulder, Colo.: Lynne Rienner Publishers, 1886.

Ethiopian Herald. "Forum Discusses Decentralization Affirmative Actions" (August 6, 2002).

Ethiopian Ministry of Foreign Affairs. "Ethiopian Government Aide Memoire." *Press Release* (November 14, 1963).

Ethiopian Nationality Law Proclamation No. 378. 2003. Accessed July 19, 2012. http://chilot
.me/2011/08/08/ethiopian-nationality-law-proclamation-no-3782003/.

Ethiopian Observer. "Emperor Haile Selassie's Speech in the Ogaden, August 25, 1956: Extracts" (December 1956).

Fearon, James, and David Laitin. "Violence and the Social Construction of Ethnic Identity." *International Organization* 54, no. 4 (2000): 845–877.

Federal Republic of Nigeria. "Chapter II, Sec. 25." *Constitution of the Federal Republic of Nigeria.* Kaduna: New Nigerian Newspapers, 1979.

———. *Constitution of the Federal Republic of Nigeria.* (1999). Accessed July 12, 2011. http://www.nigerialaw.org/Constitution%20of%20the%20Federal%20Republic%20of%20Nigeria%20(Promulgation)%20Decree.htm.

"Fighting Corruption in Kenya: Where Graft Is Merely Rampant." *The Economist,* December 16, 2004. Accessed November 1, 2012. http://www.economist.com/node/3504821.

Freedman, David. "On Types of Scientific Inquiry: The Role of Qualitative Reasoning." In *Rethinking Social Inquiry: Diverse Tools, Shared Standards,* edited by Henry Brady and David Collier, 221–236. Lanham, Md.: Rowman and Littlefield, 2010.

Gellner, Ernest. *Nations and Nationalism.* Oxford: Blackwell, 1983.

Geschiere, Peter. "Autochthony, Belonging and Exclusion: The Pitfalls of a Culturalization of Citizenship." Paper for Forum Conference on Strangeness and Familiarity, University of Groningen (October 21–22, 2010). Accessed October 11, 2011. http://www.forum.nl/Portals/Vreemdeling/publication/Strangeness-Familiarity-Peter-Geschiere.pdf.

———. *The Perils of Belonging: Autochthony, Citizenship, and Exclusion in Africa and Europe.* Chicago: University of Chicago Press, 2009.

Geschiere, Peter, and Stephen Jackson. "Autochthony and the Crisis of Citizenship: Democratization, Decentralization and the Politics of Belonging." *African Studies Review* 49, no. 2 (2009): 1–7.

Geschiere, Peter, and Francis B. Nyamnjoh. "Capitalism and Autochthony: The Seesaw of Mobility and Belonging." Public Culture 12, no. 2 (Spring 2000): 423–452.

Gilkes, Patrick. *The Dying Lion: Feudalism and Modernization in Ethiopia.* London: Julian Friedmann, 1975.

Githinji, Mwangi wa, and Frank Holmquist. "Reform and Political Impunity in Kenya: Transparency without Accountability." *African Studies Review* 55, no. 2 (2011): 53–74.

Golloba-Mutebi, Fredrick. "Who Killed Habariymana? Who Saw Him Die? What Does It Matter Now?" *East African Journal* (October 9, 2011). Accessed January 20, 2012. http://allafrica.com/stories/201110101329.html.

Gourevitch, Philip. *We Wish to Inform You That Tomorrow We Will Be Killed with Our Families: Stories from Rwanda.* New York: St Martin's Press, 1998.

Gready, Paul. "'You're Either with Us or against Us': Civil Society and Policymaking in Post-Genocide Rwanda." *Journal of African Affairs* 1, no. 21 (2010): 637–657.

Grindle, Merilee S. "Good Enough Governance Revisited." *Development Policy Review* 29, no. 1 (2001): 199–221.

Gudina, Merere. *Ethiopia: Competing Ethnic Nationalisms and the Quest for Democracy, 1960–2000.* Addis Ababa: Shaker Publishers, 2003.

Hanson, Stephanie. "Corruption in Sub-Saharan Africa." *Council on Foreign Relations* (2009). Accessed November 1, 2012. http://www.cfr.org/democracy-and-human-rights/corruption-sub-saharan-africa/p19984.

Harbeson, John. "Land and the Quest for a Democratic State in Kenya: Bringing Citizens Back In." *African Studies Review* 55, no. 1 (2012): 15–30.

Harbeson, John Willis, Donald S. Rothchild, and Naomi Chazan, eds. *Civil Society and the State in Africa*. Boulder, Colo.: Lynne Rienner Publishers, 1994.

Hassan, Mohammed. *The Oromo of Ethiopia: A History 1570–1860*. Trenton, N.J.: Red Sea Press, 1994.

Heater, Derek. *What Is Citizenship?* Malden, Mass.: Polity Press, 1999.

Helle-Valle, Jo. "Banyarunda in Uganda: Ethnic Identity, Refugee Status and Social Stigma." M.A. thesis, University of Oslo, 1989.

Herbst, Jeffrey. "The Politics of Migration and Citizenship." In *States and Power in Africa: Comparative Lessons in Authority and Control,* by Jeffrey Herbst. Princeton, N.J.: Princeton University Press, 2000.

———. *States and Power in Africa: Comparative Lessons in Authority and Control*. Princeton, N.J.: Princeton University Press, 2000.

Hickey, Sam. "Caught at the Crossroads: Citizenship, Marginality, and the Mbororo Fulani in Northwest Cameroon." In *Making Nations, Creating Strangers,* edited by Sara Dorman, Daniel Hammett, and Paul Nugent, 83–104. Leiden, Netherlands: Brill, 2007.

Higazi, Adam. "The Jos Crisis: A Recurrent Nigerian Tragedy." Friedrich Ebert Stiftung: Discussion Paper No. 2 (2011). Accessed June 30, 2011. http://library.fes.de/pdf-files/bueros/nigeria/07812.pdf.

Hintjens, Helen. "Post-Genocide Identity Politics in Rwanda." *Ethnicities* 8, no. 1 (2003): 9–10. Accessed August 28, 2012. http://etn.sagepub.com/content/8/1/5.full.pdf+html.

Hobsbawm, Eric J. *Bandits*. New York: Penguin, 1985.

Hobsbawm, Eric J., and Terrance Ranger, eds. *The Invention of Tradition*. Cambridge: Cambridge University Press, 1983.

Holm, John D., and Patrick Molutsi. *Democracy in Botswana*. Athens: Ohio University Press, 1990.

Hope, Kempe Ronald, Sr. "Corruption and Development in Africa." In *Corruption and Development: Lessons from Country Case Studies,* edited by Kempe Ronald Hope, Sr. and Bornwell C. Chikulo, 17–39. New York: St. Martin's Press, 2000.

———. 2000. Introduction to *Corruption and Development: Lessons from Country Case Studies,* edited by Kempe Ronald Hope, Sr. and Bornwell C. Chikulo, 1–13. New York: St. Martin's Press.

Hope, Kempe Ronald, Sr., and Bornwell C. Chikulo. *Corruption and Development in Africa: Lessons from Country Case Studies*. New York: St. Martin's Press, 2000.

Horowitz, Donald. *Ethnic Groups in Conflict*. Berkeley: University of California Press, 1985.

Huggins, Chris. "The Presidential Land Commission: Undermining Land Law Reform." In *Remaking Rwanda,* edited by Scott Straus and Lars Waldorf, 252–268. Madison: University of Wisconsin Press, 2011.

Human Rights Watch. "Collective Punishment: War Crimes and Crimes against Humanity in the Ogaden area of Ethiopia's Somali Regional State." New York: Human Rights Watch, 2008.

———. *Divide and Rule: State-Sponsored Ethnic Violence in Kenya*. New York: Human Rights Watch, 1993.

———. "Kenya—Ballots to Bullets: Organized Political Violence and Kenya's Crisis of Governance." New York: Human Rights Watch, 2008.

———. "Kenya. Turning Pebbles: Evading Accountability in Post-Election Violence." New York: Human Rights Watch, 2011. Accessed July 24, 2012. http://www.hrw.org/sites/default/files/reports/kenya1211webwcover_0.pdf.

————. "They Do Not Own This Place." *Government Discrimination against 'Non-Indigenes' in Nigeria* 18, no. 3A (2008): 10.

Huntington, Samuel P. *Political Order in Changing Societies*. New Haven, Conn.: Yale University Press, 1968.

Huxley, Elspeth. *White Man's Country: Lord Delamere and the Making of Kenya*. New York: Praeger, 1968.

Hyden, Goran. "Making the State Responsive: Rethinking Governance Theory and Practice." In *Making the State Responsive: Experience with Democratic Governance Assessments*, edited by Goran Hyden and John Samuel, 5–28. Washington, D.C.: UNDP, 2011. Accessed August 10, 2012. http://www.undp.org/content/dam/undp/documents/partners/civil_society/Africa%20Forum%20on%20Civil%20Society%20and%20Governance%20Assessments/Making%20the%20state%20responsive.pdf.

Hyden, Goran, Julius Court, and Kenneth Mease. *Making Sense of Governance: Empirical Evidence from 16 Developing Countries*. Boulder, Colo.: Lynne Rienner Publishers, 2004.

Ignatius, Obi E. "Broken Back Axel: Unspeakable Events in Biafra." *Xlibris*, 2011. Accessed November 12, 2011. www.xlibris.com.

Indian Society. "Module IV National Integration: Concept and Challenge." Accessed June 28, 2011. www.scribd.com/ . . . L25.

Ingelaere, Bert. "The Ruler's Drum and the People Shout: Accountability and Representation on Rwanda's Hills." In *Remaking Rwanda*, edited by Scott Straus and Lars Waldorf, 67–78. Madison: University of Wisconsin Press, 2011.

Institute for the Study of Ethiopian Nationalities. *Documents on the Establishment of the Institute for the Study of Ethiopian Nationalities* 1, no. 1 (1984): 19.

International Crisis Group. "Kenya in Crisis" (February 2008). Accessed July 25, 2012. http://www.crisisgroup.org/~/media/Files/africa/horn-of-africa/kenya/137_kenya_in_crisis_web.pdf.

International Refugee Rights Initiative. "Citizenship: Developing New Approaches to Citizenship and Belonging in Africa" (2011). Accessed November 7, 2012. http://www.refugee-rights.org/Programs/Citizenship/citizenship.html.

Iqbal, Zareen. "Kenya's New Constitution: Erasing the Imperial Presidency" (2010). Accessed November 11, 2011. http://iijd.org/news/entry/kenyas-new-constitution-erasing-the-imperial-presidency.

Isa-Odidi, Nabila. "Ethnic Conflict in Plateau State: The Need to Eliminate the Indigene-Settler Dichotomy in Nigeria." *Human Rights Brief* 12, no. 1 (2004): 18.

"Ivory Coast—The Economy." Mongabay.com. Accessed June 26, 2012. http://www.mongabay.com/reference/country_studies/ivory-coast/ECONOMY.html.

Iyob, Ruth. *The Eritrean Struggle for Independence: Domination, Resistance, and Nationalism 1941–1993*. Cambridge: Cambridge University Press, 1995.

Jackson, Robert H., and Carl G. Rosberg. "Personal Rule: Theory and Practice in Africa." *Comparative Politics* 16, no. 4 (1984): 293–307.

Jackson, Stephen. "Sons of Which Soil? The Language and Politics of Autochthony in Eastern Congo." *African Studies Review* 49, no. 2 (September 2006.): 95–123.

Jackson, Will. "White Man's Country: Kenya Colony and the Making of a Myth." *Journal of Eastern African Studies* 5, no. 2 (2011): 344–368.

Jain, Arvind K. "Corruption: A Review." *Journal of Economic Surveys* 15, no. 1 (2002): 71–121. Accessed October 29, 2012. http://onlinelibrary.wiley.com/doi/10.1111/14 67–6419.00133/pdf.

Jaycox, Edward V. K. *The Challenges of African Development*. Washington, D.C.: The World Bank, 1992.

Johnson, G. Wesley, Jr. *The Emergence of Black Politics in Senegal: The Struggle for Power in the Four Communes, 1900–1920*. Stanford, Calif.: Stanford University Press, 1971.

Johnson, Michael, and Trish Johnson. "The National Question and the Logic of Protracted Struggle." *African Affairs* 80 (1981): 181–195.

Johnson, Toni. "Boko Haram." Council on Foreign Relations, 2011. Accessed January 15, 2012. http://cfr.org/africa/boko-haram/p25739?cid=ppc-Google-bplp_.

Joireman, Sandra. *Nationalism and Political Identity*. New York and London: Continuum Press, 2003.

———. *Where There Is No Government: Enforcing Property Rights in Common Law Africa*. New York: Oxford University Press, 2011.

Jok, Jok Madut. "Diversity, Unity, and Nation-Building in South Sudan." United States Institute of Peace Special Report 287 (2011).

———. *Sudan: Race, Religion, and Violence*. Oxford: Oneworld, 2007.

Jonas, Raymond. *The Battle of Adwa: African Victory in the Age of Empire*. Cambridge, Mass.: Harvard University Press, 2011.

Joseph, Richard. *Democracy and Prebendal Politics in Nigeria: The Rise and Fall of the Second Republic*. Cambridge: Cambridge University Press, 1988.

Kabubo-Mariara, Jane. "Land Conservation in Kenya: The Role of Property Rights." *African Economic Research Consortium*, Research Paper 153 (2006).

Kanyinga, Karuti. "Kenya Experience in Land Reform: The Million-Acre Settlement Scheme" (Draft 2011). Accessed July 20, 2012. http://siteresources.worldbank.org/RPDLPROGRAM/Resources/459596–1168010635604/WBI-KenyaLandReform-WorkshopVersion.pdf.

Kasfir, Nelson. "Explaining Ethnic Political Participation." *World Politics* 31 (1978–1979): 365–388.

Keller, Edmond J. "Constitutionalism, Citizenship and Political Transitions in Ethiopia: Historic and Contemporary Processes." In *Self-Determination and National Unity: A Challenge for Africa*, edited by Francis M. Deng, 57–90. Trenton, N.J.: Africa World Press, 2010.

———. "Ethiopia: Revolution, Class and the National Question." *African Affairs* 80, no. 321 (1981): 519–550.

———. "Ethiopia: The Revolutionary Transformation of a 20th-Century Bureaucratic Empire." *Journal of Modern African Studies* 19, no. 2 (1981): 307–366.

———. "Ethnic Federalism and Democratization in Ethiopia." *Horn of Africa* XXI (2003): 30–43.

———. "The Ethno-Genesis of the Oromo-Nation and Its Implications for Politics in Ethiopia." *Journal of Modern African Studies* 33, no. 4 (1995): 621–634.

———. "Making and Remaking State and Nation in Ethiopia." In *Borders, Nationalism, and the African State*, edited by Ricardo Rene Laremont, 87–134. Boulder, Colo.: Lynne Reinner, 2005.

———. "Political Institutions, Agency and Contingent Compromise: Understanding Democratic Consolidation and Reversal in Africa." *National Political Science Review* 7 (1999): 96–115.

———. "Remaking the Ethiopian State." In *Collapsed States: The Disintegration and Restoration of Legitimate Authority*, edited by I. William Zartman, 189–205. Boulder, Colo.: Lynne Rienner Publishers, 1995.

———. *Revolutionary Ethiopia: From Empire to Peoples' Republic*. Bloomington: Indiana University Press, 1988.

———. "Secessionism in Africa." *The Journal of African Policy Studies* 13, no. 1 (2007): 1–26.

———. "The State in Contemporary Africa: A Critical Assessment of Theory and Practice." In *Comparative Political Dynamics*, edited by D. Rostow and K. Erickson, 134–159. New York: HarperCollins, 1991.

———. "The State, Public Policy and the Mediation of Ethnic Conflict." In *State Versus Ethnic Claims: African Policy Dilemmas*, edited by Victor A. Olorunsola and Donald Rothchild, 251–280. Boulder, Colo.: Westview Press (1983).

———. "Transnational Ethnic Conflict in Africa." In *The International Spread of Ethnic Conflict: Fear, Diffusion, and Escalation*, edited by David A. Lake and Donald Rothchild, 275–292. Princeton: Princeton University Press, 1998.

———. "A Twentieth Century Model: The Mau Mau Transformation from Social Banditry to Social Rebellion." *Kenya Historical Review* 1, no. 2 (1973).

Keller, Edmond J., and Donald Rothchild, eds. *Afromarxist Regimes: Ideology and Policy*. Boulder, Colo.: Lynne Reinner, 1987.

Keller, Edmond J., and Edith M. Omwami. "Federalism, Citizenship and National Identity in Ethiopia." *The International Journal of African Studies* 6, no. 1 (2007): 37–69.

Kenya Human Rights Commission. "Land Rights and Reform Agenda in Kenya: A Policy Brief and Audit." Accessed July 19, 2012. http://www.internaldisplacement.org/8025708 F004CE90B/%28httpDocuments%29/1F21DB76454E3A3EC125773E004AD8A6/$file/ Land+Rights+and+Reform+Agenda+in+Kenya+-+A+Policy+Brief+and+Audit.PDF.

Kenya Law Reports. *The Constitution of Kenya* (2010 rev. ed.). Accessed November 12, 2011. http://www.kenyaembassy.com/pdfs/The%20Constitution%20of%20Kenya.pdf.

———. *Trust Land Act* (2010 rev. ed.). Accessed August 3, 2012. http://www.scribd.com/ doc/97787585/The-Trust-Land-Act.

Kimenyi, Mwangi S., and John Mukum Mbaku. "Elections and Violence in Nigeria: The Question of Citizenship in Sub-Saharan Africa." Washington, D.C.: Brookings, 2011. Accessed October 11, 2011. http://www.brookings.edu/research/opinions/2011/04/28- nigeria-elections-kimenyi-mbaku.

Klein, Natalie S. "Mass Expulsion from Ethiopia: Report on the Deportation of Ethiopians of Eritrean Origin from Ethiopia" (1988). Accessed January 5, 2012. www.essex.ac.uk/ amendcon/story.

Kpundeh, Sahr John. *Politics and Corruption in Africa: A Case Study of Sierra Leone*. Lanham, Md.: University Press of America, 1994.

Kramon, Eric, and Daniel Posner. "Ethnic Favoritism in Primary Education in Kenya." Unpublished, 2012.

Krause, Jana. "A Deadly Cycle: Ethno-Religious Conflict in Jos, Plateau State, Nigeria." *Executive Summary*. Working Paper, Geneva Declaration, 2011. Accessed October 11, 2010. http://www.genevadeclaration.org/fileadmin/docs/regional-publications/GD-ES- deadly-cycle-Jos.pdf.

Kututwa, Noel. "African Anti-Corruption Commitments: A Review of Eight NEPAD Countries." *African Human Security Initiative* (2005). Accessed November 2, 2012. http:// dspace.cigilibrary.org/jspui/bitstream/123456789/31498/1/AHSI7.pdf?1.

Laitin, David, and Said Samatar. *Somalia: Nation in Search of a State*. London: Gower, 1987.

Lake, David A., and Donald Rothchild, eds. 1998. *The International Spread of Ethnic Conflict: Fear, Diffusion, and Escalation*. Princeton, N.J.: Princeton University Press.

Laremont, Ricardo Rene, ed. *Borders, Nationalism, and the African State.* Boulder, Colo.: Lynne Rienner Publishers, 2005.

LeBas, Adrienne. *From Protest to Parties: Party-Building and Democratization in Africa.* Oxford: Oxford University Press, 2011.

Lemarchand, Rene. *Rwanda and Burundi.* New York: Praeger, 1970.

Levine, Donald. *Greater Ethiopia: The Evolution of a Multi-Ethnic Society.* Chicago: University of Chicago Press, 1975.

Leys, Colin. *The Rise and Fall of Development Theory.* Bloomington: Indiana University Press, 1996.

———. *Underdevelopment in Kenya: The Political Economy of Neo-Colonialism.* Berkeley: University of California Press, 1975.

Lindberg, Steffan. "It's Our Time to 'Chop': Do Elections in Africa Feed Neo-Patrimonialism Rather Than Counteract It?" *Democratization* 10, no. 2 (2003): 121–140.

———. "It's Our Time to 'Chop': Do Elections in Africa Feed Neo-Patrimonialism Rather Than Counteract it?" *International Political Science Review* 22, no. 2 (2001): 173–199.

Lischer, Sarah Kenyon. "Civil War, Genocide, and Political Order in Rwanda: Security Implications of Refugee Return." *Conflict Security and Development* 11, no. 3 (2011): 261–284. Accessed August 27, 2012. http://www.tandfonline.com/loi/ccsd20.

Lofchie, Michael. "Political Constraints on African Development." In *The State of the Nations: Constraints on Development in Independent Africa,* edited by Michael Lofchie, 9–18. Berkeley: University of California Press, 1971.

Longman, Timothy. *Christianity and Genocide in Rwanda.* New York: Cambridge University Press, 2010.

———. "Limitations to Political Reform: The Undemocratic Nature of Transition in Rwanda." In *Remaking Rwanda,* edited by Scott Straus and Lars Waldorf, 25–47. Madison: University of Wisconsin Press, 2011.

Lynch, Gabrielle. "The Wars of Who Belongs Where: The Unstable Politics of Autochthony on Kenya's Mt. Elgon." *Ethnopolitics* 10, nos. 3–4 (2011): 391–410.

MacArthur, Julie. "How the West Was Won: Regional Politics and Prophetic Promises in the 2007 Elections." *Journal of Eastern African Studies* 2, no. 2 (2008): 227–242.

MacLean, Lauren M. *Informal Institutions and Citizenship in Rural Africa: Risk and Reciprocity in Ghana and Cote d'Ivoire.* New York: Cambridge, 2010.

Mamdani, Mahmood. "Beyond Settler and Native as Political Identities: Overcoming the Political Legacy of Colonialism." *Comparative Studies in Society and History* 43, no. 4 (2001): 651–664.

———. *Citizen and Subject: Contemporary Africa and the Legacy of Late Colonialism.* Princeton, N.J.: Princeton University Press, 1996.

———. "Ivory Coast: A UN Failure." *Aljazeera* (2011). Accessed June 25, 2012. http://www.aljazeera.com/indepth/opinion/2011/04/20114258205629868.html.

———. *When Victims Become Killers.* Princeton, N.J.: Princeton University Press, 2001.

Manby, Bronwen. *Citizenship Law in Africa: A Comparative Study.* New York: Open Societies Foundation, 2010.

———. *Struggles for Citizenship in Africa.* London: Zed Books, 2009.

Manning, Patrick. *Francophone Sub-Saharan Africa 1880–1995.* Cambridge: Cambridge University Press, 1998.

Marcus, Harold. *The Life and Times of Menelik II: Ethiopia, 1844–1913.* Oxford: Clarendon Press, 1975.

Markakis, John. *Ethiopia: The Last Two Frontiers.* London: James Curry, 2011.

Marshall, T. H. "Citizenship and Social Class." In *The Citizenship Debates,* edited by Gershon Shafir, 93–112. Minneapolis: University of Minnesota Press, 1950.

———. *Class, Citizenship and Social Development.* Garden City, N.Y.: Anchor, 1965.

Marshall-Fratani, Ruth. "The War of 'Who Is Who?' Autochthony, Nationalism and Citizenship in the Ivorian Crisis." In *Making Nations, Creating Strangers,* edited by Sara Dorman, Daniel Hammett, and Paul Nugent, 29–67. Leiden, Netherlands: Brill, 2007.

Maxon, Robert M. *Kenya's Independence Constitution: Constitution-Making and End of Empire.* Lanham, Md.: Fairleigh Dickinson Press, 2011.

Mayersen, Deborah. "'A Political Monopoly Held by One Race': The Politicisation of Ethnicity in Colonial Rwanda." In *Directions and Intersections: Proceedings of the 2011 Australian Critical Race and Whiteness Studies Association and Indigenous Studies Research Network Joint Conference,* edited by Damien W. Riggs and Clemence Due, 167–180. Australian Critical Race and Whiteness Studies Studies Association, 2011.

Mbaku, John Mukum. *Corruption in Africa: Causes, Consequences and Cleanups.* Lanham, Md.: Lexington Books, 2007.

McAdam, Doug, Sidney Tarrow, and Charles Tilly. *Dynamics of Contention.* Cambridge: Cambridge University Press, 2001.

McGovern, Mike. *Making War in Côte d'Ivoire.* London: Hurst and Co., 2011.

Meyer, Katie. "Kenya: Healing the Nation." *Peace Magazine* 24, no. 2 (2008): 16–19. Accessed October 13, 2011. http://peacemagazine.org/archive/v24n2p16.htm.

Mgbako, Chi. "Ingando Solidarity Camps: Reconciliation and Political Indoctrination in Post-Genocide Rwanda." Fordham Law Legal Studies Research Paper. *Harvard Human Rights Journal* 18 (2005): 201. Accessed August 31, 2012. http://ssrn.com/abstract =1719138.

Moi, Daniel Arap. *Kenya African Nationalism: Nyayo Philosophy and Principles.* London: Macmillan, 1996.

Momoh, Abubakar. "The Pathology of Citizenship in Nigeria." In *The Citizenship Question in Nigeria,* edited by I. Muazzam, 59–114. Kano: Centre for Research and Documentation, 2009.

Moore, Jina. "Africa's Continental Divide: Land Disputes." *The Christian Science Monitor.* January 30, 2010.

Mouffe, Chantal. "Democratic Citizenship and Political Community." In Miami Theory Collective (ed.), *Community at Loose Ends,* 70–82. Minneapolis: University of Minnesota Press, 1991.

Moyo, Dambisa. *Dead Aid: Why Aid Is Not Working and How There Is a Better Way for Africa.* New York: Farrar, Straus and Giroux, 2009.

Moyo, Jeffrey, "No Reforms in Zimbabwe as Mugabe Continues to Intimidate and Crack Down on the Judiciary and the Media." *NTA Newstime Africa* (April 22, 2013).

Mueller, Susanne. "The Political Economy of the Kenya Crisis." *Journal of Eastern African Studies* 2, no. 2 (2008): 185–210.

Mutunga, Willy. *Constitution-Making from the Middle: Civil Society and Transition Politics in Kenya, 1992–1997.* Nairobi: SAREAT, 1999.

Ndegwa, Stephen N. "Citizenship and Ethnicity: An Examination of Two Transitional Moments in Kenyan Politics." *The American Political Science Review* 91, no. 3 (1997): 599–616.

Ndungu, Paul N. November "Tackling Land Related Corruption in Kenya." Unpublished. (2006). Accessed May 4, 2012. http://siteresources.worldbank.org/RPDLPROGRAM/ Resources/459596–1161903702549/S2_Ndungu.pdf.

Neuberger, Benjamin. *National Self-Determination in Postcolonial Africa*. Boulder, Colo.: Lynne Rienner Publishers, 1986.

Newbury, Catherine. *The Cohesion of Repression: Clientship and Ethnicity in Rwanda, 1860–1960*. New York: Columbia University Press, 1988.

———. "High Modernism at the Ground Level: The 'Imidugudu' Policy in Rwanda." In *Remaking Rwanda*, edited by Scott Straus and Lars Waldorf, 223–239. Madison: University of Wisconsin Press, 2011.

Newitt, Malyn, Patrick Chabal, and Norrie Macqueen, eds. *Community and the State in Lusophone Africa*. London: King's College, 2003.

Nkrumah, Kwame. *Neocolonialism, the Last Stage of Imperialism*. New York: International Publishers, 1966.

Nnoli, Okwudiba. "Ethnic Violence in Nigeria: A Historical Perspective" (2003). Accessed January 4, 2012. http://www.indiana.edu/~workshop/papers/nnoli_021003.pdf.

Nyamnjoh, Francis B. "From Bounded to Flexible Citizenship: Lessons from Africa." *Citizenship Studies* 11, no. 1 (2007): 73–82.

———. *Insiders and Outsiders: Citizenship and Xenophobia in Contemporary Southern Africa*. London: Zed Books, 2006.

Nyerere, Julius K. *Freedom and Development*. London: Oxford University Press, 1967.

———. *Freedom and Socialism*. Dar es Salaam: Oxford University Press, 1968.

Nyukuri, Barasa Kundu. "The Impact of Past and Potential Ethnic Conflicts on Kenya's Stability and Development." A paper prepared for the USAID Conference on Conflict Resolution in the Greater Horn of Africa June, 1997. Accessed January 4, 2012. http://payson.tulane.edu/conflict/Cs%20St/BARASFIN1.html.

Nzongola-Ntalaja, Georges. "Citizenship and Exclusion in Africa: The Indigeneity Question." Keynote Address at a National Workshop on Citizenship and Indigeneity Conflicts in Nigeria. Organized by the Centre for Democracy and Development (CDD), Abuja, Nigeria, February 8–9, 2011.

———. *The Congo: From Leopold to Kabila: A People's History*. London: Zed Books, 2002.

Ogeik Peoples' Development Organization. "Dynamics of Conflict in the Mau Forest Complex: Towards an Early Warning and Monitoring System" (2011). Accessed November 3, 2012. http:// www.ogiekpeoples.org/pdf/EW%202%20-%20Mau%20forest%20 Complex.pdf.

Ojo, Bamidele A. *Problems and Prospects of Sustaining Democracy in Nigeria: Voices of a Generation*. Huntington: Nova Science Publishers, 2001.

Okuk, James. "The GoSS Mission in US and Question of Sudanese Citizenship." South Sudan News Agency. (2010). Accessed July 7, 2010. http://www.southsudannewsagency.com/opinion/articles/the-goss-mission-in-us-and-question-of-sudanese-citizenship.

Olsen, Gorm Rye. "Europe and the Promotion of Democracy in Post Cold War Africa: How Serious Is Europe and for What Reason?" *African Affairs* 97, no. 388 (July 1998): 353–357.

Omotoso, Femi. "Indigeneity and Problems of Citizenship in Nigeria." *Pakistan Journal of Social Sciences* 7, no. 2 (2010): 146–150.

Ongugo, Paul, Jane Njuguna, Emily Obonyo, and Gordon Sigu. "Livelihoods, Natural Resource Entitlements and Protected Areas: The Case of Mt. Elgon Forest in Kenya." Kenya INFRI Collaborative Research Centre. Accessed November 2, 2012. http://mail.cbd.int/doc/case-studies/for/cs-ecofor-ke-02-en.pdf.

Onoma, Ato Kwamena. *The Politics of Property Rights Institution in Africa*. Cambridge: Cambridge University Press, 2010.

Oommen, T. K. "Introduction: Conceptualizing the Linkage between Citizenship and National Identity." In *Citizenship and National Identity: From Colonialism to Globalization,* edited by T. K. Oommen, 13–53. London: Sage, 1997.

Osaghae, Eghosa. "Colonialism and Civil Society in Africa: The Perspective of Ekeh's Two Publics." *Voluntas* 17 (2006): 233–245.

Ostien, Philip. "Jonah Jang and the Jasawa: Ethno-Religious Conflict in Jos, Nigeria." *Muslim-Christian Relations in Africa* (2009). Accessed December 8, 2011. www.sharia-in-africa.net/media/publications/_ethno-religious.

Ottaway, David, and Marina Ottaway. *Ethiopia: Empire in Revolution.* New York: Africana, 1978.

Ottaway, Marina. *Africa's New Leaders: Democracy or State Reconstruction?* Washington, D.C.: Carnegie Endowment for International Peace, 1999.

Otunnu, Ogenga. "Rwandese Refugees and Immigrants in Uganda." In *The Path of a Genocide: The Rwanda Crisis from Uganda to Zaire,* edited by Howard Adelman and Astri Suhrke, 1–30. New Brunswick, N.J.: Transaction Publishers, 2000.

Owusu, Maxwell. *The Uses and Abuses of Political Power: A Case Study of Continuity and Change in the Politics of Ghana.* Accra: University of Ghana Press, 2006.

Oyelaran, Olasope, and Michael Olu Adediran. "Colonialism, Citizenship and Fractured National Identity: The African Case." In *Citizenship and National Identity: From Colonialism to Globalism,* edited by T. K. Oommen, 173–198. New York: Sage Publications, 1997.

Parham, Margery. *The Government of Ethiopia.* London: Faber and Faber, 1948.

Preparatory Committee for the Founding of the People's Democratic Republic of Ethiopia. "Ensuring the Rights of Nationalities." Addis Ababa: Preparatory Committee for the Founding of the People's Democratic Republic of Ethiopia. (September 1987).

Prime Minister of the Federal Democratic Republic of Ethiopia. *The System of Regional Administration in Ethiopia.* Addis Ababa, 1994.

Prunier, Gerard. *The Rwanda Crisis: History of a Genocide, 1959–1994.* London: Hurst & Co., 1985.

Przeworski, Adam. "Some Problems in the Study of the Transition to Democracy." In *Transitions from Authoritarian Rule: Comparative Perspectives,* edited by Guillermo O'Donnel, Philippe C. Schmitter, and Laurence Whitehead, 47–63. Baltimore: Johns Hopkins University Press, 1988.

———. *Sustainable Democracy.* Cambridge: Cambridge University Press, 1995.

Przeworski, Adam, Michael E. Alvarez, Jose Antonio Cheibub, and Fernando Limongi. *Democracy and Development: Political Institutions and Well-Being in the World, 1950–1990.* New York: Cambridge University Press, 2003.

Radelet, Steven. *Emerging Africa: How 17 Countries Are Leading the Way.* Washington, D.C.: Brookings Instructions Press, 2009.

Reed, William Cyrus. "Exile, Reform and the Rise of the Rwandan Patriotic Front." *Journal of Modern African Studies* 34, no. 3 (September 1996): 482–483.

Regassa, Tsegaye. "State Constitutions in Federal Ethiopia: A Preliminary Observation." Unpublished paper, 2004.

Reid, Richard J. *Frontiers of Violence in North-East Africa: Genealogies of Conflict since 1800.* New York: Oxford University Press, 2011.

Report of the Independent Review Commission on the General Elections Held in Kenya on 27 December 2007. Accessed November 1, 2012. http://www.communication.go.ke/media.asp?id=719.

Republic of Kenya. *Report of the Commission of Inquiry into the Illegal/Irregular Allocation of*

Public Land (2003). Accessed January 2, 2012. http://www.africog.org/reports/Mission%20Impossible%20Incomplete.pdf.

Reyntjens, Filip. "Waging War Abroad: Rwanda and the DRC." In *Remaking Rwanda: State Building and Human Rights after Violence,* edited by Scott Straus and Lars Waldorf, 132–151. Madison: University of Wisconsin Press, 2011.

Robinson, Amanda Lea. "National Versus Ethnic Identity in Africa: State, Group, and Individual Level Correlates of National Identification." *Afrobarometer* (2009). Working Paper 112. www.afrobarometer.org/index.php?option=com_docman.

Robinson, Pearl T. "The National Conference Phenomenon in Francophone Africa." *Comparative Studies in Society and History* 36, no. 3 (1994): 575–610.

Rodney, Walter. *How Europe Underdeveloped Africa.* Washington, D.C.: Howard University Press, 1981.

Rogowski, Ronald. "How Inference in the Social (but Not the Physical) Sciences Neglects Theoretical Anomaly." In *Rethinking Social Inquiry: Diverse Tools, Shared Standards,* edited by Henry Brady and David Collier, 77–83. Lanham, Md.: Rowman and Littlefield, 2010.

Rostow, W. W. *Stages of Economic Growth: A Non-Communist Manifesto.* Cambridge: Cambridge University Press, 1960.

Rubenson, Sven. *Survival of Ethiopian Independence.* London: Heinemann, 1976.

Rutten, Marcel, Alamin Mazrui, and François Grignon, eds. *Out for the Count: Democracy in Kenya.* Kampla: Fountain Publishers, 2001.

Sadiq, Kamal. *Paper Citizens: How Illegal Immigrants Acquire Citizenship in Developing Countries.* Oxford: Oxford University Press, 2009.

Samatar, Abdi Ismail. *An African Miracle: State and Class Leadership and Colonial Legacy in Botswana Development.* Portsmouth: Heinemann, 1999.

———. "Ethiopian Federalism: Autonomy versus Control in the Somali Region." *Third World Quarterly* 25, no. 6 (2004): 1131–1154.

Scott, James C. *Weapons of the Weak: Everyday Forms of Peasant Resistance.* New Haven, Conn.: Yale University Press, 1985.

Sebarenzi, Joseph. "Justice and Human Rights for all Rwandans." In *Remaking Rwanda: State Building and Human Rights after Violence,* edited by Scott Straus and Lars Waldorf, 343–353. Madison: University of Wisconsin Press.

Segal, Edwin S. Review of Peter Geschiere, *The Perils of Belonging: Autochthony, Citizenship, and Exclusion in Africa and Europe.* In *Anthropological Quarterly* 82, no. 2 (2009): 607–610. Accessed November 11, 2011. http://www.forum.nl/Portals/Vreemdeling/publication/Strangeness-Familiarity-Peter-Geschiere.pdf.

Sellassie, Sergew Habte. *Ancient and Medieval Ethiopian History to 1270.* Addis Ababa: United Printers, 1972.

Serra-Horguelin, Arnault. "The Federal Experiment in Ethiopia: A Socio-Political Analysis." *Travaux Documents: Centre d'etude D'Afrique Noire* (1999), 64.

Shivute, Peter. "The Rule of Law in Sub-Saharan Africa—An Overview." In *Human Rights and the Rule of Law in Namibia,* edited by Nico Horn and Anton Bösl, 213–219. New York: Macmillan, 2009.

Siegel, R. P. "Corruption and Sustainability: Like Oil and Water Do Not Mix." *Triple Pundit.* (2012). Accessed November 2, 2012. http://www.triplepundit.com/2012/01/corruption-sustainability-like-oil-and-%20water-mix/.

Simon, H. A. *Reason in Human Affairs.* Stanford, Calif.: Stanford University Press, 1983.

Siringi, Elijah M. "Forest Conflict amidst National Controversy in Kenya: Lessons of the

Mau Forest Complex." *Environment and Natural Resources Journal* 8, no. 1 (2010): 9–22. Accessed November 2, 2012. http://www.en.mahidol.ac.th/journal/2010_v8_n1/2_siringi_f.pdf.

Sisk, Timothy. *Democratization in South Africa: The Illusive Social Contract.* Princeton, N.J.: Princeton University Press, 1995.

Sklar, Richard. "Democracy in Africa." *African Studies Review* 26, nos. 3–4 (1983): 11–24.

———. "Democracy in Africa." In *Political Domination in Africa,* edited by Patrick Chabal, 30–51. Cambridge: Cambridge University Press, 1986.

Smith, Anthony. *Ethno-Symbolism and Nationalism: A Cultural Approach.* New York: Routledge, 2009.

Smith, Daniel Jordan. *A Culture of Corruption: Everyday Deception and Popular Discontent in Nigeria.* Princeton, N.J.: Princeton University Press, 2007.

Smith, Lahra. *Making Citizens in Africa: Ethnicity, Gender and National Identity in Contemporary Ethiopia.* Cambridge: Cambridge University Press, 2013.

Smock, Audrey. *Ibo Politics: The Role of Ethnic Unions in Eastern Nigeria.* London: Oxford University Press, 1971.

Somerville, Keith. "Violence, Hate Speech and Inflammatory Broadcasting in Kenya: The Problems of Definition and Identification." *Ecquid Novi: African Journalism Studies* 32, no. 1 (2011): 82–101.

Southall, Roger. "The Ndungu Report: Land and Graft in Kenya." *Review of African Political Economy* 32, no. 103 (2005): 142–151. Accessed April 27, 2012. http://dx.doi.org/10.1080/03056240500121065.

Stepan, Alfred. "Towards a New Comparative Politics of Federalism, (*Multi*)Nationalism, and Democracy: Beyond Rikerian Federalism." In *Arguing Comparative Politics,* edited by Alfred Stepan, 315–362. Oxford: Oxford University Press, 2001.

Straus, Scott. *The Order of Genocide: Race, Power, and War in Rwanda.* Ithaca and New York: Cornell University Press, 2006.

———. "Seeing Like a Post-Conflict State." In *Remaking Rwanda,* edited by Scott Straus and Lars Waldorf, 4. Madison: University of Wisconsin Press, 2011.

Straus, Scott, and Lars Waldorf. "'It's Sheer Horror Here': Patterns of Violence during the First Four Months of Côte D'Ivoire's Post-Electoral Crisis." *African Affairs* 110, no. 440 (2011): 481–489.

Suberu, Rotimi T. *Ethnic Minority Conflicts and Governance in Nigeria.* Ibadan: Spectrum Books, 1996.

———. *Federalism and Ethnic Conflict in Nigeria.* Washington, D.C.: US Institute of Peace, 2001.

———. *Public Policies and National Unity in Nigeria.* Ibadan, Nigeria: Development Policy Center, 1999.

Tarrow, Sidney. *Power in Movement: Social Movements and Contentious Politics.* New York and Cambridge: Cambridge University Press, 1998.

Taylor, Scott. *Culture and Custom of Zambia.* Westport, Conn.: Greenwood Press, 2008.

Tiemessen, Alana Erin. "After Arusha: Gacaca Justice in Post-Genocide Rwanda." *African Studies Quarterly* 8, no. 1 (2004): 57–76. Accessed August 31, 2012. http://www.africa.ufl.edu/asq/v8/v8i1a4.htm.

Tilly, Charles. "The Emergence of Citizenship in France and Elsewhere." *International Review of Social History* 40 (December 1995): 223–236.

Transparency International. *Corruption Perception Index.* (2011). Accessed January 5, 2012. http://cpi.transparency.org/cpi2011/.

Tronvoll, Kjetil, and Oyvind Aadland. "The Process of Democratization in Ethiopia: An Expression of Popular Participation or Political Resistance." *Human Rights Report No. 5* (1995): 47. Oslo: Norwegian Institute of Human Rights.

Trust Africa. "Report of Workshop on Citizenship and Identity in Africa." Addis Ababa, June 9–12, 2003. Accessed April 18, 2012. http://www.trustafrica.org/documents/report3_identity.pdf.

Union of Oromo Students in North America. "A Brief History of Oromo Resistance against Abyssinian Colonialism, 1855–1900." *Waldaansso: Journal of the Union of Oromo Students in North America* 3 (August 1979): 3–5.

United Nations. "Outreach Programme on the Rwanda Genocide and the United Nations" (2005). Accessed August 31, 2012. http://www.un.org/en/preventgenocide/rwanda/about/bgjustice.shtml.

———. "Universal Declaration of Human Rights" (1948). Accessed November 10, 2012. http://www.un.org/en/documents/udhr/history.shtml.

Van der Meeren, Rachel. "Three Decades in Exile: Rwandan Refugee 1960–1990." *Journal of Refugee Studies* 9, no. 3 (1996): 257.

van Hoof, Paul J. M. "Local Governance Assessment in Southern Africa: The Dynamics behind the Façade." In *Making the State Responsive: Experience with Democratic Governance Assessments,* edited by Goran Hyden and John Samuel, 158–176. Washington, D.C.: UNDP, 2011.

Wallerstein, Immanuel. "Citizens All Citizens Some: The Making of the Citizen." *Comparative Studies in Society and History* 45, no. 4 (2003): 650–679.

———. "The Range of Choice: Constraints on the Government Policies of Independent African States." In *The State of the Nations: Constraints on Development in Independent Africa,* edited by Michael Lofchie, 19–36. Berkeley: University of California Press, 1971.

Wallis, William, and David White. "Kenya: Officials, Banks in $1bn Corruption Probe." *Financial Times* (December 15, 2003). Accessed November 1, 2012. http://www.corpwatch.org/article.php?id=9429.

Watson, Catherine. "Exile from Rwanda: Background to Invasion." *The U.S. Committee for Refugees: Issue Paper:* 5 (February 1991).

Weekly Review. "Indigenous and the Natives" (July 9, 1993).

Weiner, Myron. "Political Integration and Political Development." In *Political Modernization: A Reader in Comparative Political Change,* edited by Claude Welch Jr., 150–166. Belmont, Calif.: A.Wadsworth, 1969.

Whitaker, Beth Elise. "Blurring the Line: The Politics of Citizenship in the Ivory Coast." Paper presented at the Annual Meeting of the African Studies Association, 2011.

———. "Citizens and Foreigners: Democratization and the Politics of Exclusion in Africa." *African Studies Review* 48, no. 1 (2005): 109–126.

Whitaker, C. Sylvester, Jr. *The Politics of Tradition: Continuity and Change in Northern Nigeria, 1946–1966.* Princeton, N.J.: Princeton University Press, 1970.

Widner, Jennifer A. *Building the Rule of Law.* New York: Norton, 2001.

———. *The Rise of a Party-State in Kenya: From "Harambee" to "Nyayo."* Berkeley: University of California Press, 1992.

Williams, Gareth, Alex Duncan, Pierre Landell-Mills, Sue Unsworth, and Tim Sheehy. "Joint Governance Assessment: Lessons from Rwanda." In *Making the State Responsive: Experience with Democratic Governance Assessments,* edited by Goran Hyden and John Samuel. Washington, D.C.: UNDP, 2011.

Woods, Dwayne. "The Tragedy of the Cocoa Pod: Rent-Seeking, Land and Ethnic Conflict in Ivory Coast." *Journal of Modern African Studies* 41, no. 4 (2003): 641–655.

World Bank. "Implementing Affirmative Action in Public Services: Comparative Administrative Practice" (2003). Accessed June 1, 2012. www.worldbank.org/publicsector/bnpp/report%20012405.doc.

Wrong, Michela. *It's Our Turn to Eat: The Story of a Kenyan Whistle-Blower.* New York: HarperCollins, 2009.

Young, Crawford. *The African Colonial State in Comparative Perspective.* New Haven, Conn.: Yale University Press, 1994.

———. "Comparative Claims to Political Sovereignty: Biafra, Katanga, Eritrea." In *State versus Ethnic Claims: African Policy Dilemmas,* edited by Donald Rothchild and Victor A. Olorunsola, 199–232. Boulder, Colo.: Westview Press, 1982.

———. "Nation, Ethnicity and Citizenship: Dilemmas of Democracy and Civil Order in Africa." In *Making Nations, Creating Strangers,* edited by Sara Dorman, Daniel Hammett, and Paul Nugent, 241–264. Leiden, Netherlands: Brill, 2007.

———. *The Politics of Cultural Pluralism.* Madison: University of Wisconsin Press, 1976.

———. *The Postcolonial State in Africa: Fifty Years of Independence, 1960–2010.* Madison: University of Wisconsin Press, 2012.

Young, Robert R. C., ed. "Neocolonialism." *Oxford Literary Review* 13, no. 1 (1991).

Zangon-Kataf, "Human Rights Watch Interview, November 16, 2005." In *They Do Not Own This Place:* Government Discrimination Against Non-Indigenes in Nigeria. *Human Rights Watch* 18, issue 3, Part 1 (April 2006).

Zolberg, Aristide. *One-Party Government in the Ivory Coast.* Princeton, N.J.: Princeton University Press, 1964.

Zorbas, Eugenia. "Reconciliation in Post-Genocide Rwanda." *African Journal of Legal Studies* 1, no. 1 (2004): 29–52.

Index

EDMOND J. KELLER has been studying and researching on African politics for almost forty years. He earned his Ph.D. in political science at the University of Wisconsin and has been a postdoctoral fellow at the Institute for Development Studies (Nairobi), the Bureau of Educational Research (Nairobi), the UN Economic Commission for Africa (Addis Ababa), the Institute of International Studies, UC Berkeley, and the Africa Institute of South Africa (Pretoria). His most involved research has been in East Africa (Kenya, Uganda, Tanzania, Ethiopia), but he has done work in three-quarters of all the countries in sub-Saharan Africa. He is the past president of the African Studies Association and the 2008 Distinguished Africanist of the African Studies Association. He has regularly served as a consultant for governmental (USAID, U.S. House of Representatives, U.S. Senate) and nongovernmental organizations (Oxfam-America, World Bank, the Carter Center, African American Institute, National Democratic Institute, UN Development Program, UNECA). His books include *Revolutionary Ethiopia: From Empire to People's Republic* (Indiana University Press, 1988) and *"Trustee for the Human Community": Ralph Bunche and the Decolonization of Africa* (Ohio University Press, 2010).

9 780253 011848